On
Cultivating
Liberty

Selected Books by Michael Novak

Ascent of the Mountain, Flight of the Dove
·
Belief and Unbelief
·
The Spirit of Democratic Capitalism
·
Business as a Calling: Work and the Examined Life
·
*Freedom with Justice: Catholic Social Thought
and Liberal Institutions*
·
Free Persons and the Common Good
·
The Catholic Ethic and the Spirit of Capitalism
·
Choosing Presidents
·
The Experience of Nothingness
·
The Guns of Lattimer
·
The Joy of Sports
·
The New Consensus on Family and Welfare (EDITOR)
·
The Open Church
·
*Taking Glasnost Seriously: Toward an
Open Soviet Union*
·
*This Hemisphere of Liberty: A Philosophy
of the Americas*
·
To Empower People: From State to Civil Society (EDITOR)
·
Toward a Theology of the Corporation
·
Unmeltable Ethnics
·
Will It Liberate: Questions about Liberation Theology
·
*The Fire of Invention: Civil Society and the Future of the
Corporation*

On Cultivating Liberty

Reflections on Moral Ecology

MICHAEL NOVAK

Edited by Brian C. Anderson

ROWMAN & LITTLEFIELD PUBLISHERS, INC.
Lanham • Boulder • New York • Oxford

ROWMAN & LITTLEFIELD PUBLISHERS, INC.

Published in the United States of America
by Rowman & Littlefield Publishers, Inc.
4720 Boston Way, Lanham, Maryland 20706

12 Hid's Copse Road
Cumnor Hill, Oxford OX2 9JJ, England

British Library Cataloguing in Publication Information
Available

Library of Congress Cataloging-in-Publication Data

Novak, Michael.
    On cultivating liberty : reflections on moral ecology /
Michael Novak ; edited by Brian C. Anderson.
        p.   cm.
    Includes bibliographical references and index.
    ISBN 0-8476-9405-4 (cloth : alk. paper)
    1. Liberty. 2. Liberty—History. I. Anderson,
Brian C., 1933– . II. Title.
JC585.N69   1998
323.44—dc21   98-45128
                                                CIP

Printed in the United States of America

∞ ™ The paper used in this publication meets the minimum
requirements of American National Standard for Information
Sciences—Permanence of Paper for Printed Library Materials,
ANSI Z39.48–1984.

Contents

III. Afterword

A CKNOWLEDGMENTS

The author and editor would like to thank the following publications, where versions of some of the chapters first appeared:

The Review of Politics (chapter 1)
Commentary (chapter 3)
Crisis (chapter 4)
Society (chapter 6)
First Things (chapters 7, 8, and 9)
National Review (chapter 11)
America (chapter 13)

More detailed publication information is included at the beginning of each chapter.

· Introduction ·

MICHAEL NOVAK: MORAL ECOLOGIST OF LIBERTY

Brian C. Anderson

Michael Novak is best known for his wide-ranging exploration of the ideal and practice of "democratic capitalism." Novak's journey through political economy—understood in the most capacious sense— began with the architectonic *The Spirit of Democratic Capitalism* in 1982, developed with *The Catholic Ethic and the Spirit of Capitalism* in 1993, and continued with two recent books, *Business as a Calling* and *The Fire of Invention*, that looked at democratic capitalism from within.[1]

Novak's writings on democratic capitalism, which grew out of a long self-education described in the auto-biographical "Errand into the Wilderness" included in this volume, seek to take back the moral high ground socialism claimed for most of the twentieth century. Socialists, with many fellow-traveling liberal intellectuals in tow, had long excoriated the capitalist societies for their many failures—from economic inequality to pervasive consumerism. As Novak painstakingly argued, however, socialists unfairly compared the *ideal* of socialism with the *practice* of democratic capitalism; had they bothered to look closely at the *reality* of actually existing socialism, they would have discovered what the British political theorist John Gray felicitously called "the system of ruins."[2]

Conversely, capitalism's enemies paid no attention to the moral goods democratic capitalism promised, and in many cases realized: rule of law, the intrinsic dignity of the individual, the encouragement of creativity, economic prosperity, and the challenge and moral decency of a life in business. We can safely say in post-Marxist 1998 that Novak won the argument, though the socialist idea continues to burn, albeit more dimly, on college campuses and in academic publishing houses across the globe. Now the contention has increasingly shifted to finding out what *kind* of capitalism works best. Among the possibilities: the "American" model of openness to innovation; the "Rhine" model of risk-averse social democracy; or an "Asian" capitalism more communitarian than either of its worldly rivals.[3]

But Novak's work extends far beyond the defense of market institutions to encompass a global vision of the free society—in all its dimensions, political, moral, and cultural, as well as economic. The purpose of *On Cultivating Liberty* is to highlight this broader dimension of Novak's thought by publishing a range of essays—two appearing here for the first time, and several in substantially expanded versions—on, to borrow a title from Novak's 1987 Notre Dame lectures, "how to make a republic work."[4]

For if the free society won its debate with socialism, it hasn't won its debate with itself: to build or preserve a free society requires vigilantly tending to what Novak calls "the moral ecology" to prevent moral relativism from corrupting it. The essays collected here offer a sharp corrective to the moral deregulation that threatens democratic societies, despite their immense productivity and unprecedented liberties, with fragmented families, escalating crime, an overextended government that enervates the human spirit, and, at the limit, what Pope John Paul II calls "the culture of death"[5]—a cheapening of human life that attacks society's vulnerable: the unborn, the infirm, the elderly. The free society, Novak warns, will only survive if it grounds itself in an order of moral truth that transcends it.

Without unduly anticipating what follows, let me pull on three major threads that run through *On Cultivating Liberty*'s essays—each a crucial part of Novak's social thought as a whole.

Man's nature: dignified and sinful. As Novak stresses, man is made in the image of God—capable of reflection and choice, remarkable acts of creativity, communal solidarity, and a life well, and virtuously, led. But man is fallen, too, immersed in the sin that mocks his pretensions and from which none of us ever completely frees himself. This dual aspect of human nature has political and economic implications: anti-utopianism (no earthly city will ever be the city of God); an emphasis on unintended consequences (given human blindness due to sin and finitude, the social world can't be programmed like a computer); the need for political and economic institutions that cultivate man's creative and rational side and that discourage his weaknesses, but that always remain sensitive to the human capacity for good *and* evil. (See "Twice Chosen: Irving Kristol as American"; "Errand into the Wilderness.")

Liberty and truth. Nihilism has been "the dark underground river of the twentieth century" (see "Truth and Liberty: The Foundations of the Republic"). Liberal theorists, many of whom bravely resisted the totalitarian temptation, haven't been as successful in escaping the twin seductions of the nihilistic view of freedom: that no moral constraints, whether natural or supernatural, limit the will; and that the will is sovereign, lord and master of all it surveys, a pure force of self-invention, at no time more commanding than when it rejects reason. To Novak, this is a dramatically false, and ultimately self-destructive conception of liberty. Upon its relativistic base, no republic can stand. Novak's alternative understanding of liberty as *ordered*—as self-government—links many of the essays included in this volume, and brings together thinkers as diverse as Irving Kristol and Pope John Paul II, both profiled below.

From state to civil society. The twentieth century has witnessed an unprecedented growth in state power—closely related to the abandonment of liberty as self government. This growth has taken monstrous forms, with the emergence of totalitarian regimes that exacted a terrifying cost in human suffering; and it has taken more benign forms, in the emergence of the social democratic "mixed" regimes that managed, at least for a time, to combine political and intellectual liberties with some redistribution of economic wealth. But even in its benign forms, the growth of the state has had deleterious results: it replaced the vibrant associations of civil society with stultifying government bureaucracy, and sapped economic productivity—to such an extent that Europe's social democracies can no longer afford their over-generous welfare systems. (See "The Crisis of the Welfare State"). Novak's response to the expansion of the state is to call for a reinvigoration of civil society, that realm of associations between individual and state where men and women pursue their interests and learn, as Tocqueville argued, how to be citizens of a democracy. ("See "Civil Society and Self Government.")

To highlight these three themes, though, is not to deny the existence of other rich veins running through *On Cultivating Liberty*: grappling with the "boredom" of democratic capitalist societies; controversially articulating a "Whig" tradition of political thought, open to progress, but respectful of the past, running from Thomas Aquinas to F.A. Hayek; exploring the tension-filled intersection between religion and democracy, the centrality of the family to the free society, and the permanence of tragedy; and making many more forays in neoconservative political theory. The picture that I hope emerges by the end of the volume is of a complex thinker, working toward a synthesis of classical insights into the possibilities and limits of human nature and destiny and modern institutional advances protecting the individual from arbitrary power in politics, economics, and morality and culture.

The idea for *On Cultivating Liberty* occurred to me when I still worked with Michael Novak at the American Enterprise Institute. (I was assistant to Novak for three years, from September 1994 through October of 1997, when I left to become Senior Editor of the Manhattan Institute's *City Journal*. It was a tour of duty I will remain eternally grateful for, and I learned much from it.) Though Novak's body of work had grown to enormous size, many of his best essays, published in leading journals like *Commentary* and *First Things* or delivered as conference papers in Europe or Latin America— particularly on political theory and intellectual history— had not yet appeared in book form. With Novak's encouragement, I pursued the project, and the essays selected, I'd like to think, tell a coherent story about the threats facing the free society as the millennium closes.

On Cultivating Liberty is divided into three sections.

The first, "Liberty: The Virtue and the Institutions," collects several of Novak's most important essays on the free society, written over the past decade and a half. The section moves from the foundations of liberty (chapters one and two) to specific historical and institutional questions of the free society (chapters three through five) and concludes with a remarkable 1982 meditation on the family—the school of practical wisdom and fierce enemy of all projects to engineer the human soul. The second section, "Liberty: The Tradition and Some of its Heroes" is exactly that—a look at some of the most profound theorists of freedom, arranged in the order that Novak first encountered them. The third section, "The Afterward," consists of Novak's intellectual autobiography, "Errand into the Wilderness," which traces his disaffection with the Left, his immersion in political economy, and how he understands his work. In addition, I've included a "Readers' Guide" to Novak's major writings, co-authored by Rev. Derek Cross in honor of Novak's sixty-fifth birthday in 1998. (Rev. Cross wrote all but the last three entries.)

I'd like to thank, first of all, Michael Novak for his unflagging support. Steve Wrinn of Rowman & Littlefield was an extremely patient, though impressively enthusiastic, editor for the second time (he was my editor for my 1998 book *Raymond Aron: The Recovery of the Political*). Two American Enterprise Institute interns made helpful suggestions: Jon Kravis and Tom Gilroy. Cathie Love typed more than she wanted to do, and did so with her usual proficiency. Flavio Felice, an Italian student of Novak's thought, offered many insights in conversations in Washington and Krakow. Daniel J. Mahoney continues to be a source of profound judgment. And last, but not least, let me thank my wife Amy and our delightful son Luke, who, at seven months, really didn't want his dad working on this book.

· I ·

LIBERTY:
THE VIRTUE
AND
THE INSTITUTIONS

· 1 ·

TRUTH AND LIBERTY: THE FOUNDATIONS OF THE REPUBLIC

Few centuries have been as sanguinary as the twentieth. Leaving behind as their monuments the ruins of concentration camps and the work camps of the Gulag Archipelago, temporarily discredited, fascism and communism may have slouched into the shadows. Still, the forces of liberty have not succeeded in laying the foundations for a world of free republics. During the twentieth century, both in Europe and in the United States, the moral life of the free societies has been severely weakened. Families are a shadow of what they used to be. Traditional virtues and decencies, a sense of honor, and respect for moral character have given way to vulgar relativism. Thus, the dark underground river of the twentieth century has not been fascism nor communism but their presupposition: nihilism. And nihilism has not yet been abandoned.

First presented as a lecture at the Henry Salvatori Center, Claremont McKenna College, Claremont, California, April 18–20, 1996; first published in *The Review of Politics*, winter 1997.

LIBERTY: THE VIRTUE AND THE INSTITUTIONS

The Problem of Nihilism

Even before fascism and communism arrived, many in Europe began to hold that humans may make themselves and the world around them whatever they wish. Gradually they denied that the human intellect has purchase on moral reality. *Choosing* matters, they insisted: *will*, not intellect. Such convictions made political nihilism plausible.

This vulgar nihilism systematically infected the souls of the "sensitive spirits"—artists, social critics, journalists, professors; in general, those who set standards, the guardians of culture. Even among liberals in the twentieth century who rejected dictatorship and the state-directed economy, many accepted (and still today accept) two nihilist claims: that there are no constraints rooted in creation, nature, or intellect that the will must heed; and that to be free is to exercise pure will, even apart from the guidance of the intellect.

As Woody Allen still today summarizes these claims: "The heart wants what it wants."[1] The U.S. Supreme Court exemplified them in *Casey*: "At the heart of liberty is the right to define one's own concept of existence, of meaning, of the universe, and the mystery of human life."[2] This is pure nihilism. If I am free to make up my own universe, no law binds me. Nihilism means never having to be judged, and in this it gives the illusion of total freedom and unfettered autonomy. It allows one to indulge whatever desires pull one's heart.

Under Nazism and communism, these were powerful allurements. Not to have a judge (not even an inner "impartial spectator") felt, at first, like "liberation." To follow one's imperious desires wherever they listed yielded a feeling of mastery. One felt that one belonged to a master race, privy to a secret knowledge, those who know about the nothingness. Even Albert Camus found that his own early nihilism, fashionable in the cafes of the 1930s, deprived him of any arguments against the Gestapo agent who strangled one of his friends with a piano wire.[3] For to yield to nihilism was to give up the concept and criterion of truth.

That may not seem like much. Many sober liberals, from Arthur M. Schlesinger, Jr., to Richard Rorty, today recommend it.[4] Only on the basis of relativism, they say, is democracy safe. On the other hand, Vaclav Havel and other heroes of the struggle against totalitarianism attest that only on the basis of personal fidelity to truth, at great cost, were they able to overcome the oppressive public Lie.[5] Solzhenitsyn wrote that one word of truth is more powerful than all the arms of the most heavily armed regime.[6]

Which is it, then? Does liberty need relativism, or does liberty need truth?

Three Concepts of Liberty

Political philosophers commonly use the term liberty to signify a relation between the individual and the regime in which the individual lives and acts. In this political context, the term may signify the degree to which the regime is not coercive, the space that it allows to the individual for self-determination. Isaiah Berlin in his famous essay "Two Concepts of Liberty" defined this way of thinking about liberty as "negative liberty."[7] The regime merely does not coerce, gets out of the way, stays within its own limits. At first blush, this might appear to be the liberal approach to liberty.

By contrast, Berlin's second concept of liberty appertains to state-oriented political philosophies of the communist, socialist, social democratic, and national socialist types; in other words—the nonliberal regimes. Here the governing insight is that individuals left to their own devices may in many cases be *formally* free to do something (not coerced otherwise by the regime) but not at all *able* to do it—lacking money, training, or other means and assistance. At least in certain fundamental areas and up to certain general standards of decency, proponents of this view argue, individuals need to be *enabled* to do things before they can be said to be truly free. Moreover, it is the duty of the regime so to enable them. The state must play a positive role. True freedom comes from this positive enablement, and hence true freedom is called "positive liberty," that is, state-enabled liberty.

Between the two world wars, many liberals in Britain and America were tempted to abandon the classical liberal ideal of negative liberty, in favor of the socialist ideal of positive liberty; and in this widespread cultural crisis of conscience Isaiah Berlin's essay shed much-needed light. Nonetheless, to Berlin's two concepts of liberty a third must be added,[8] if we are to properly understand the project of republican politics—the project of self-government.

By the project of self-government is meant government of the people, by the people, for the people, exercised chiefly through civil associations, but also through representative government, and a freely constituted state properly limited, divided, and checked. As distinguished from positive liberty and negative liberty, this republican project calls forth a concept of liberty as self-government. This third concept of liberty, further, forms a bridge between political philosophy and moral philosophy. "Self-government," for example, refers both to a type of regime and to the internal organization of personal moral life.

This third concept of liberty also forms a bridge between modern and ancient concepts of liberty, which to some influential political philosophers seem otherwise separated by a wide chasm. Ancient philosophers such as Aristotle, Plato, Seneca, and Cicero believed that a sound republic is "man writ large," a reflection of human nature, premised on a virtuous citizenry. By contrast, it is said, modern regimes are based not on virtue—which they judge to be too high and unrealistic an aim—but on lower and humbler bases more likely to be realized, such as interest and utility. If in the ancient view statecraft is a kind of soulcraft, the modern regime is designed to appeal very little to the soul, and perhaps not at all.[9]

Those who draw this contrast between ancient and modern political science have strong evidence on their side. Nonetheless, political reality and political thought move through history like wandering rivers and on many levels at once, maintaining continuities not always apparent on the surface. Honest atheists have often been obliged to confess that they hold today to certain Jewish and Christian concepts despite themselves—such as compassion, the idea of progress, conscience, and the unparalleled worth of the human individual. Bertrand Russell, Jean-Paul Sartre, Albert Camus, Leo Strauss and others have observed such buried movements near the bottom of their thoughts.[10] Alexis de Tocqueville wrote that religion—and he clearly meant Judaism and Christianity—is the primary political institution of democracy.[11] Without religion, he held, belief in the inviolable rights and transcendent worth of individuals would not be indefinitely sustainable. I take his point to be not that in any one generation the masses need religion, while the intellectually strong do not, but that even the latter would over time begin to doubt whether human beings have rights in any sense that does not also apply to animals and trees and rocks, and so for democracy atheism is an untrustworthy support.

Thus, I want to suggest that in the twenty-first century we shall see a new departure in political philosophy, which is at the same time something of a return to something older than the modern. In those parts of the world in which democratic regimes and capitalist economies have been imperfectly achieved, the crisis of the coming century will be experienced, at least at first, as primarily moral and cultural. For democratic and capitalist regimes are not sustainable except under certain moral conditions and among citizens of specifiable moral habits. For their survival, they will have to tend again to central virtues.

Consider just a few: When telling falsehoods and untruths becomes the fashion, when cheating and goldbricking grow in ascendancy; when loyalty, honesty, and fidelity to promises lose point; when rules are routinely violated as long as violators can get away with it; when judges are susceptible to bribes or threats, and officials make no ruling on its merits but only on what it is worth to them; when nepotism, familism, and favoritism overpower justice and fairness; when citizens (as in many countries today) prefer to yield all their responsibilities to leaders, even if they are rogues and thugs; when no one takes pride in their daily work, and all essentially pretend to work; when no one trusts anyone else, nor accepts another man's word, nor cooperates with others except while exercising the strictest watchfulness—in such cases of moral degradation, the institutions of the commercial republic sputter and fail, and self-government dissolves.

The Social Ecology of Self-Government

Because republican self-government and the free economy grew up among a religious and moral people, political philosophers and economists took for granted the existence of such tacit moral preconditions—the functioning of specifiable moral dispositions, tendencies, and habits such as those just noted (by their absence) above. So pervasive were these habits that they seem natural, rather than merely second-nature—that is, part of a learned social inheritance, shaped painstakingly over many centuries by populations willing to correct their bad instincts, inclinations, and habits over time and to replace them with better, in lifelong struggles of self-improvement. Dramatic personal efforts, multiplied throughout millions of families, made the institutions of democracy and the inventive economy practicable.

To allude to Reinhold Niebuhr's great line: The moral strengths of citizens make democracy (and capitalism) possible; their moral weaknesses make democracy (and capitalism) necessary.[12] Such "modern" institutions of republican self-government as checks and balances, bicameral legislatures, divided powers, and the like (though many of these, also, have ancient and medieval precedents) are not constructed in such a way that they depend on the perfect virtue of citizens. Recognizing the realism of the Jewish and Christian teaching on "original sin," the only Christian doctrine (Niebuhr also suggested) that one does not learn by belief but by experience, the American Founders in particular took pains to line up self-interest against self-interest and power against power, so that the self-love of each would become a sentinel over that of others. According to a twelfth-century monastic maxim, "Self-love dies a quarter-hour after the self."

In a word, political philosophers need to explore again the moral preconditions of democracy and capitalism, and to specify in practical detail the moral habits indispensable to their functioning. Though indispensable, these moral habits are not, given human weaknesses, sufficient; and, therefore, the checks and balances, division of offices, and other remedies for human weakness devised by our American Founders (and subsequent generations) also have their role. But institutional arrangements alone cannot keep the machinery of self-government functioning, apart from the quite substantial virtues learned and practiced by citizens. It is chimerical to think, James Madison once wrote, that without virtue in its citizens a republic can long survive.[13]

But how, as Madison asked, can a people incapable of governing its appetites in its private life possibly be capable of self-government in its public life? This is likely to be the central political problem of the twenty-first century: How to arrest the declining moral habits of our peoples. Put otherwise, How are we to instruct our children, and ourselves, in the virtues required for the survival and prospering of republican and capitalist institutions?—the virtues required, secondly, to make the free society worthy, attractive, and morally delightful in itself? (Displaying this task in two steps rather than in one makes evident that virtue is also an end in itself, not merely an instrumental means to the survival of a free society.)

Liberty in this sense consists in an act of self-government by which we restrain our *desires* by temperance and related habits, and curb our *fears* by courage, steadfastness, and related habits. We do so *in order to reflect soberly, deliberate well, and choose dispassionately and justly* on the merits of the case under consideration, in such a way that others can count on our commitment and our long-term purpose. Such practices of self-government are found in a recurrent and habitual way only in persons of considerable character. It is the great fortune of the United States that our first President,

George Washington, was understood by all who knew him to be the prototype of this sort of liberty—the man of character, a man one could count on, decisive, self-starting, a leader, by his very virtues worthy of the admiration and affection of his countrymen, a model for the liberty the nation promised to all who would wish to earn it.[14]

Liberty of this sort comes neither by the positive nor the negative actions of the state, although the Constitution of the American Republic allows it scope and depends upon its widespread realization. The liberty of self-government must be acquired, one person at a time. This personal task is rendered easier when the whole surrounding public ethos teaches it, encourages it, and proffers many examples of it—as well as proffering many examples of the self-destruction wrought by its absence. In this sense, personal liberty is much favored or impeded, depending upon the social ecology of liberty.

But it is fruitless to talk of a recovery of virtue if our society has lost all concept of truth. As the ancient proverb says, it is, in fact, the truth that sets us free (John 8:31–32). No truth, no liberty.

But What Is Truth?

I will insist that the Hebrews have done more to civilize men than any other nation. If I were an atheist, and believed in blind eternal fate, I should still believe that *fate* had ordained the Jews to be the most essential instrument for civilizing the nations. If I were an atheist of the other sect, who believe or pretend to believe that all is ordered by chance, I should believe that *chance* had ordered the Jews to preserve and propagate to all mankind the doctrine of a supreme, intelligent, wise, almighty sovereign of the universe, which I believe to be the great essential principle of all morality, and consequently of all civilization.

—John Adams[15]

John Adams, the second president of the United States, here makes a profound point: Civilization depends on truth, and so does morality. If (contrary to Moses) there is only opinion—your opinion, my opinion, everybody else's opinion—but no truth, then there is no inherent reason why slavery is not equal to liberty, or coercion to equality. If all opinions are equal, Mussolini's are equal to Jefferson's and Adolf Hitler's to Bertrand Russell's.

By contrast, if (as Moses teaches) there is a Creator who understands all of us, who knows all things, who loves all things, who created all things, and who is also an undeceivable Judge, then however rich or powerful some persons might become, they still cannot escape God's judgment. Put another way, against power and wealth and position, other persons can appeal to truth—and to justice. More strongly still, if God is our judge, then civilization is possible. Since in that case truth counts, then human beings have the possibility of entering into rational conversation with one another, trying to persuade one another in the light of truth. As Thomas Aquinas commented, civilization is constituted by conversation.[16] Barbarians club one another; civilized people persuade one another by argument.

The reality of God, from this point of view, provides a barrier against relativism, the cult of power, and the influence of money. God sees through all these things, and humans are thereby encouraged to do the same.

On the other hand, if there is no God, as Adams insists on underlining, if Western civilization is rooted in the biblical God of the Jews (and through the Jews, the Christians) only by mere contingency, we are a quite fortunate civilization, sheerly by chance. Whether by chance or design, our liberty from power, wealth, deception, position, and tyranny in all their forms derives from our commitment to the priority of truth, even if that commitment has come about by chance. (To hold that it does come about by chance, however, is of course to render this commitment absurd—useful, but absurd.)

At this point, I want to make my point crystal clear. As readers of my earlier books *Belief and Unbelief* and *The Experience of Nothingness* will corroborate, I have long resisted making the argument that belief in God is a necessary prerequisite for the defense of the free society. I took this position in order to prevent the use of the idea of God as a mere means, that is, an instrument of worldly ambition. I did so even though the ambition in question seeks the noblest political end of all: the slow and patient pursuit of the ideal of the free republic, the only political ideal worthy of the liberty endowed in human nature. Therefore, I am not arguing here that only a theist—but no atheist or agnostic—can justify his or her commitment to the cause of a free society. The fact is, such self-proclaimed individual atheists as Sidney Hook and others have done so, both before the bar of their philosophical peers and (one supposes) to the satisfaction of their own consciences.

Admiration for Sidney Hook, Milton Friedman, and others has led me, therefore, to frame for myself the following distinctions: (1) Experience shows that atheists as individuals, in association, or as a category of citizens are often good, loyal, and even outstanding citizens. Many have served the common good of the nation in exemplary fashion. (2) Since the Constitution declares the state incompetent in the realm of conscience, there is no contradiction between being an atheist and being a good citizen. (3) Some atheists are stalwart defenders of truth, against relativism; of reason, against emotivism, bigotry, and ignorance; and of responsible and ordered liberty, against libertinism and license—and more effective in this defense than many religious people. (4) Some atheists have followed Hobbes, Locke, and others in offering an intellectual defense of "natural rights" against totalitarianism, brute power, and nihilism. They do so entirely on atheistic grounds. Nonetheless, (5) experience also shows that this defense is a Maginot Line which the swirling tides of history easily overwhelm. On the one side, atheistic arguments fail to convince religious people (a not inconsiderable constituency on the side of liberty). On the other side, for many atheists such arguments crumble before the Nietzschean critique of reason.

For such reasons, it does not seem to me likely that a *whole society over several generations* can find a sustainable intellectual basis for the free society on an atheistic premise. Atheism unsupported by Jewish and Christian tradition can tell us neither why individual rights are inviolable, nor why each individual person is of incommensurable value. It can, at best, supply a rationale based upon utility; but that defense was easily turned by Hitler into "Truth is determined by the victors." In this sense, Western atheists and agnostics have been more dependent than they have ever wanted to admit upon Jewish and Christian convictions, narratives, and dramatic forms. That was Friedrich Nietzsche's point in showing that rationalism without God is an absurdity.[17]

As if to verify Nietzsche's point, the calm rationalism of Sidney Hook, not only comfortable but reigning victorious in American universities for the first three-quarters of the twentieth century, did not survive the century.

Hook's students, before the century's end, were nearly everywhere dethroned, ridiculed, and mocked by "postmodernists." The great-grandchildren of the Enlightenment, alas, suddenly abandoned reason. With it, they also abandoned respect for truth and ordered liberty.

The history of liberty, Lord Acton found, is coincident with the history of Judaism and Christianity.[18] In no other world religions does one find the view that the human person should be valued above all other creatures in the universe. No other has taught that the responsible liberty of the human person is the central drama of the universe and the bright red thread of human history.

Relativism—Once Again

Nonetheless, surveying the wreckage of the twentieth century, in which the Jewish-Christian narrative line of history was overthrown, Pope John Paul II noted in his two recent encyclicals *Centesimus Annus* (1991) and *Veritatis Splendor* (1993) that cultural elites again today are promoting relativism, skepticism, and agnosticism. This time their argument is that these are the best foundation for democratic forms of political life. In rebuttal, the pope notes how often in the first nine decades of the twentieth century the turn to relativism led to capitulation to superior power. "If there is no ultimate truth to guide and direct political activity, then ideas and convictions can easily be manipulated for reasons of power. As history demonstrates, a democracy without values easily turns into open or thinly disguised totalitarianism."[19] People who reject the fiction that truth is whatever a majority says it is root freedom in truth, not fashion. Far from being unreliable from a democratic point of view, such persons are the granite on which democracy is based.

The pope makes a further useful point: In actual practice, the concept of truth is appealed to again and again in concrete democratic life; namely, in appeals to "truthfulness in the relations between those governing and those governed, openness in public administration, impartiality in the service of the body politic, respect for the rights of political adversaries, safeguarding the rights of the accused against summary trials and convictions, the just and honest use of public funds, the rejection of equivocal or illicit means in order to gain, preserve or increase power at any cost," and the like.[20] Even from a pragmatic point of view, the concept of truth is indispensable to democratic habits. This is observable fact. Without a people's commitment to truth in all these senses, liberty is unsustainable.

Still, several questions remain. When confronted with the pope's words about truth and liberty, Milton Friedman wrote sharply and to the point in *National Review*: "Whose truth?"[21] More fully, Friedman wrote:

> As a non-Catholic classical liberal, I find much to praise and to agree with in this letter addressed to the members of the Catholic faith. My stress on its political character, on the dominance of good will and high motives over substantive content is not a criticism. For the Church is a political as well as a religious institution, and this is a political document. But I must confess that one highminded sentiment, passed off as if it were a self-evident proposition, sent shivers down my back: "*Obedience to the truth* about God and man is the first condition of freedom." Whose "truth"? Decided by whom? Echoes of the Spanish Inquisition?

"*Whose* truth?" might be a relativist's question, meaning (or implying) that "your" truth is different from "my" truth, and that truth is always just somebody or other's perception. In other words, there really is not any truth; no objective standards measure which opinions are closer to or further from the reality of things. In that case, nothing exists but subjective perceptions and values. The human subject is not mastered by evidence; the subject is sovereign over the evidence. It would not be easy to discern this purely relativist view at work in Milton Friedman's expositions of evidence in economics.[22]

It is possible, of course, to make a distinction between the truths known through the use of scientific method and the "truths" known through moral reason or (more commonly today) moral "perception." For some authors, the term "reason" is restricted to the use of the mind under the rules of scientific method. Beyond that narrow range, they say, the rest is subjective. Everything else reflects merely private values, personal perception, and choice. This view, once widespread but now thought naive, is called positivism.

In the theoretical order, the impossibility of formulating the positivist position in a positivist way brought its early formulations into disrepute. More importantly, in the practical order, the universal condemnation of Nazi war criminals shows that positivism is in practice untenable. What the Nazis did may have been legal and under orders—that is, positivistically correct—but even a moral cretin should have come upon the knowledge that it was morally intolerable.

Pascal, of course, had tried to make a related claim in his aphorism: "The heart has its reasons which the reason knows not of."[23] But that is too weak a version of a stronger point: Human reason has many more uses than the two uses beloved of positivists, logic and scientific method. These include important uses in politics, practical daily life, the arts, conversation, friendship, and the moral life. In such contexts, good uses of reason can be distinguished from bad (rationalization, for instance), and some statements are understood by those with experience to ring true, while others do not ring true. Without an understanding of the distinction between truth and falsehood in these contexts, we could not use the word "realism" or distinguish it from "foolishness" or "illusion." But we do use these words, every day; and even apart from using the words, we quietly make the discriminations they express amid the many things we see and hear.

For example, we observe that some people are more expert in their observations and behaviors than others. We judge leaders and statesmen—de Gaulle, Churchill—by the perspicuity of their reason in political matters. We know some people who regularly manifest bad judgment, and lack common sense.

As is clear, Milton Friedman is neither a relativist nor a positivist. Yet his question, "Whose truth?" does bring out an important point. What we look to when we use the term *truth* is a standard that is in no one's possession. No one "holds" the truth in his grasp. On the contrary, a person may be possessed *by* the truth, in the grip of the evidence in such a way that he or she cannot deny it, once having taken it in. Indeed, such a person cannot, perhaps, be shaken from the evidence, even under torture. Truth possesses us, we do not possess it. We come under it, not it under us.

Such reflections show why writers concerned with discovering the truth, such as John Stuart Mill, have expressed confidence in appeals to tolerance, civil discourse, and an open marketplace of ideas. They believe that the truth about any particular matter, great or small, is likely to elude the grasp of any one seeker. Each seeker may be moved by one fragment of truth; other fragments emerge in the open contestation of ideas, under fair rules of argument. As Reinhold Niebuhr used to warn himself: There is always some truth in the errors of others and some error in my truth.[24] The standard of evidence is beyond all of us. We need to listen hard—even where we would rather not listen—to learn all that we might learn about reality, especially moral reality.

It is obvious that the term *truth* can be used in many different senses, not all of them acceptable. In the context of a moral and political concept such as human liberty, classically considered, the word *truth* is commonly used by religious people (Jews and Christians notably) in three senses. Consider, for example, the familiar refrain beloved of Americans, "The truth shall make you free." On the first level, this means that fidelity to the Almighty is fidelity to the very light that infuses everything that is and makes it intelligible (*i.e.*, intelligible in itself and in its relation to all other things). The practical payoff is this: fidelity to the evidence of things is the only way to avoid being ensnared by power, money, or other seductions that would turn one's eyes away from evidence. One might not always know in any particular dilemma exactly what *is* true, good, just, right; but one does wish to avoid being swayed by improper partiality.

An atheist, of course, can interpret all this more simply by appealing to a commitment to honest inquiry (or, in the language of some, "the impartial spectator" theory). The Jewish or Christian believer can be that simple, too, but in fact holds that such a commitment is not simply to a methodological principle. It is a commitment to a Person with Whom humans are in covenant, to the One-who-*is*, whose name (for Jews) it is better not to speak or write, lest it be taken to be like all other names rather than above all names. It is a commitment to an undeceivable but loving Judge.

On the second level, "The truth shall make you free" is taken as an operational axiom: Be alert for deception and illusion; seek to understand rightly; beware of the Evil Spirit whose name is the Prince of Lies; know that there are many more insights than there are sound insights. The former come frequently to the top of the head, especially among bright people; the latter are grounded in a virtually unconditioned review of all the evidence. In other words, be of steady and sober judgment, develop habits that strengthen one's ability to perceive quickly and keenly, deliberate wisely, and judge in a manner that is far more often than not (no one is perfect) "spot on," right in the bullseye. People under illusions or driven by errant passions are distant from reality, and their freedom is thereby diminished.

On a third level, "The truth shall make you free" signifies what is implicit on the first two levels; namely, that if one is to be ruled by evidence, not go off half-cocked, then one must deploy all the habits and dispositions necessary to act by self-mastery (by self-government, not by momentary passion or whim). To be free does not mean for humans what it means for the other animals—at least, as Tocqueville points out, not in America.[25] Two cats that frisk, run, bat each other, roll over and run again may seem to be free, but they are in fact doing no more than following the law of their own instincts. Cats do what their instincts tell them, when they tell them. They do what they want, when they want. The trouble is that humans have a far more complicated set of instincts.

From the earliest days, American preachers (Tocqueville notes) drew the distinction between animal freedom and human freedom. Humans must *order* all their instincts, get them into a proper harmony and alignment, order them "sweetly," if they can, in the order laid out for them by the Creator; and if one or another of their wants, desires, or instincts is out of order, ornery, recalcitrant, they must take it by the horns, if necessary, in as many of the little battles of daily life as it takes until it learns by second nature, if not first, where it belongs. Such battles are likely to continue all through a pilgrim's life, as *Pilgrim's Progress* taught millions.[26] In any case, the American conception of liberty is "ordered liberty," a liberty of self-mastery, self-discipline, self-government.

George Washington was a model of this new type of liberty, recognized by all, as were many other Founders: Franklin, Madison, Jefferson, Charles Carroll and, four generations later, Abraham Lincoln. These were men who went through many struggles, but came out at the end men whose word you could trust; whose commitments you could count on; whose judgments about men and affairs were shrewd and often startlingly profound (for all their plainness of statement); whose deliberations showed the work of reason in a great repertoire of various movements and a great range of mood and observations; and whose decisions hewed closely to enduring truths about the human person. Tocqueville called theirs "the new science of politics," and this science of theirs was both ancient and original (as is man himself).

In other words, the third meaning of "the truth shall make you free" is that liberty is constituted by acts of sober reflection and well-deliberated choice. Such acts spring from persons of serious and trustworthy character, whose commitments may be counted on. These acts are free because they are directed by the compass of enduring moral realism, as best these agents can discern it. To live by moral realism (the full truth about humans) is to live an examined and deliberate life. No other, such persons hold, is worth living. To be a slave to illusions is to lose touch with reality, and no longer to be either a sensible or a free person.

Liberty apart from enduring moral truth is illusion. Truth that does not issue in responsible action is sterile.

Conclusion

Thus, our argument has come full circle. Liberty and truth form a beneficent circle. The truth makes us free. And the one thing a free person is not free to do—unless in betrayal—is to turn his or her face against the evidence. The evidence binds, and makes us free from all else. This, at least, is how I read Jefferson, who implies that our minds must be free from every coercion except one: the coercion effected upon the mind by evidence. The mind that is coerced by nothing but the evidence is free; the mind coerced by anything but truth is unfree.

The rationale for defending liberty—especially "the free marketplace of ideas"—is to come closer to the truth. The rationale for defending truth is that it makes us free.

Without such moral foundations—without, that is, a commitment by a preponderance of citizens to the moral habits that make "liberty" and "truth" more than words on paper; that make them, that is, dependable dispositions in the moral life of the nation—it is hard to see how a republic, any republic, can long endure. Our rights are not protected by words on paper, but by habits that exhibit respect for truth and love for ordered liberty.

Keeping the meaning of truth and liberty clean and clear, like white stones in a sparkling stream of the Montana Rockies, is the task of every generation. It is, we might say, a matter of moral ecology.

· 2 ·

Seven Whig Amendments to the Liberal Conception of Liberty

Enormous piles of bodies were heaped up in the twentieth century by National Socialists and International Socialists in their massive efforts to show that liberalism (or liberal individualism) is a mistaken, decadent, and corrupting political philosophy. In the name of the two most potent forms of collectivism in our time, Hitler's legions put to systematic death some sixteen million persons, and Lenin's and Stalin's followers put to death (by Solzhenitsyn's count) fifty-six million.

Nonetheless, the fierce assault on liberal individualism by the organized forces of collectivism should not drive philosophers of liberty into the blind defense of everything that goes by the name of liberalism. In the first place, if we consider but three nations—the United States, Great Britain, and France—those who gave concrete meaning to the term "liberal" in each of those

Based on lecture given at the Conference on Liberalism in the 21st Century, Naples, Italy, June 4–7, 1997, under the sponsorship of the Italian review *Liberal*.

countries, the chief theoreticians and the leaders of actual political movements, fall into three quite different national traditions. Among the names that Americans must conjure with in establishing the national liberal tradition are James Madison, Thomas Jefferson, Alexis de Tocqueville (for his *Democracy in America*), and Abraham Lincoln. With the notable exception of Tocqueville, the theoretical and practical works of these men are not central to discussions of political philosophy in France or Great Britain. Nor do the French mean by *liberal* the same lineage of theory and history that Britons do.

In the second place, as we turn the leaf over into a new century—in fact, into a new millennium—philosophers are within their rights, even obligated, to weigh carefully what has heretofore passed as liberalism. Perhaps they can reconstitute a better thing around the surviving core that it passes forward from the fires of history.

My aim here is to propose a *Whig* context (in the sense in which Thomas Aquinas has been called the first Whig) in which to place the surviving core of the liberal tradition. This reconstituted way of understanding the project of building free societies—that is, the liberal project rightly understood—redresses serious intellectual and practical deficiencies in most manifestations of liberalism. A Whig understanding of the liberal project brings liberalism closer to the facts of the human condition in the harsh light of the twentieth century, and better roots the liberal project in older and richer traditions.

1. Preliminary Distinctions

The liberal party in philosophy has long thought of itself as the party of liberty. Indeed, the liberal party of France, in seeking to construct a huge public symbol of its ideal that would rival the Eiffel Tower, the Pyramids, and other wonders, commissioned the Statue of Liberty, which was successfully erected in New York Harbor in 1886, at the gateway to the New World. At the philosophical core of the liberal party, this symbol says, stands a philosophy of liberty.

Much depends, therefore, on getting this philosophy of human liberty correct; yet the terrain around the concept of liberty is notoriously slippery. For some generations, especially in the beginning, it was easier, perhaps, for liberals to define those views they were against, than to state clearly and adequately what they meant by liberty; easier to state what they wanted freedom *from* than what freedom *is*. It is easy to get important matters wrong, and many did. Some liberals hated the past; they wanted to erase it: *Ecrasez l'infâme!* Others carelessly threw away fragments of wisdom their own project desperately needed. Coming to an accurate understanding of human liberty would have been more useful to the liberal project.

In seven separate respects that I have been able to detect, existing theories and practices of liberalism fall short of human needs. But before recounting these, I need to make some preliminary distinctions. First, the primary context of my thinking and imagination is the United States. Those whose primary context is elsewhere will need to draw analogies and make adjustments.

Second, we must distinguish between two arenas in which a philosophy of liberty must be deployed: the first concerns the role of the state in the free society; the second concerns the liberty of civil society. The second is my subject here. (At another time, I might wish to outline some serious inadequacies in current liberal understandings of the state, at least in the U.S.,[1] but not here.)

Third, we must distinguish between discussing liberty

in wholly secular terms, and a more realistic discussion which would take account also of religious terms. Many philosophers of liberty are non-religious, and some are even anti-religious. Without prejudice to their convictions, it is more concrete to include religious perspectives within any discussion of liberalism, since many free persons and free communities are quite religious, and since liberty of conscience is usually regarded as the first liberty. Furthermore, there are sound empirical reasons, even if one is not oneself a Jew or Christian, for assenting to Lord Acton's observation that the idea of liberty of conscience, as both a personal and a political reality, is historically coincident with the advent, rise, and spread of Jewish and Christian ideas and understandings. For these reasons, it is proper and often necessary to introduce Jewish and Christian ideas into a concrete real-world discussion of liberty, and this may be done without apology.

Finally, my subject here is not political liberalism but philosophical liberalism. In the United States today, the political liberal is criticized and (sometimes) opposed by the communitarians (Amitai Etzioni), the civic republicans (Charles Murray), the libertarians (Milton Friedman), the neoconservatives (Irving Kristol), the economic conservatives (Jack Kemp), and the cultural conservatives (William Bennett). In general, political liberals favor expanded government, equality, redistribution, and the relief of insecurity (for unemployment, low wages, health, old age, disabilities, and the like). Their closest soul mates in Europe are probably social democrats.

Philosophical liberalism, however, is a set of beliefs about the individual, liberty, and choice that may be shared by both political liberals and political conservatives. The classic statement of philosophical liberalism is encapsulated in the "one very simple principle" of J.S. Mill's *On Liberty*:

> The sole end for which mankind are warranted, individually or collectively, in interfering with the liberty of action of any of their number is self-protection. . . . The only part of the conduct of any one, for which he is amenable to society, is that which concerns others. In the part which merely concerns himself, his independence is, of right, absolute.

Here we have the image of man as a solitary agent "unencumbered" by any human relations except the moral imperative "Do no harm." Here we have no social animal, no political animal, no creature of sympathy and historic communal faith, nor family member, nor citizen—only a naked and self-directed will. One may contrast this liberal self with the self of my newly married friend who, when I telephoned to ask him if he wished to go to a baseball game with me the next night, said to me: "I must ask my wife. I am now two." Making up his mind means making up two minds.

My interest at present is primarily in philosophical liberalism. However, I wish to discuss it in the context of that larger sense of politics, not partisan politics, whose purpose is to construct a free and open society rather than a repressive society. My subject is not political liberalism. It is philosophical liberalism in a political context.

2. Correcting the Flaws of Liberalism

Many thinkers—Irving Kristol, Alasdair MacIntyre, John Gray, among others—have over the years described various deficiencies in key statements of liberal philosophy. An unusually vivid public statement of such inadequacies recently appeared in Judge Robert Bork's best-seller, *Slouching Towards Gomorrah*. From such writers, I have learned to distinguish at least seven of the inadequacies of liberalism as it is currently discussed and practiced in the United States. The first four consist of a more or less systematic *neglect*. Liberals neglect the moral and intellectual habits required for *rationality*; the moral and intellectual habits required for *choice* (the difference between commitment and preference); the *community* necessary for the formation of strong and self-determining individuals; and the *totalitarian tendencies* of individual will and collective will, even when the latter is exercised by a minority. The "tyranny of the majority" can also, under certain conditions, be supplanted by a "tyranny of a minority." For example, when well-placed elites "manage" the majority.

The next two inadequacies consist of frequently observed *unworthy tendencies* among public liberals: a narrow *intolerance* toward religious believers; and the *arrogance* implicit in a claim to being distinctively "enlightened."

The seventh is the historically unnecessary, dangerous, and self-mutilating *separation between secularist and religious defenders of liberty* to which, for example, Friedrich Hayek called attention in his inaugural address at the first meeting of the Mont Pelerin Society in 1947, in his criticism of excessive rationalism:

> It is this intolerant and fierce rationalism which is mainly responsible for the gulf which, particularly on the Continent, has often driven religious people from the liberal movement. . . . I am convinced that unless this breach between true liberal and religious convictions can be healed there is no hope for a revival of liberal forces. There are many signs in Europe that such a reconciliation

is today nearer than it has been for a long time, and that many people see in it the one hope of preserving the ideals of Western civilization. It was for this reason that I was specially anxious that the subject of the relation between Liberalism and Christianity should be made one of the separate topics of our discussion.

Instead of elaborating negatively on the deficiencies of the liberal philosophy, it may be more fruitful to amend it, in order to strengthen and correct it. For the basic insight of liberalism is just and true—that what is distinctive about the human animal is its capacity to reflect and to choose, and therefore to bear responsibility for his or her own destiny. Theologically, this is the sense in which the human is made in the image of God, to be provident as God is provident. This is also the sense in which Karol Wojtyla as philosopher spoke of "the acting person" as an acting *subject*, and described liberty of conscience as the first of human rights. This is, finally, the sense in which Lord Acton, the great historian of liberty, described the idea of liberty as coincident with Christianity—found only in, and nowhere else except in, cultures profoundly affected by Christianity. Historians will recall that it is precisely on this ground that Thomas Aquinas so fiercely resisted the Averroists, and saw in their denial of personal responsibility for reflection and choice a radical undercutting of the possibility of Christian faith. (Nothing reveals more clearly than this medieval debate the difficulties Islamic philosophy has confronted ever since in developing a philosophy of liberty.)

The amendments to be introduced to the liberal philosophy of the person may be collectively described as a "Whig" modification of the idea of freedom, after Lord Acton, who described Thomas Aquinas as "the first Whig" and who himself is probably best described as a

Whig and a critic of liberalism. Emphatically, however, Acton belonged to—made his own—the party of liberty, for he saw the development of institutions suited to human liberty as the main interpretive thread of history.

3. The Whig Modifications of Liberalism

Not so many years ago a popular book in the United States described an African lion as born free, and for at least two centuries the imagination of Europeans and Americans has associated liberty with the wild animal (or the human) brought up outside civilization. Many people seem to associate liberty with instinct and, specifically, animal instinct. Others associate liberty with lack of constraint—not simply physical constraint such as jail or manacles, but even the constraints of custom, convention, the opinion of others, laws, rules, regulations, social pressures, taboos, stigmas, guilt feelings. A third step is taken by others, who suggest that liberty consists in getting free of mind, self-consciousness, reasons, and purposes, so as to attain a sort of pre-rational, feral innocence, perhaps of the type that Nathaniel Hawthorne brought to dramatic life in *The Marble Faun*. Sometimes these steps are compressed into a simple theory of pleasures and pains, as in the less complicated of the accounts of utilitarians. Liberty is thereby reduced to a preference for pursuing pleasures and avoiding pains—a preference that is almost automatic, even though it may require subtle calculations, in order to weigh complex situations in which some pleasures and some pains are irremediably mixed, and more than one person is involved.

A thought-experiment shows how woefully simpleminded such accounts of liberty are. Suppose that science and technology have advanced so far that those portions of the brain that produce pleasures and pains have been precisely identified and subtly wired, in such a fashion that our children from an early age can be equipped with a lightweight belt that allows them to press buttons to increase the amounts of pleasure that they feel and to blot out all pain. Would you want your children, say, from the age of three or four equipped with such belts? (This thought-experiment was proposed by Charles Murray in *In Pursuit of Happiness and Good Government*, a sustained reflection on human happiness.) I would most certainly not; the very idea seems repulsive. States of blissful feelings and pleasures so infallibly and effortlessly produced are utterly remote from what I would wish for my children. What gives me pride is seeing my children seize responsibilities, overcome setbacks, and pursue noble intentions through obstacles and difficulties. Performances like that yield more pride than a father can say. Such judgments about the constitution of true liberty seem widespread, transcultural, true to experience, and deeply etched in human nature.

Humans seem not to be born free but to be born to struggle to attain freedom. Pleasures and pains are neither irrelevant nor the heart of the matter. What matters is taking responsibility. That, in turn, requires reflection and commitment over time; that is, a sustained willingness to bear quite considerable pain for the sake of the particular type of pleasure that arises from attaining a difficult objective. That objective, moreover, must sometimes be "worthwhile" in some important sense; not only worth the pain endured in reaching it, but in some way altering the self, so as to make one more able to act in other and new respects. It is not liberty, Lord Acton wrote, to do what we want; it is liberty to do what we ought.

Humans are the only creatures known to us who do

not fulfill the law of their own nature by following their instincts. Or, rather, our instincts are more numerous and more complicated than the instincts of other animals. We share with the other animals the full range of animal instincts, but in addition we have the capacity to reflect on our own instincts and our own behavior, to reflect upon possible futures, and to choose among these futures. We are able to reflect and to choose, to choose in the sense not only of selecting preferences but also in the sense of making long-range commitments. We can set goals. We can perceive, imagine, and conceive of goals at quite a long distance from where we now are. We can set for ourselves lifetime goals, and establish intentions that will serve us through better and worse, in sickness and in health, until death puts an end to our temporal striving.

It is sometimes asserted that modern science put an end to teleology. Whatever might be said to be the case in the field of cosmology—and given recent work in physics, perhaps that is less than has been believed—such a conclusion is wholly unwarranted in the field of human action and freedom. Both as a personal achievement and as a social project liberty is inherently teleological. Over most of the earth, we have not yet built free societies. In our personal lives, each of us struggles to become free persons to a greater degree today than yesterday. We struggle to free ourselves from ignorance, errant passions, and reflexive faults of many sorts, that prevent us from acting as we ought to act and as we deeply desire to act. Things we ought to do we do not, and things we ought not to do we do, despite our best intentions. We find it hard to be both all we want to be, and all we know we ought to be. (Our spouses and our children are wont to inform us of our shortfalls, should these be obscure to ourselves.) The vocation of becoming free women and men is no easy vocation. We honor it daily more in the breach than in the achievement.

There are at least four reasons why liberty is so difficult to attain in personal life as well as in our social conditions. Liberal theorists have been neglectful of these reasons. With respect to each of them, the Whig tradition introduces an amendment to the liberal conception of liberty.

The first of these amendments is fuller emphasis upon *the complexity of the rational elements in human choice*, specifically reflection and deliberation. When I am faced with a decision about how to choose a line of action in an important matter, I find it highly useful to consult with persons in my circle whose own choices in life I have had reason to admire. They have the facility of remaining calm, dispassionate, and clear-eyed, assessing various goods, obstacles, interests, powers, difficulties, possibilities, likely sequences of events, probable countermoves by others, likely unintended consequences, and other contingencies. They tend to see more angles than others, and in a more farsighted way. What impresses me is the evenness of temper they maintain, their sobriety, and their calm and unpanicky habits of analysis. Persons of sound judgment—persons with practical wisdom—are the best of possible friends, and their counsel is of immeasurable value.

One soon learns from such friends that the array of good habits necessary for sufficient reflection and clear-sighted deliberation is like a full quiver of arrows. Many sound habits of mind and a well-ordered will are required. Otherwise, one's choices are likely to be intemperate, blinded by passion, obscured by indecent haste, untutored by an instinct for likely consequences. This, of course, is an indirect way of saying that to act as a rational creature is no simple task, and that to learn the art of self-government is to learn the full range of virtues required for rational choice. Put another way, rationality in action implies the prior task of acquiring the many good habits needed for wise reflection and deliberation attuned to reality.

The second Whig amendment to the liberal conception of liberty concerns the richness of the concepts of choice and will. Choice is not a simple idea, easily reduced to *preference*, as in a preference for vanilla over chocolate, a red over a blue automobile, or the like. In the matter of liberty, we must enrich the concept of choice to include commitment for the long term, even the commitment of an entire lifetime, through good times and bad, in pleasures and in pains, facing setbacks and failures and obstacles and enemies. Choice as commitment requires a different frame of mind and a different measure of deliberation and resolution than choice as preference. In some matters, all of us find ourselves unhappy when we are wishy-washy, fickle, irresolute, too easily swayed by our surroundings, or too quick to abandon our aims when difficulties arise. Put starkly, we are too often lazy, risk-averse, and unwilling to endure adversity. It is not always our ideas that fail us. We see clearly enough what we should do. We even express it beautifully. The problem is that we tend to agree with the last person to advise us, and are easily blown off course. Or we follow the course of least resistance.

These experiences confront us with the role of will in our choices. When we know what we want, we go after it doggedly, except when certain temptations—which we love too much—prove irresistible. As our reason requires a set of good habits to function well, so does our will. Without these strengths, neither our practical intelligence nor our resolution always work as those of free persons ought to work. Lame, they prevent us from walking erect as free persons ought to walk.

The third Whig amendment to the liberal idea of liberty is to note that *liberty is arrived at not in solitary isolation but in community*. It takes strong communities—families, first of all—to form free persons. In the end, it is entire lands—that is, cultures—that form the free and the brave. Liberty is a long school. Many teachers are needed to instruct every individual self. Some of these teachers are the heroes and wise ones and scholars of the past. Others are among one's family and friends. For if one did not see examples of truly brave and noble persons, how would one learn how to behave under adversity or in the midst of temptation? One also needs counsellors, words of warning, and words of encouragement. One needs persons who make one feel ashamed to fall short, and others to suggest that we have not yet done enough and that self-satisfaction is premature.

For most of us, it is very hard to swim against the stream all day long and every day. That is why those blessed with brave and true companions know their good fortune. When all around are floating in decadence and dishonesty, surrendering to circumstance, and going along in order to survive, only a few are likely to resist, and these are likely to seem to others mad. The power of the raised eyebrow is the most powerful moral weapon in the world. That is why the American prisoners in their solitary cells in Hanoi worked so hard at their rudimentary signal system, as Admiral Stockdale has illuminatingly recounted. They needed to build up their common ability to hold true to one another and to themselves. Liberty is a communal achievement, because the human being is inherently relational. We are not solitary atoms, we are members of one another. Soldiers near death fight so as not to let their comrades down. Even those who fight alone fight not for themselves, but in and with the community of spirit in which they habitually dwell (even in solitude). In liberty, to stretch a metaphor, the human being is not a biped but a multiped.

The fourth Whig amendment to the liberal conception of liberty is to note *fatal weaknesses in defining liberty solely in terms of will*—as in doing whatever one wills, following one's own sweet will, and *just do it*! This is true whether the context is individual or social. The will alone, cut free from practical intelligence and good judgment, is cold, heedless, cruel, totalistic, often self-destructive and destructive of others. Mussolini is the historical figure who first defined the word totalitarian, which is constituted, he said, by *la feroce volontà*. That says it exactly; totalitarianism is unchecked will. (Hell itself is probably best defined as the eternal isolation of the will in its own self-love.) Even in democracies, the tyranny of a majority is an ever fiercer tyrant than tyranny by a single individual. It is less intelligent, less constrained, madder in its passions, and even less easily touched by mercy. This form of tyranny is a perpetual threat to democratic experiments.

The will alone, single or social, knows no truth; it knows only power. For this reason, liberal definitions of liberty that stress *choice*, in the sense of will alone, and fail to include reference to the knowledge of the true and the good, are not exactly without compass but, rather, on a direct slope of descent into a world of heartless totalitarian power.

4. The Final Three Whig Amendments

The fifth Whig amendment to the liberal conception of liberty is to recognize and respect the religious roots of liberty; put otherwise, to *cease identifying the liberal party as the anti-religious party*. Religious ideas do not work in history as premises in logic or postulates in geometry; they work as yeast in dough. For their aim is not so much to change logic as to change personal and social life. To fulfill this aim, meditation, reflection, and the slow process of self-criticism are needed. Thus, the conviction that the one God is the Creator of all and made every woman and man in his image became the main ground in history for the growing sense of the dignity of every human person, even among slaves and the poor and the vulnerable. That the Creator calls all humans to himself, and is also the indeceivable Judge of all, further became the main historical ground for the idea that truth is weightier than power and interest, and that *therefore*, it is the truth that sets us free. Against every power and interest, the human being rightly appeals to truth. It is the same for the idea that every person is responsible for his own free choices in life, on which he or she will be judged. It is under the tutelage of Judaism and Christianity that, in due course, the operation (and the nature) of conscience emerged in human consciousness, and also the idea that the power of the state is limited in the realm of the sacred.

Such religious ideas are not antiliberal; they are, to say the least, the main historical grounds of liberal convictions. Lord Acton, as we have seen, made a stronger claim; viz., that the history of liberty is coincident with the history of Christian cultures. In modern Europe, alas, an adversarial relation developed between the party of liberty and the church. By contrast, in America the churches were among the staunchest supporters of the cause of liberty, as Tocqueville pointed out, and precedent-making innovations in practices of religious liberty took root. In America, Tocqueville writes, religion and liberty were friends, much to the benefit of both. To this day, religious belief and practice in the United States thrive as in few other places; and the party of liberty has a preponderance of religious members.

The sixth Whig amendment to the liberal project is to note *the ideological arrogance implicit in the self-description of "the Enlightened,"* as well as the imputation that their opponents belong to the forces of darkness. This is an unfortunate form of Manicheanism imported into the world of ideas.

Moreover, the notion that one can defend reason and liberty apart from the conviction that truth derives from the Creator and Judge has turned out to be a weak reed, just as Nietzsche predicted. Usually, we use the word "truth" as a characteristic either of propositions or of the reality of things. But the suppressed implication of this usage, as Nietzsche saw clearly, is that truth is in the end personal; it is grounded in God. Take out God and truth floats free, flimsily related if at all to either propositions or things. It comes then to seem rooted in nothing more than our own desires and projects. It thereby loses its original force. We are thus once again (after an exceptional interval of two millennia) left embedded in a world whose moving forces are power and interest. This is the ground Mussolini seized in his definition of totalitarianism as *la feroce volontà*. Intellect is in the end impotent, and will reigns supreme. Fifty years after Mussolini, the philosopher of Charlottesville (Richard Rorty) may describe our condition as nihilism with a happy face. But nihilism offers no protection against thugs and criminals in power. Against them, on the grounds of nihilism, our descendants will be able to offer no defense in the name of truth, justice, or even solidarity.

Whigs hold that God is truth, and that it is truth that makes us free. The idea of truth is indispensable to the idea of liberty. And a recognition of the reality of truth is next door, at least, to the recognition of the reality of God. (All persons of good will, who seek the truth with their whole hearts, are "saved" even according to the teaching of the Catholic Church, at Vatican II.)

Furthermore, because the relationship of every person to his Creator and Judge belongs to the realm of the sacred, that relationship is inviolable by others, whether by private persons or by officials of the state. The state is simply incompetent to infringe upon this relationship. Total respect for this relationship is the primordial and most fundamental human right, grounded in the ultimate source of human dignity: the incommensurable, incommunicable, inalienable, and immortal value of every person in the eyes of the Creator. If one accepts the reality of God, one is bound to respect the rights of conscience of atheists, agnostics, and skeptics, and is properly blamed for any failure to do so.

Conversely, if one does not accept the reality of God, one may or may not respect "rights" supposedly grounded in truth or in the human relation to truth. Some regimes do, and some don't. Among atheist regimes today, notably but not solely China, the persecution of persons on grounds of conscience is an extensive and dreadful reality. (Among Islamic nations, some religious and some secular, the struggle for the soul of Islam on the issue of freedom of conscience is intense. Political forces, often not truly interested in Islam, adopt a religious disguise to overpower those who insist that Islam, as religion, is bound to defend liberty of conscience, out of respect for the sacred working of Allah in the souls of individuals.)

I do not doubt that there is a wholly secular way to construct a defense of liberty of conscience, at least in the political sphere. Many writers in the West, following

Thomas Hobbes and John Locke (if Locke is interpreted as a wholly secular thinker), do just that. Of these arguments, the best I have encountered argues from fear of torture and tyranny. Since everyone rightly fears what might be imposed upon them through systematic torture, all have a supreme interest in denying to civil power any rights over conscience or ideas, and this denial becomes part of the social compact establishing civil society. Vigilance on the part of active civic associations is required to assure that this compact is adhered to. This argument seems to me workable, so far as it goes. Yet serious dangers lurk within it.

The appetites of powerful secular elites, particularly when they gain working control over the media, the law schools, the courts, and major law firms—to name only a few central institutions with great power in democracies—may, or may not, be checked by rival elites of commensurate power. Such appetites, unchecked, may subtly and steadily become engines of a new secular conformity, imposing a tyranny of a powerful minority over key institutions of a republic. Thus, lawyers who are opposed to abortion, or euthanasia, or some other agenda of dominant elites, may be denied positions in key law firms, on the courts, or in other important civil locations. Further, a regime of public laws may slowly be imposed upon the whole society that is radically hostile to religious believers. That this is a process already far advanced in the United States is the gravamen of Robert Bork's powerful argument in *Slouching Towards Gomorrah*, and in articles and books by others, to the effect that purely secular liberal principles, unchecked and unmoderated by respect for religious believers, have already been turned inside-out into a systemic illiberalism. In France, Pierre Manent and Philippe Bénéton have made analogous arguments.

In short, we have arrived at a new situation, in which in many nations (on the one hand) secular liberalism is dominant, and has revealed its own shortcomings and limitations, and in which (on the other hand) religious believers have come to internalize (perhaps with amendments as herein sketched) the value of many liberal insights, practices, and institutions. It is even possible that religious peoples have learned more from the liberal project than secularists have learned about the liberal potentialities of religious belief. Several of the documents of Vatican Council II—*The Church in the Modern World*, *Religious Liberty*, and others—and the writings of John Paul II, in particular *Centesimus Annus* and *Veritatis Splendor*, bear this out on the religious side. More and more liberal writers, too, have begun writing with greater appreciation of religious contributions to liberal perplexities, such as Irving Kristol, Charles Murray, Charles Taylor, Michael Sandel, and many others.

The seventh Whig amendment of liberal conceptions of liberty flows from the last two. Whigs hold that *it is wrong, and injurious to liberty, to instill and to foment separation between religious and secular partisans of liberty*. The party of liberty needs both religious and secular supporters. In order to achieve cooperation among religious and secular partisans of liberty, powerful historical currents will have to be reversed. Of these, perhaps, one key feature may be singled out for immediate attention—the ideology of mutual hostility. For some generations, liberals who are secular have taken pride in their antagonism to religion. Some have even proclaimed that their fundamental project consists in building a philosophy, an ethic, and societies that reject Judaism, Christianity, and religion in general. For their part, some believers and churchmen have for generations made it their mission to oppose the insufficiencies and (as they see them) the errors of liberalism. Suppose that much of this mutual antagonism is misplaced; that many writers, on both sides, are working with caricatures of the other. Could we not then make significant progress in the near term simply by making more careful distinctions, and by agreeing that we, all of us together, face a new and unprecedented situation? Is it not time to see how we can come to each other's assistance, and make special efforts to include each other in our public discussions, in order to make certain that mutual respect will replace mutual hostility?

I do not think that any wise person today would assert that the cause of liberty within our own countries is secure in the face of the third millennium, just now about to dawn. In the world as a whole, terrible crimes against persons and consciences are still abundant, and vast social uncertainties stare us in the face. Even in the best of circumstances, institutions of liberty are fragile. Any one generation might, quite freely, elect to sabotage or to abandon those institutions, or might easily reject (or forget) the hard-won principles that underlie them. Worse still, habits of self-government in private life might yield to decadence and dissolution, thereby precipitously diminishing the probabilities of successful self-government in public life. A vulgar relativism, like an invisible gas, might infiltrate the lungs of the free and the brave, collapsing their will to resist some new soft despotism. This despotism would arrive among them quietly bearing sweet promises to care for them in the intimate details of their lives, so long as they agree to live once more as serfs.

5. Conclusion

These seven Whig amendments to liberal conceptions of liberty are friendly amendments, and have the wisdom of centuries to commend them. If there is something hard and challenging about them, then, given the difficult times that lie ahead in the coming two generations, that fact may tell in their favor.

If liberty is a cause worth dying for, it is surely a cause worth thinking about as carefully as we can. For liberty is a moral project—even a religious project—and the first moral obligation, Blaise Pascal taught us, is to think clearly. To say what liberty is, is to say what man is, under these stars, with the wind on our faces. If Judaism and Christianity are correct, man is the noblest project of the Creator. And man's liberty is the target toward which hurtles day by day

L'Amor che move il sole e l'altre stelle!

If Judaism and Christianity are not correct, still, human liberty is the most precious of the gifts we inherit from our ancestors, and infinitely worthy of our care.

· 3 ·

BOREDOM, VIRTUE, AND DEMOCRATIC CAPITALISM (OR) THE END OF HISTORY

Late in May 1989, the bicentennial of the French Revolution, Chinese students in Shanghai openly defied a communist regime, carrying before them a white plaster replica of the Statue of Liberty. During that same spring, both the Soviet Union and Poland were experiencing their first relatively free elections under communist domination. In Hungary, moves toward democracy and capitalism were proceeding both in public argument and in tentative, practical action. Symbolically, at least, the institutions and ideals of the liberal society were gaining adherents rather rapidly.

No wonder, then, that so many people have begun saying that these institutions and ideals are now sweeping everything before them. For it does indeed appear that of the three great systemic ideas of the twentieth century—communism, fascism, and democratic capital-

---

First prepared for lectures in Sidney and Melbourne, Australia, and in Hong Kong in 1989, and revised for publication in *Commentary*, September 1989, in part as a response to Francis Fukuyama's now famous end of history thesis.

ism—only the last is still vigorous and growing. Just as fascism collapsed in the ashes of its cataclysmic defeat in 1945, so also, not quite forty-five years later, communism seems to have died, even in the minds of party elites. I want to emphasize: has died as an *idea*; in other words, not necessarily as a residual reality—a militarily dangerous reality, at that.

In a stimulating essay published in the Summer 1989 issue of the *National Interest*, Francis Fukuyama even goes so far as to draw the conclusion that "history," in Hegel's sense, has arrived at its appointed end. By this he means that the entire world is being driven by trial and error away from faulty ideas about the future shape of human life ("The Thousand Year Reich," "The Workers' Paradise") and toward their antithesis: a society based on a democratic polity and a capitalist economy.

So far so good, says Fukuyama. But he also sees a downside:

> The end of history will be a very sad time. The struggle for recognition, the willingness to risk one's life for a purely abstract goal, the worldwide ideological struggle that called forth daring, courage, imagination, and idealism, will be replaced by economic calculation, the endless solving of technical problems, environmental concerns, and the satisfaction of sophisticated consumer demands. In the post-historical period there will be neither art nor philosophy, just the perpetual caretaking of the museum of human history. I can feel in myself, and see in others around me, a powerful nostalgia for the time when history existed. Such nostalgia, in fact, will continue to fuel competition and conflict even in the post-historical world for some time to come. Even though I recognize its inevitability, I have the most ambivalent feelings for the civilization that has been created in Europe since 1948, with its North

Due Date
Receipt

Call Number	JC585 .N69 1999
Title	On cultivating liberty : reflections on moral ecology /
Item Barcode	22113000445713
Due Date	03/02/15 11:59:59 PM

Call Number	JC153 .L85 1952
Title	The second treatise of government /
Item Barcode	22113001346092
Due Date	03/02/15 11:59:59 PM

Set up your library account today so that you can view checked out items and renew any that are coming due.

Atlantic and Asian offshoots. Perhaps this very prospect of centuries of boredom at the end of history will serve to get history started once again.

In this lament, Fukuyama echoes the single most persistent criticism of democratic capitalism, even among its friends: that it is spiritually deficient. It may work, they say. It may produce abundance. It may put an end to famine, curb disease, enable the average age of mortality to jump from eighteen in the year 1800 to seventy-five in 1986. It may even generate unprecedented liberties. But, they say, all this is for naught, since under democratic capitalism human beings live vacuous and empty lives.

Such a judgment springs from what logicians call a category mistake—and a horrific one. A democratic capitalist regime is not the kingdom of God. It is not a church, or even a philosophy, and it is only in an outward sense "a way of life." A democratic capitalist regime promises three liberations by institutional means—liberation from tyranny and torture; liberation from the oppression of conscience, information, and ideas; and liberation from poverty. The construction of a social order that achieves these is not designed to fill the soul, or to teach a philosophy, or to give instruction in how to live. It is designed to create space, within which the soul makes its own choices, and within which spiritual leaders and spiritual associations may do their own necessary and creative work.

Indeed, one of the chief differences between a democratic capitalist society and a fascist or communist society is that the first is in no sense a religion. Fascism and communism are pseudo-religions; they aim to shape and to invigorate the whole soul; they attempt to merge the individual into a movement and a common purpose as a drop is merged in the ocean. Such societies are collectivist and totalitarian by design, for the sake of the inner unity of all, an inner unity that can be (for a while) very satisfying. No one who has watched on film Hitler's Nuremberg rallies can doubt the willingness of many hearts and minds to be inflamed with one common purpose.

By contrast, the institutions of democratic capitalism do not cause those who live under them to merge their own identities in a common sea; rather, they encourage each individual in his own, individually charted, "pursuit of happiness."

Nonetheless, there are, for all that, two fields of spiritual value and moral virtue associated with democratic and capitalist institutions (two, that is, in addition to the higher values and virtues that such institutions cannot themselves supply, but for whose practice they leave space and provide indirect support). The first consists of those spiritual values and moral virtues called forth by democratic capitalist institutions, and the second is made up of those without which its institutions could not possibly survive.

It is, of course, broadly agreed that traditional societies (precapitalist, predemocratic, prepluralist) had their own distinctive virtues. In ancient Greece and Rome, as well as in medieval and Renaissance Europe, the cardinal virtues were temperance, fortitude, justice, and prudence (practical wisdom). Whole lists of other virtues praised by Aristotle and Cicero were for centuries also widely celebrated.

With the invention of democratic capitalism in America, new demands were made upon the citizens, for which new virtues were required. The school for learning these virtues was long, but as Tocqueville noted, the American people learned them during the many years between the founding of Plymouth Colony in 1620 and the Revolution of 1776.

In the absence of direct rules from Great Britain, the American colonist had first to develop the habits of self-reliance, community-building, and self-government that may be summarized under the heading of *civic responsibility*. When they left behind the comfortable hostels and taverns of Leyden, the first boatloads of "pilgrims" (so they styled themselves, although their pilgrimage was to no known sacred place) recognized that there would be no homes, shelters, barns, or warm hearths waiting for them: all these they would have to build. At first, they tried a form of communism—ownership and labor in common. That soon failing, they turned to a regime of private property.

For a people often accused by sociologists of "excessive individualism," their primary task, repeated again and again across a vast continent, was the building of new communities where no such communities had existed before. They depended very much upon the ambition of their most imaginative and able members, but they also depended upon the capacities of all for freely given cooperation and coordination. Civic responsibility required individual initiative and a spirit of cooperation in equal parts.

The second new virtue called forth by this new type of society was *personal economic enterprise*. It is the function of enterprise to break from received ways of doing, making, and distributing goods and services. In this respect, enterprise seems to be a peculiarly capitalist virtue. Not unknown in previous history, in a capitalist system it becomes, so to speak, the red-hot center, the dynamo, the ignition system, of development. It is the very principle of economic progress.

Enterprise is, to deepen the notion, both an intellectual and a moral virtue. Its intellectual moment consists in a discovery heretofore neglected and in some sense original, usually concerning either a new need of the community which might be served, or a new method for doing so. Its moral moment consists in the effort, ingenuity, and persistence required to bring that insight into reality. Enterprise consists, in other words, of noticing possibilities that others fail to see and, second, of practicing the skills and aptitudes necessary to their realization.

Related to enterprise is the more general virtue of creativity. For personal economic enterprise is not socially sustainable unless would-be entrepreneurs are supported by a social intelligence covering many areas—law, banking and finance, governmental administration, the arts, journalism, education, scientific and industrial research, and even religion and philosophy.

In fact, the virtue of creativity is so central to the capitalist society that, contrary to most of our dictionaries and economic textbooks, which tend to take their definitions of capitalism from Marx (of all sources), I define it as the economic system whose institutions are designed to nourish creativity in every sphere of life. As every virtue is accompanied by characteristic vices, so capitalist societies are often swept by a lust for novelty for its own sake; but such vices help to define the contours of the virtue. Perhaps Jean-Jacques Servan-Schreiber in *The American Challenge* might be credited with calling public attention in recent years to this aspect of capitalist development, noting, for example, that half the business of U.S. chemical companies in 1967 was based on products that had not even existed ten years earlier. But Ludwig von Mises and Friedrich von Hayek had long been making the same point.

Capitalism, then, is the economic system whose central animating dynamic is invention, discovery, enterprise—in short, creative mind. Such a system *uses* private property, markets, and the incentive of profits, of course, but these ancient institutions alone do not define it. For traditional, precapitalist societies (such as biblical Jerusalem) also had private property, markets, and profits, as do the precapitalist societies of contemporary Latin America and Africa, and parts of Asia. Thus, the recognition of intellectual property, as in the patent and copyright clause of the U.S. Constitution of 1787 (Article 1, Section 8), was a decisive moment in the history of modern capitalism. As the prime analogue of property, this clause supplanted land with the inventions of the mind. It thereby helped to set in motion not only an immense transformation in the productive capacities of the human race, but also the process which today, through computers, electronics, and miniaturization, is placing the irradiations of the human mind in more and more of the things we produce and use: in our cameras, our autos, our communications, our financial methods, etc. Under capitalism, the material world is becoming, so to speak, more and more mind.

A fourth, and often overlooked, virtue of the democratic capitalist regime is a special kind of communitarian living. It is often said that socialist societies strengthen bonds of community, whereas capitalist societies engender "excessive individualism." Empirically, however, existing socialist societies often appear to place the quiet of the graveyard over most of the forms of genuine community that humans have known. By contrast, capitalist societies abound in many varieties of frank and friendly association, in a great deal of teamwork, in habits of openness and easy companionship that are marvelous to see and to experience.

It is true that community in the sociologist's sense, *Gemeinschaft*—that long and close binding of village life over many generations with persons of the same faith and interests and family connections—is less possible in dynamic and mobile societies. Nonetheless, the ancient dictum that humans are social animals is clearly validated in capitalist societies. There is said to be much loneliness in such societies, but, granting that a certain loneliness is inherent in personal liberty, most economic activities under contemporary capitalism—with their committees and their meetings and their consultations— are nothing if not associational.

Finally, there is *competitiveness*, which is universally recognized as a quality called forth by capitalist societies, but is almost always treated as a vice. Yet competitiveness is both a sentinel of economic fairness and a defense against monopolistic collusion, not only in the economic sphere but also in the realms of morality and religion, not to mention politics. As a famous passage in *The Federalist* puts it:

> The great security against a gradual concentration of the several powers in the same department consists in giving to those who administer each department the necessary constitutional means and *personal motives* to resist encroachments of the others. The provision for defense must in this, as in all other cases, be made commensurate to the danger of attack. Ambition must be made to counteract ambition. The *interests of the man* must be connected with the constitutional rights of the place. It may be a reflection on human nature that such devices should be necessary to control the abuses of government. But what is government itself but the greatest of all reflections on human nature? If men were angels, no government would be necessary. If angels were to govern men, neither external nor internal controls on government would be necessary. [Emphasis added]

Apart from calling forth these (and other) new virtues, democratic capitalist societies are rooted in certain spiritual values without which they could scarcely have been imagined, let alone have come into existence.

From the beginning the claim was made of democratic capitalist societies that they were built to the pattern of "the system of natural liberty." The implication was that such a system would belong to all humans, wherever they might be. It would be adaptable to local customs, histories, traditions, and cultures, provided only that these opened the institutional ways to universal human capacities for reflection and choice—in politics, economics, and the realm of conscience and culture. The system was not designed for Jews or Christians only, or for Anglo-Saxons or Frenchmen; it was designed for all human beings.

This claim is not forfeited by the historical fact that the insights and practices which originally led to the development of the necessary institutions arose first in lands deeply shaped by the teachings of Judaism and Christianity. That democratic capitalism was embryonically realized first in such lands was, of course, "no accident." Judaism and Christianity are, in an important way, religions of history and, consequently, religions of liberty. Although no one sees God, and no one can form an idea of God commensurate with His reality, humans are led by the Bible to imagine that He sees, chooses, acts. And humans, according to the Bible as well, are made in His image. In their capacity to reflect and to choose—and to create, in the sense appropriate to their limits—they are made like unto Him. Time itself is imagined as revealing the narrative of His compact with them—a compact into which they have freely entered. History is the story of how humans live out their end of this bargain.

In this philosophical-theological vision, every single human being has dignity, is in a way sacred, because of his capacity to reflect and to choose; a covenant freely entered into is the highest model to which human communities aspire. Civilization is imagined to be an ideal city in which humans address one another, not through force or coercion, but through the conversation of reason.

It was out of such beliefs that the words of Thomas Jefferson in the Declaration of Independence ultimately flowed:

> We hold these truths to be self-evident: That all men are created equal; that they are endowed by their Creator with certain unalienable rights; that among these are life, liberty, and the pursuit of happiness; that to secure these rights, governments are instituted among men, deriving their just powers from the consent of the governed; that whenever any form of government becomes destructive of these ends, it is the right of the people to alter or to abolish it, and to institute new government, laying its foundation on such principles, and organizing its powers in such form, as to them shall seem most likely to effect their safety and happiness.

To say, however, that a "system of natural liberty" seems to flow directly from the convictions of Jews and Christians about human nature and destiny, is to say neither that free societies are limited solely to those who hold such beliefs, nor that the details of such societies actually were or could have been worked out only by believing Jews and Christians. Indeed, many of the insights and many of the practical institutional experiments that were indispensable to the eventual development of democratic capitalist societies were first championed by the pagan cultures of Greece and Rome and, later, by some who had set their faces against Judaism and Christianity. Furthermore, in recent decades, the success of Japan and of other societies outside the Judeo-Christian orbit in emulating the democratic capitalist model of development has afforded conclusive proof of the American Founders' claims concerning *natural* liberty: that is, a liberty belonging and available not solely to Jews or Christians, but to all.

What then of the future?

In 1949 there were only forty-eight nations to sign the Universal Declaration of Human Rights of the United Nations, whereas today the list of nations has expanded to 166. Many experiments in ideology and system-building have been tried, and their dismal outcomes have been observed. In particular, the death of the socialist ideal—at least within socialist nations, if not among many intellectuals and clerics in the capitalist world—seems to have cleared the way for fresh assessments and for the firm establishment of a number of propositions:

1. Even under the power of states, secret police, and torturers, individual conscience exerts its strength, and instills an awareness of inalienable rights in the soul.
2. Some form of democratic-republican governance is the most reliable protection for these rights, the best institutional means for "securing" them.
3. A free economy is a necessary, but not sufficient, condition for the successful practice of democracy.
4. A free moral and cultural life—freedom of conscience, information, and ideas—is indispensable both for democracy and for economic development.

5. A free economy, giving rightful place to personal economic initiative and human capacities for creativity, is the best systemic means for achieving some rapid liberation from poverty.

6. The cause of the wealth of nations is, most of all, the creative mind—invention, discovery, personal and associative enterprise—and the free institutions that support it.

That all this should be on the way to universal recognition and acceptance is wonderfully heartening, but too high a note of optimism is not yet to be sounded. Human beings always say they want liberty, Dostoyevsky warned, but the first thing they do, once they obtain it, is hand it back. Moreover, much that is promising never comes to fruition; and horrible evils sometimes spring from what appears to the naked eye as a highly civilized and prosperous people—as from Germany in this century.

Even apart from such possible disasters, the essence of democratic capitalism, organized around the creative mind, is a precarious instability. The most stable societies on earth, liberal societies, are always changing. It would take only a generation of citizens who have forgotten their founding principles and all the lessons of experience to set in motion a precipitous and calamitous slide.

Thus, even on the highly dubious Hegelian assumption that history can come to an end, it is surely a little premature to announce that it has. Institutions that carry through the three liberations of politics, economics, and culture remain still to be erected over most of the earth's surface. And even where these institutions already exist, their future depends precisely on the capacity to replenish the spiritual abundance that gave them birth. But to this there is an upside. For far from facing the boredom and the vacuity that writers like Fukuyama fear, those who live under democratic capitalist regimes still have as much work before them—spiritual and spiritually nourishing work—as they and their forebears ever had to accomplish in the past.

· 4 ·

CIVIL SOCIETY AND
SELF-GOVERNMENT

After the fall of the evil collectivist regime that insisted on "the scientific study of atheism," and that so dominated world history in the twentieth century, what is to be said about the construction of a normal, decent, human society? This question is of vital import for the young democracies of East and Central Europe; it is also crucial for more "seasoned" experiments in democracy.

1. Atheism v. Atheists

A sound analysis must start at the beginning. The foundational error of communism—the error that led Leo XIII to predict in 1891 that communism could not and would not work, that it was not only evil but futile—was its atheism. More exactly perhaps, its *dialectical materialist* atheism. For one can imagine—one has some-

---

This essay was first delivered as a lecture for the Civic Institute in Prague, where its theme of the turn from state to civil society had a powerful resonance; it was later published in an abridged form as "The Future of Civil Society" in *Crisis*, October 1996.

times encountered (in the American philosopher Sidney Hook, for example)—an atheist who is not a materialist but a humanist. Such atheists have a sense of irony and tragedy, and an instinct for community and compassion; and they grasp and defend the rules of right reason. The atheist who is also a humanist often acts like a Christian saint, and like Dr. Rieux in *The Plague*, may be recognized, in the phrase of Albert Camus, as a "secular saint."

"Take our moral philosophers, for instance," Camus once wrote, "so serious, loving their neighbor and all the rest—nothing distinguishes them from Christians, except that they don't preach in churches" (*The Fall*). As I wrote in an early book of mine, *Belief and Unbelief*, it is not always easy to distinguish the practical actions of a Jewish or Christian believer from those of an unbeliever who is a humanist. In the end, it is only God who judges the souls of women and men.

Still, atheism is a fundamental error about the possibilities open to humankind. Like a guillotine, it cuts off horizons that are in fact open. It foreshortens the human perspective. The religious impulse is as universal and deep in humans as the love for music—even deeper. At the same time, it is possible for humans, even those who love music, not to have an ear for it, not to be able, on their own, to carry a tune accurately (I am one such). Similarly, it is possible for those who respect religion, and know its power and its rightful place, not to have an ear for it, as Friedrich Hayek confessed in *The Fatal Conceit* that he, alas, did not.

For reasons such as this, it is important for believers not to pass judgment on the state of soul of professed atheists. Some of them may in the depths of their consciences be as faithful to the light of honesty, compassion, and courage as it is given to them to be. With such light as they have, they may be in God's eyes more pleasing in their fidelity than those to whom religious faith is given, but whose actual fidelity is less concrete.

In trying in draconian fashion to force humans to believe that they are no more than random and temporary units of matter, destined for immediate oblivion, communism was obliged to deny far too many daily experiences. Looking at the curve of one's infant granddaughter's ears, looking into the innocence and wonder in her eyes, basking in her smile, one is tempted to such wonder and rejoicing as cannot be stifled. All around us, as the sociologist Peter Berger has put it, are "rumors of angels." To be on constant guard against these inbreaking intimations of the infinite, even the divine, requires a fierce and heroic discipline—and, in the end, one that is as self-mutilating as that imposed upon youthful Spartan militants of old or, in our own time, on the Nazi *Einsatzgruppen* (extermination units) inured to the cruelty commanded of them.

Let me put this in another way. Among many of those confined to the prisons and torture chambers of the twentieth century, who entered prison as atheists or agnostics, there were not a few who decided at a certain moment *not under any circumstances to continue cooperating with the lie*. Such persons learned through terror the difference between the lie and truth, and no matter the consequences entrusted themselves to truth. So long as their minds were intact, they came to recognize, no one could separate them from this truth—this commitment never again to cooperate with lies. In such truth, they found shelter against injustice, cruelty, and brutal power. And many came to believe, in Solzhenitsyn's words, that one word of truth is more powerful than all the arms of the world. In 1989, that miracle year, so truth proved to be. And in this agonized way many came to the threshold of hope. In the experience of many, no God appeared to them in the darkness. And yet they knew, at last, what it is like to believe in God—to trust in the light, against the lie.

They were aware of being in the presence of a darkling light, an imperative, a calling, which they did not wish to refuse. For some, the force they felt inwardly remained nameless. For others, it slowly became recognizable as what is meant by the classic Jewish and Christian terms for the unknown, unseen God. No one has seen God, St. John tells us. Only by this do you know if you love God: if you have love for one another—i.e., not by what you see, but by what you are led to do. Belief does not show itself to us by presenting us with an object, but by involving us in action in and with a subject from whose presence we draw strength.

Thus, in trying to cut humans off by force from the transcendent origin of their own knowing and loving, communism undid itself. Its project was futile from the first. In its very prisons and torture cells, it turned itself inside out. Its official materialism forced into evidence a nonmaterial love for truth, as opposed to the enforced official lies. And this, in turn, awakened silent reflection on the human significance of the indestructible instinct for truth in the human heart, no matter the material consequences. Why would anyone do something so lacking in pragmatism as to remain faithful to that instinct? What does that instinct say about the nature and existence of man? Despite itself, communism awakened wonder.

In that silent wonder, a new vision of the future of humanity was awakened, after and beyond communism, which had proved itself metaphysically shallow and experientially unlivable—a vision of a new "city on the hill," a new city of man (which *might* also be a city of

God, if conceived of in an intelligent way, avoiding the mistakes of the past. The possibility of building a new city on the ruins of communism was no longer foreclosed).

What will this new civilization of man look like? That is the primary question dogging the imagination of all European civilization, at the very heart of Europe in the new democracies, but also in the whole world.

After establishing beyond the shadow of a doubt that atheism is like a snake's skin, unable to contain the bursting dynamism of the human mind, communism made one other thing clear: that a city organized solely as a state is bound to be tyrannical, airless, suffocating, and doomed to debility. Thus there was awakened at the heart of Europe a spontaneous outcry for the air and oxygen of "the civic forum."

2. Civil Society

As has been recognized since the time of Adam Ferguson in Scotland (1723–1816), civil society is a larger, more supple, airy, sun-filled social reality than the iron rods and stiff, formal structures designated by the term "state." Civil society is constituted by conversations among free persons, associating themselves in a thousand inventive ways to accomplish their own social purposes, either with or entirely independent of the state. Civil society is the internet, the web, that self-governing citizens construct for themselves over time, sometimes tacitly and un-self-consciously, and at times with full explicit purpose and deliberate voluntary choice. Village associations, regional societies, national (or even international) voluntary associations such as the Boy Scouts, Red Cross, professional organizations of economists and filmmakers and the like—all these and multitudes more, from stock associations and commercial boards and organized markets under written and unwritten rules, to athletic leagues and the international Olympics, constitute civil society in all its imaginative vitality.

But civil society is not an unambiguous term. Under the Austro-Hungarian Empire, for example, the term "civil society" sometimes connoted an informal network of aristocratic and other hereditary powers, who exercised considerable political authority behind the veils of state power. In other words, "civil society" was a euphemism for informal power parallel to, undergirding, and sometimes actually directing (as if with a puppeteer's strings) the exercise of an often weaker state power. Civil society in this sense was a cover for real power. To it and to its hereditary and often tacit laws, the emperor himself frequently bowed.

The Habsburg talent, it has often been said, lay in forging informal consent among the disparate parts of the empire, chiefly through leaders whose authority derived from tradition. These the emperor did not so much command as gently and sagaciously herd toward tacit consensus, for their own mutual self-interest, and in the name of the practical common good of their subjects. That there was good faith and practical wisdom in these arrangements is evidenced by their longevity, and also by the relative loyalty they evoked in their subjects over many generations.

Nonetheless, such a regime was necessarily less meritocratic than suits modern ideas of liberty and self-realization; less permeable by upward mobility than satisfies "subjects" longing to become "citizens"; and less open to the ideals of a new sort of city, the democratic city, which Tocqueville observed providence bringing about in America. These new democratic ideals, Tocqueville predicted, would later move the souls of Europeans and others around the world. He was at least partly right. From the ashes of the ancien régime left by the two world wars, a regime more in tune with "the system of natural liberty" has everywhere been struggling to be born. Accurate emphasis falls upon *struggling*.

Thus, we must be careful to point out that what we mean by "civil society" today is not the civil society of the old Habsburg era, the civil society of the ancien régime as experienced in say, Spain, but a civil society conceived of after the American model. The ideal we seek need not be (should not be) exactly like the American model, but should certainly be closer to it than to the ancien régime past.

But what is the American model? Many commentators, especially those on the Continent but also those Americans infected with Continental ideas of a socialist, Rousseauian, collectivist cast, think that what dominates the American imagination is *the individual*, the Lone Ranger, the lonely cowboy riding carefree on the prairie, the free and unconnected atomic self, the do-as-he-pleases outlaw on the frontier beyond the laws of the city. By contrast, Europeans, a visitor observes, tend to fear the independent individual; they visibly prefer people tied down by a thousand gossamer Gulliver's threads of tradition, custom, and unquestioning willingness to do as things have always been done. Europeans prefer solidarity, in this sense (not the only sense): communal intensity.

Americans experience this difference in virtually every European hotel they check into; they encounter many things that cannot be done, because they have never yet been done. Turned toward them frequently is a highly visible (and irritating) European complacence, that this is the way things ought to be—and that Americans should learn better manners. A specter haunts Europe still—the specter of the free individual questioning the rationality of custom, tradition, and habit; the individual who is communitarian, but not wholly defined by his community.

Nonetheless, despite its reputation, the American character is not the exact opposite of the European character—is not purely individualistic—but communitarian without being intensely communal. The true inner heart of America, as Tocqueville grasped right at the beginning, is the art of association. In America, fifty years after the ratification of the Constitution of 1787 (itself a model of the art of association), Tocqueville observed thousands of associations, societies, clubs, organizations, and fraternities invented by a self-governing people unaccustomed to being told by the state (or even by custom) what to do and when to do it. At the time of the Revolution in France, he wrote, he did not think there were ten men in all of France who were capable of practicing the art of association as most Americans practiced it.

In the new science of politics, Tocqueville added, the art of association is the first law of democracy. This art does not belong to Americans only. It is rooted in the social nature of man. Its source does not lie in the authority of the state (as in France) or of the aristocracy (as in Britain), but in the capacity of all citizens to originate cooperative activities with their fellows, without being commanded from above. The American is not the individual par excellence, but the practitioner of association par excellence. The American is through and through a social being. Virtually nothing significant gets done in America apart from free associations, of a virtually infinite number of kinds. In this view, the primary agency of the common good is civil society; the state is secondary. The practice of forming associations for civic purposes is called civic republicanism.

In America, even the churches come to be conceived of as associations, formed out of the decisions of individuals either to associate themselves with historical communities or to form new sects never seen before. In practice, this conception of churches as associations has gained considerable plausibility, even for Catholics and Jews, who did not historically think of their communions in so individualistic a way. After all, when immigrants arrived in America, they could choose whether or not to continue in the faith they brought with them in the habits of their hearts. A great many chose not to. Nonetheless, probably a majority of both Christians and Jews elected to re-create communities of faith in the New World, in continuity with their fellows in Europe.

In America, however, this choice did not mean continuing to worship in a building older than six or more centuries, as it would have meant in their native villages in Europe. In America, if there were to be any churches, the people would have to build them themselves—and priests would have to be found to lead them in worship. America was a missionary land. There was no church structure, already there, for them to inherit. Voluntarily, without state help, they would have to build church organizations themselves, beyond the reach of European habits and methods and ways of thinking.

Even so, the meaning of "association" is not the same for Catholics and Jews as it is for Protestants. For Protestants, sects are formed by the free choice of individuals banding together. For Jews and Catholics, the community of faith does not originate in their personal free choices but in the authority of God; they freely join in a covenant that long preexists their personal response to it. Their individual choice is not constitutive, but responsive. This difference in understanding entails two different understandings of such other concepts as autonomy, the relation of the individual to the community, and the relation of conscience to tradition. (Tradition is the community of the living, the dead, and those yet to come; it is, as Chesterton called it, "the democracy of the dead.")

The religious "establishment" in the United States, insofar as it existed, was in many colonies before the Revolution of 1776 the Church of England, and in some others one or another of the Protestant sects descending from the dissidents who had abandoned the Church of England either in Britain or on coming to America; and in Pennsylvania, the Quakers, Moravians, and Amish. Catholics and Jews were regarded as "different," but on the whole they were shown toleration and even, as President Washington put it in a letter to the Jewish community of Newport, Rhode Island, more than toleration, respect.

The American understanding of "church" and even "religion," however, has contained from the beginning certain deficiencies, which have lately become apparent. To these deficiencies we will shortly return.

3. Four Characteristics of Civil Society

The American conception of civil society, meanwhile, may be outlined swiftly in four propositions:

1. "Civil society" is a larger and deeper concept than "state." Civil society is a moral reality conceptually prior to the state. To revolve power from the state to civil society is at the heart of the experiment in self-government. Self-governing citizens try to meet their social needs first through creating their own social organizations, and only as a last resort, when all else fails, through turning to the state. Turning to the state is considered a morally inferior, although sometimes necessary, way of proceeding—a falling away from the project of self-reliance and self-government.

2. *The primary social institution of democracy is religion.* "The first political institution of democracy," Tocqueville wrote, is the churches and synagogues. The reason for this is twofold.

First, as Vatican Council II stressed, freedom of conscience is the first of all freedoms; it lies deeper than, and beyond the reach of, political institutions. ("Congress shall make no law respecting an establishment of religion, or prohibiting the free exercise thereof"—the First Amendment. "Nor shall any religious test ever be required as a qualification to any office or public trust under the United States"—Art. VI.) The inner forum of conscience is beyond the reach of the political power, and morally prior to it. That is the meaning of the two American maxims: "One nation under God" and "In God we trust." Even for atheists, the term "God" in these public maxims is intended as a sentinel protecting the realm of conscience (including the consciences of atheists) from the power of the state.

Second, as the historian of liberty Lord Acton noted, the concept and practice of liberty are in historical fact coincident with the history of Judaism and, even more so, Christianity. The decision of the Council of Jerusalem to baptize the Gentiles, without demanding that they first be circumcised, cut the link between birth as a son of a Jewish mother and faith, therefore invoking liberty of spirit as the primary condition of faith. The ideal of liberty in its full range, from liberty of conscience to liberty of speech, and including civil and political liberties, does not appear in Muslim, Hindu, Buddhist, Confucian, Shinto, or Animist cultures.

Thus, to weaken the churches and synagogues is to dilute the source of convictions about personal liberty from which the concept and practice of civil society flow. Here, surely, is one reason why the Communists were determined to destroy the churches and synagogues. Judaism and Christianity depend on, and defend like tigers, liberty of conscience.

Another reason why church and synagogue are central institutions of civil society is that they encourage their members to take up their social responsibilities in other civic institutions.

3. *The separation of church and state, yes, but also the inseparability of politics and religion.* As the twenty-first century approaches, after the experience of communism, one urgent need is as clear as Bohemian crystal: the need for a limited state; under the rule of law; with multiple checks and balances; and also other protections to rein in the power of the state. Among these protections is the disestablishment of the churches. The power of the state should not be enhanced by its identification with religion. Churches need to be free from state power. This is the case even in countries like Poland or Spain where the vast majority are Catholic.

Nonetheless, the separation of the coercive power of the state and the spiritual/moral *power* of the churches, as institutions, does not mean that the concrete human being should become schizophrenic. It would be a violation of integrity for a human person to be split down the middle between being a political animal on one side and, in a separate compartment, a privatized spiritual/moral animal. The separation of church and state does not entail sealing off, in the minds of individuals, watertight compartments between religion and politics. On the contrary, the deepest motives for loving liberty, respecting the dignity of the person, and feeling identification with the life of the earthly city are religious. Psychologists (Allport, e.g.) find that religion is rooted more "deeply" in the psyche than politics; most people change their religion much more reluctantly than their politics. Religion is a matter of conviction; politics, a matter of practical judgment. On its many levels of consciousness, the human soul ought not to be divided against itself.

Therefore, public policy inquiries that affect both the polity and religion stir the souls of individuals in complex ways. Whether the issue is abortion, euthanasia, sex education, the roles of females and males, family life, or a host of other difficult questions, the intelligent person is likely to struggle with two different sets of criteria— moral and religious, on the one side, and political or social, on the other side. Tangled issues on both sides must be clarified, and then a judgment reached that does justice to both.

It is wise, of course, not to confuse political reasoning with religious reasoning; even in the same person, these two modes are not the same. But the person of integrity cannot abandon either one. There are cases in which practical wisdom demands that one or the other must be given precedence. (Some things judged to be immoral are, for practical motives, not made illegal; they are tolerated, lest worse evils result.) It is always a mistake, however, to simplify one's decision making simply by cutting one side of one's mind out of the discussion and ramming through a partially considered decision.

4. Religion has a rightful place in the public square. Religion and politics do not meet only in the privacy of the heart; they also meet—and sometimes clash—in the public square. Here both the Protestant and the secular (libertarian) points of view sometimes fail to do justice to the realities involved. In many cases, it is imagined that religion is a mostly private matter, best confined

within the closet of the individual's soul (or "preferences," as libertarians might be inclined to say). In their
view, the "liberal society" depends upon a bargain: religion will be tolerated, even respected, but only so long
as it is confined within the private closets of the heart,
and agrees never to enter the public square. As the
French political philosopher Pierre Manent has recently
written, the secular project

> does not affirm, with 'the foolish' of Scripture, that 'there
> is no God.' Not only does it say nothing about God, but it
> says nothing, or very little, about the world, and even
> about man. However, by positing that the political body
> has for its only rule or law the will of the individuals who
> compose it, it deprives the law of God of all political au-
> thority or validity, whether the latter is conceived as ex-
> plicitly revealed, or solely inscribed in the nature of man.
> . . . The man of the enlightenment implies, or presup-
> poses, that there is no God, or that He is unconcerned
> with men, since he rejects, or at most considers as 'pri-
> vate' and optional obedience to the law of God.

For Jews, Catholics, and others, this type of liberalism
is oppressive, for in their understanding religion has a
social and public dimension, just as each human being
has. True religion does not consist solely in prayers conducted in private, but also in helping the widow, feeding
the hungry, caring for the poor—and building up the city
of man. Religion requires action in the world. Religion
requires vitality, civil argument, and cooperative action
in the public square. The individualistic and privatizing
understanding of religion, whether of certain Protestants
or of some libertarians, is too cramped and narrow. Religion ought not to be established; but neither ought it to
be confined in merely private places. Religious persons
must be free to express their arguments in the public

square, and to take part in public actions. They ought to do so with conspicuous civility, but they ought to do so.

The public square should not be naked or empty. It should ring with civil argument about how a free people ought to order its life together. In that argument, religious people ought to have a voice—in practice, many voices.

4. Avoiding Two Mistakes of the Past

Both secular and religious thinkers need to be crystal clear that the relation between church and state in the twenty-first century cannot be, and should not be, the same as their relation prior to the advent of communism. This is particularly the case with the new democracies of Eastern and Central Europe, who have emerged from under the rubble of state socialism. In such countries, the church once owned much land and many buildings put up in the past, many of which were unjustly confiscated by the communists in 1948. A democratic state ought not to be complicit in the continuation of this injustice.

Further, the church once enjoyed many privileges that harken back to an aristocratic period. Not all such reminders of the past ought to be abolished; Great Britain has successfully blended ancient traditions with modern adaptations. It is usually a mistake to try to wipe the slate of history clean—another "fatal conceit," born of "the murderous spirit of abstraction." Nevertheless, care must be taken not to claim for the church in a democratic age trappings deemed appropriate for earlier ages but scandalous by democratic standards.

On the other side, a libertarianism that weakens social bonds in the name of the atomic individual (another abstraction) is in practice a form of statism. It reintroduces "democratic centralism" by the ironic route of ideological individualism. It renders the individual helpless and needy. It tempts the omnivorous state to reoccupy empty civic space. Apart from civil society, supported by solid institutions (especially those with international anchors), there is no power that keeps the state within its proper limits. Among these anchors are international associations of economists and other scholars, as well as the churches, the Red Cross, etc.

Thus, those nonbelievers who remember abuses prevalent in unhappy arrangements from the past, especially in the field of church-state relations, must not fashion from such memories blinders that restrict their vision of the future.

In the post-Marxist period opening in front of us, a new future in the relations between the state and the church is already taking shape. As a particular aspect of those relations, the Polish theologian Maciej Zieba writes:

> A clear definition of the political role of the Church in a democratic society is necessary. The Church may opt to become the subject of a political game, participating in the mechanisms of legislation, exercising power in the state. But it could also consciously resign from a share in concrete legal solutions and political games and concentrate on the metapolitical sphere. The Church's proper action in that sphere would be the renewal and building of social consensus, in the light of moral values and the vision of the human vocation proclaimed by the Gospel.

5. The Great Reversal

Earlier, I mentioned weaknesses in the U.S. practice of church-state relations. One of these weaknesses is the assumption that religion belongs in the closet of privatized sentiment—not of conviction, but only sentiment; not a fruit of the critical mind, but only of the feelings. Actually, in this formulation, two mistakes are intertwined: first, that religion is a merely private internal matter; second, that religion is relativized, has nothing to do with mind or truth, but only expresses a preference or a feeling, without grounding in a judgment about reality. Here the writings of Pierre Manent offer light.

At the founding of the democratic experiment, toward the end of the Enlightenment, democracy seemed strong and religion weak. Democracy commanded that religion accept certain demands: Religion would be tolerated if it agreed to be individualized, privatized, and relativized. Not only on pragmatic grounds, but for serious reasons of its own (having to do with the dignity of persons and an ideal of charity—caritas—as the form of human community), the Jewish and Christian communities agreed to play by the rules democrats prescribed.

But what has happened? Within two centuries, democracy has been diminished into a contest among special interests and a formalism of correct procedure. Democracy says little or nothing about man. It lacks a vision or even a clear statement of the criteria that any vision of a good society for free women and free men would have to meet. By affirming that it is sovereign over human nature and that it is, little by little, its own creator, with no plan laid down in advance, democratic humanity basically declares that it wills itself, without knowing itself. The churches, not without "a benevolence tinged with irony," as Pierre Manent puts it, accept this. Nonetheless, Manent continues,

The political submission of the Church to democracy is, perhaps, finally, a fortunate one. The Church willy-nilly conformed herself to all of democracy's demands. Democracy no longer, in good faith, has any essential reproach to make against the Church. From now on the church can hear the question which it alone poses, the question *Quid sit homo*—What is man? But democracy neither wants to nor can respond to this question in any manner or form. On democracy's side of the scale, we are left with political sovereignty and dialectical impotence. On the Church's side, we are left with political submission and dialectical advantage. The relation unleashed by the Enlightenment is today reversed. No one knows what will happen when democracy and the Church become aware of this reversal.

Finding the proper relation between state and civil society, and especially between the state and the church, is still a work in progress. No country seems to have gotten it quite right, just yet. But there is no question, compared to the youthful pride of two hundred years ago, that the arrogance of the democratic state has been curbed. Cynicism regarding politicians grows. The social assistance state and its budgetary resources are in crisis. Public and private morals tumble into decline.

The free society is a noble cause, but it is maintained only through constant vigilance. And such vigilance depends upon a firm idea of the possibilities and duties of humankind, the conditions demanded by natural liberty, and a commitment to distinguishing lies from truth. No one may "possess" the truth, but all must be committed to pursuing evidence wherever it leads; in that sense, all must remain open to truth. Truth is as necessary to liberty as air to fire.

In one of history's sweetest ironies, it is today a pope, Pope John Paul II, who publicly defends reason and the idea of truth in the face of deconstructionists, postmodernists, and other children of the Enlightenment, who are nowadays renouncing both reason and truth, and basing themselves on a metaphysic that recognizes only raw interests and disguised power. The pope defends reason, which the Enlightened scorn. The pope speaks for truth discernible by reason, while the Enlightened deny the possibility of truth, and clothe themselves in the interests of class, race, gender, and power. Speaking for reason and truth, this philosophical pope writes:

> If there is no transcendent truth, in obedience to which man achieves his full identity, then there is no sure principle for guaranteeing just relations between people. Their self-interest as a class, group or nation would inevitably set them in opposition to one another. If one does not acknowledge transcendent truth, then the force of power takes over, and each person tends to make full use of the means at his disposal in order to impose his own interests or his own opinion, with no regard for the rights of others.

In summary, it appears that Tocqueville was right in saying that without belief in a Creator to Whom everything that is is intelligible, because He understood it before He created it, and everything is graced and good because He loves it, the foundations of democracy are weak and likely to fail. As Pope John Paul II writes:

> Only God, the Supreme Good, constitutes the unshakable foundation and essential condition of morality, and thus of the commandments, particularly those negative commandments which always and in every case prohibit behavior and actions incompatible with the personal dignity of every man.

It has not yet dawned on democratic humanists that the ecology of liberty rests upon a certain limited range of understandings both about human nature and about "the system of natural liberty." Without a concept of truth, people cannot reason with each other or converse with each other in the light of evidence. Without a commitment to truth, reason is irrelevant, only power matters. As civilization is constituted by conversation, so conversation is rooted in fidelity to truth: not the "possession" of truth, but openness to the light of appropriate evidence.

The democratic state depends upon a lively civil society, full of civil argument and vital conversation, conducted under the light of evidence. This, too, is one of the reasons why civil society depends upon religion (certain types of religion). Religions, certainly those that speak of the Creator and Final Judgment, keep alive in consciences standards of truth beyond their own preferences.

· 5 ·

THE CRISIS OF THE
WELFARE STATE

In the end each nation is no more than a flock of
timid and hardworking animals with government
as its shepherd.

—Alexis de Tocqueville[1]

For Alan Greenspan, Chairman of the Federal Reserve
Board in the United States, the decisive economic
event of our time was the collapse of the Berlin Wall in
late 1989. The outside light which then flooded East
Germany revealed the outcome of the forty-year experiment in socialist economics, in stark contrast to the capitalist economics in West Germany. Both parts of Germany had shared the same culture and history; both had
been reduced to ruins by World War II; both had had to
start over from ground zero. "It is as near as social scientists ever get to observing a controlled experiment,"
Greenspan says. For the hypothesis that socialist economic theory is superior to Western theories of political
economy, the results were devastating.

First delivered at a conference on welfare reform in Rome,
Italy, sponsored by the publishing house Mondadori in 1997;
revised for publication in a symposium of the Institute of Economic Affairs in London, U.K., in 1998.

Ten years after the fall of the Wall, even though heavily subsidized, East Germany is still a very poor cousin of West Germany. The most dramatic costs of the socialist experiment are measured in the loss of human capital, including the work ethic, entrepreneurship, and habits of risk, trust, and creativity.

Moreover, the collapse of "real existing socialism" in its stronghold in the former Soviet Union has had a ripple effect through the structures of international socialism elsewhere. For it demonstrated to all that as an economic theory socialism is seriously flawed, and that the socialist analysis of capitalist economies was also incorrect.

This collapse of the economic principles of socialism affected not only communism but all those other doctrines and ideals that rest in part on socialist economic theories, including social democracy. Communist and socialist parties around the world hurried to change their official names, usually to some euphemism such as "social democratic." Yet even in those parties having a genuine claim to the good name of social democracy, birth rates are falling; senior citizens are living longer; advances in health care grow ever more costly; and the ratio of active workers to pensioners has already dropped to nearly three to one or worse, and is projected to continue dropping rapidly.[2] In these circumstances social democratic parties are adopting economic policies favoring enterprise, job creation, profits, reinvestment and personal incentives.

1. The New Terrain

Thus, the election of Tony Blair in Britain in 1997, and the conception of New Labour which enabled him to triumph, far from vindicating social democracy, in fact confirmed its transformation, and in a way that has important consequences for Britain, Italy and, indeed, all of Europe. Many commentators in Europe and elsewhere have noted that the triumph of Tony Blair may in one sense be regarded as the triumph of Margaret Thatcher. Blair's New Labour has adopted a political project (and a social ideal) inconceivable for Labour fifteen, ten, or even five years ago. After her election in 1978, Margaret Thatcher demonstrated that the world had changed fundamentally and radically. By launching Great Britain on a trajectory of growth and opportunity that lasted, with some inevitable setbacks, for twenty years, the Iron Lady weaned New Labour from a sterile and punitive redistributionism, on the one hand, and from the enervating Nanny State, on the other. She taught Blair the importance of growth, opportunity, and incentives. Only so could Tony Blair ride to triumph.

It appears that many (although not all) on the European Left have learned this lesson, including the recently elected Socialist Party in France. Leaders of the European Left are accustomed to lead social change, not to follow, and in the main to change their own course rather than to fail. As long as they can protect (as they see it) the ends they have in view—equality, compassion, amelioration of the lot of the poor, etc.—they fairly easily adjust to new means: new tactics, new strategies, even new visions of the future.

Consider the words of John Gray of the London School of Economics, on occasion one of the most perceptive political thinkers in Europe, writing in *The Times Literary Supplement* (May 9, 1997):

Europe's social democratic regimes were established during an era of closed economies. They rested on the capacity of sovereign states to limit the free movement of capital and production through exchange controls and tariffs. They cannot survive in an environment in which capital and production exercise unfettered global mobility.

Tony Blair, Gray argues, is important because several years ago he grasped how deeply Europe's social democracies are mired in policies that belong to an irrecoverable past. The muck and mire in which social democracy is stuck, according to Gray, consists of three parts. First, once technological innovation begins wiping out entire occupations (and even industries), a labor market anchored in institutions of job security is not sustainable. Second, pension schemes that tie benefits to a single employer offer flimsy security in this new era, in which no one can be sure of having the same job across a working lifetime. Third, welfare institutions that are designed primarily to compensate people for failure and punish them for success, "are supremely unfitted for an age of globalization." From these points Gray concludes: "Unless Europe's social democracies reform themselves deeply and swiftly, they will be blown away by the gale of global competition."

If John Gray is correct, the premises of the social compact that followed after World War II have been thrown into doubt. No wonder there is much social pessimism on the Continent. No wonder the prospect of "globalization" agitates many intelligent Europeans. Their deepest worry is not just high unemployment. Nor is it the towers of debt mounting on all sides. It is a growing doubt about the basic postwar settlement.

After generations of denigrating capitalism, especially American capitalism, many of the Continent's intellectuals are for the first time doubting their traditional understanding of the word "social"—socialism, social democracy, social justice, social compact. Suddenly, they do not like one form of socialization; they do not like "globalization."

In the United States, by contrast, one most often hears optimism about globalization. (To be sure, we have our own doomsayers, economic nationalists wedded to the memories of an isolationist Fortress America. Noisy though they be, however, they do not command either political party.) The rising stock market reveals the current American temper well enough, but an anecdote may sharpen the picture. When in May 1997, the Dow Jones Industrial average stood at an all-time high of 6500 and the papers were predicting an imminent serious "correction," two economic journalists made a bet in the presence of a dozen others, that by the last day of the year 2000 the market would stand at 11,000; and no one at the dinner thought the bet unreasonable. The basis for their bet: globalization.

Several months later, the Asian crisis became evident and then the Russian crisis, then the Latin American crisis. The market shot above 9000 by July 1998, when a severe correction set in. Thus, talk of rose-colored opportunity may be wildly mistaken. Anecdotes prove nothing. They do illustrate, however, a recurrent experience: regarding globalization, the difference in psychological climate between the United States and the Continent is palpable. (Britain, with its far-flung Commonwealth connections, may share something of the U.S. optimism, while still being close enough to the Continent to share the sense of strain.)

As long ago as 1835, Alexis de Tocqueville pointed out that, compared to Europeans, Americans delight in risks, opportunities, adventures, dreams. Even today, Americans delight in the striking economic success (despite the recent "Asian crisis") of capitalist models among what

Gray called "the highly literate and numerate societies of East Asia," and look now for new opportunities as the lessons behind that crisis are learned. They also delight in "the enormous expansion of world markets consequent on the Soviet collapse and economic reform in China," and in the remarkable advances in leading sectors of Latin America (such as Chile). Some Americans conclude that, for the first time in history, the vast natural resources of the entire planet—in remote Russia, in China—will come on stream for the benefit of the common good of all humanity.

How can one explain this optimism to Europeans? In 1979, recall, President Carter and many others saw only malaise, "stagflation" and decline. Since Ronald Reagan launched foundational economic reforms in 1981, however, the U.S. economy has grown by more than one-third—added the equivalent of the whole economy of Germany, East and West, to its base—and given birth to new technologies and whole new industries never seen before. The computer industry, in 1981 insignificant, is now the nation's largest. The ranks of America's employees have swollen by more than thirty million; the unemployment rate is the lowest in thirty years. This optimism about economic prospects is not partisan; Clinton and Gore have made it their own.

2. The Cultural Crisis

Given our economic dynamism, we in the United States are nonetheless preoccupied with a different sort of crisis: a cultural crisis. Whereas in Europe the *social contract* of the era since World War II is in need of urgent reform, in the United States most analysts argue that we need urgent *cultural* reform. We need cultural reform

not only in the realm of movies and television and popular music, but also in the arena of public and private
moral life. Indeed, most Americans concur that the free
society, to maintain its vitality, depends upon a healthy
moral ecology (if one may so speak). *A free society is
primarily a moral achievement.* Free institutions cannot
be maintained, certainly their vigor cannot be maintained, on just any moral basis whatsoever. How can a
people incapable of self-government in personal life,
James Madison once asked, prove capable of self-government in public life?

From both sides of the Atlantic, therefore, although
from different patterns of evidence, our common civilization is becoming aware of mortal dangers. The structural constitution of the modern state faces two witherin-
gly severe tests over time, and if it fails to meet either of
those tests, the state may all too easily shatter on the
rocks. The first test is the test of outer reality—
economics, what is happening in other states, technological developments, globalization, etc. The second test is
the test of inner reality—what is happening to the morality and the morale of citizens. Europe most fears the first;
America the second.

A few words about the second test, the inner test, may
be useful because less familiar in public discourse. Two
decades ago, on a given Monday the Shah of Iran pre-
sided over the fifth largest army in the world, and by the
subsequent Friday, after a sudden Islamic uprising, his
army laid down its arms and he was deposed: A lesson
in the power of the human spirit over arms. One decade
ago, the events of June 1989 in Beijing and then of No-
vember 1989 in Hungary, Czechoslovakia, East Germany, Romania and elsewhere, again demonstrated the
great power of spiritual factors.

Another aspect of the cultural crisis might best be revealed in a parable. In California in the late 1960s, Gunnar Myrdal assured a public seminar that social democracy (the apple of his eye) would never weaken the virtues of the Swedish people. Years later, he issued a sorrowful public statement that, regrettably, the morals of Sweden had been weakened, perhaps irreparably; many were calling in sick when they were not sick, or declaring disability for "bad backs," etc. Similarly in the U.S.: "The state is pushing all that money out there," runs the new rationalization. "It would be naive of me not to claim my share." Dependency on state subsidies has grown in the last thirty years. That is not, of course, the only source of moral corruption in our time (along with being the source of much good); the cultural sources of corruption are many.

That the morals of the people of the United States have been corrupted for the worse during our lifetime is abundantly evident in innumerable statistical profiles: violent crime up 600 percent since 1965; births out of wedlock up 600 percent, etc. Robert Bork presents some of these indicators in *Slouching Towards Gomorrah*.[3] The Secretary of Health of the United States estimated in 1990 that 40 to 70 percent of all premature deaths in the U.S. are behavioral—that is, due to avoidable, self-damaging personal behaviors (excessive drinking, drugs, disordered sex, smoking, failing to exercise, poor diet, habits of violent behavior, etc.). Independent of a moral analysis (even if from plural points of view), the public policy costs of these unprecedented trends are stubborn and immense. The costs of crime prevention, health, and welfare have rocketed upwards. Deficits burdening future generations are incurred. Worse, current taxpayers are coerced into subsidizing self-destructive behaviors on the part of others.

Although consensus is widespread among policy experts both in Europe and in the United States about the *financial crisis* of the welfare state—its fiscal unsustainability and the impending implosion of accumulated debt that will greet a new generation in the not-too-distant future—it is the *spiritual* crisis of the welfare state that is the more severe. For the most important form of capital is human capital: the active, intelligent, creative citizen. If we are destroying our human capital, our civilization is in mortal danger.

Even years ago, Alexis de Tocqueville gave early warning about the triumph of the ideal of equality over liberty: "I am trying to imagine under what novel features despotism may appear in the world," he wrote in 1835. He imagined a type of "orderly, gentle, peaceful slavery," which under the name of equality has come to be accepted as endurable. Moved by compassion for its subjects, government

> provides for their security, foresees and supplies their necessities, facilitates their pleasures, manages their principal concerns, directs their industry, makes rules for their testaments, and divides their inheritances. It covers the whole of social life with a network of petty, complicated rules that are both minute and uniform, through which even men of the greatest originality and the most vigorous temperament cannot force their heads above the crowd. It does not break men's will, but softens, bends, and guides it; it seldom enjoins, but often inhibits, action; it does not destroy anything, but prevents much being born; it is not at all tyrannical, but it hinders, restrains, enervates, stifles, and stultifies so much that in the end each nation is no more than a flock of timid and hardworking animals with the government as its shepherd.[4]

This is the nightmare that haunts Americans.

3. Accusations against the Welfare State

It is obvious to us in the United States—certainly, to those of us born into poor families, in the midst of the depression of the 1930s—that the welfare state has done much good; indeed, has been in many ways indispensable. From programs of rural electrification to building new college campuses (on the average of one every two weeks from 1948 until 1978); from programs of farm credit to mortgage assistance; from food stamps to employment and work training programs; from income supplements (Social Security) to Medicare for senior citizens—in countless ways, federal and state governments have helped virtually all citizens to find better lives.

The argument today is not then, *whether* to have welfare programs but of what *kind*, in order to meet new conditions and to correct deficiencies and unintended consequences that sixty years of experience (since Franklin Delano Roosevelt's "New Deal") have brought to light. In addition, a sharp distinction is often made between the philosophy underlying the New Deal and the quite different philosophy underlying the "Great Society" launched by President Lyndon B. Johnson in 1964. The New Deal was based—to state the issue much too roughly—on traditional American values; the Great Society, it is alleged, introduced a new morality. Under the former, for instance, some 98 percent or so of recipients of Aid to Families with Dependent Children were widows; under the latter, nearly all benefits now go to divorced, separated, and (no questions asked, no demands made) never-married women. The spirit of the Great Society programs is both to be "nonjudgmental" and to hand out benefits without concern for reciprocity from the recipient, as if in plain and simple "entitlement."

Because of such practices, accusations such as the following have become more frequent: First, the benefits of the welfare state are too easy to obtain and too attractive to resist. We come to feel (by a multitude of rationalizations) that the state "owes" us benefits, to which we are as "entitled" as anybody else. Whether we need it or not, we would be foolish not to take what is so abundantly offered. In this way, the welfare state corrupts us—and loses control over its own mounting expenditures.

Second, in an exaggerated reaction against "individualism," U.S. liberals (in Europe, social democrats) not only tend to overemphasize "community," but also too uncritically to identify "community" with the "public sector" (the state). To act as the primary agent of community, they typically prefer the official programs of the administrative state to existing voluntary programs. Some do this even while warning themselves against the dangers embedded in bureaucratic methods (that these deny the subjectivity of the person, for example). They say that a national project generates a greater sense of "belonging" to a caring national community.

Two results seem to follow. First, the subjective sense of personal responsibility slowly atrophies, eventually breeding the "sluggishness" in welfare states on which, for instance, the Second Vatican Council commented in 1965, even while praising the welfare state.[5] Next, the administrative state steadily swallows up most of the functions that used to be exercised by civil society.[6] Mediating institutions become enfeebled.[7] Thus, the principle of subsidiarity is continually violated, as the higher levels crush the lower.

One of the most respected social commentators in the United States, Irving Kristol, cites Hegel on the descent from the virility of Republican Rome to the decadence of Imperial Rome: "The image of the State as a product of his activity disappeared from the soul of the citizen." It is far worse today, Kristol holds:

> Today, it is the mission of the welfare state to convince the citizen that he is the product of the state's activity,

> that he is an importuning subject of the state, no longer a
> citizen in the classical sense. The fully developed welfare
> state is a modern version of the feudal castle, guarded by
> moats and barriers, and offering security and shelter to
> the loyal population that gathers round it.[8]

The peoples of the welfare state have traded the inheritance of liberty that had been won for them at enormous cost in exchange for a promise of security—a promise that can no longer be met.

The welfare state softens the morals of some of its recipients, one accusation goes; another says that it penalizes the creativity and hard work of those who pay for it, too; a third, that it discourages employers from creating new jobs.

Statistics do not directly reveal how subtly this last process works. Permit me again to tell a story. In 1997, an Italian professor was talking with his barber, asking him why, since he was so busy, the barber didn't hire more help. The barber stopped cutting his hair and became agitated. "I would like to hire somebody!" he insisted. "But I have taken my pencil and counted up the costs. By the time I pay wages, and every kind of benefit, and every kind of tax, I end up losing money, and that doesn't count headaches and aggravation or my time! I would like to hire someone, I am getting old, but I can't! *Che stupidaggine!*"

Among the new critics of the welfare state is a surprising one: the pope (surprising because in Europe Catholic social thought is widely believed to be closer to social democratic thought than to *laissez-faire)*. The opinions of a pope may cut little ice in Britain, but since Catholics in several European nations tend to lean in a social democratic direction, papal criticisms of the welfare state, such as the following, shed an interesting light on the coming crisis:

By intervening directly and depriving society of its responsibility, the Social Assistance State leads to (1) a loss of human energies and (2) an inordinate increase of public agencies, which (3) are dominated more by bureaucratic ways of thinking than by concern for serving clients, and (4) are accompanied by an enormous increase in spending.[9] [enumeration added]

In displacing the action of human charity, in other words, the Social Assistance State displaces the "little platoons" that give life its properly human scale, and generates a "mass society," impersonal, ineffectual, counter-productive, and suffocating of the human spirit. In displacing the vitalities of a thick and self-governing civil society, the Social Assistance State diminishes the realm of responsible personal action.

Without question, the modern welfare state has done much good, particularly for the elderly, and yet in many nations its results for younger adults, and especially for marriage and family life, have been highly destructive. The proportion of children born out of wedlock has hit unprecedented levels in many nations, including the United States, Great Britain, and Sweden.[10] Many take this to be the most devastating piece of evidence in the case against the welfare state. Quite unintentionally, contrary to its intention, social democracy seems to injure families even in cultures in which the family has been the primary basis of strength. "Fifty years ago," adds Irving Kristol, "no advocate of the welfare state could imagine it might be destructive of that most fundamental social institution, the family. But it has been, with a poisonous flowering of those very social pathologies—crime, illegitimacy, drugs, divorce, sexual promiscuity—that it was assumed the welfare state would curb if not eliminate."

4. The Family and Welfare

It was precisely to examine such accusations that the Seminar on Family and Welfare, carefully chosen to represent both the right and the left, met together for more than one year. After considerable effort, we reached consensus on what had been achieved by welfare programs during the preceding twenty years, between 1965 and 1985—what had gone right, and what had gone wrong.[11] We also reached agreement on a long list of recommendations for reform. We hoped that we might turn the thinking of both major political parties in a new direction.

No one could deny that the lot of the elderly (those over sixty-five) had improved enormously since 1965. By 1985 a huge majority of those over sixty-five lived in their own homes (a sign of their health and independent spirits) and most of their homes were mortgage-free. The percentage living in poverty had been reduced to single digits, and this residuum was due mainly to failures to connect to existing programs, of which they were not taking advantage. The elderly were certainly living longer; by 1985, in fact, there were millions more of them than in earlier generations. Indeed, a new concern suddenly emerged for what were now called the "elderly elderly," the suddenly enlarged cohort of those over eighty-five.

The picture is quite different for young adults, whose situation was far worse in 1985 than in 1965. Violent crime was far worse; family structure was far more deeply wounded; the morale of many was far less hopeful. Moreover, our seminar discovered that the worst sufferings usually ascribed to "poverty" were, in fact, associated with family breakup. This discovery arose accidentally. In correlating various statistical tables, our research noted that: (a) of all married-couple families in the U.S., only 6.7 percent were poor. In other words, the simple fact of being married gave Americans a 93 percent chance of not being poor. These chances were further improved by two more factors: (b) completion of secondary school (which is both wholly subsidized and mandatory) and (c) full-time employment at any job, even a minimum wage job.

This glimpse of the stunning effectiveness of such fundamentals as marriage, education, and employment in reducing poverty was next matched by a closer inspection of the disabilities involved, in the United States, at least, in the lot of being a single mother. Such single moms and their children were the largest group of the U.S. poor and the fastest-growing group. In addition, their children were at far greater risk of not finishing school; not being employed or even employable; having a greater number of health problems; and being involved in the criminal justice system. The picture was far better, of course, for divorced and separated mothers, who tended to be rather more mature at the time of the divorce and separation. Such older single women tended in far higher proportions to find jobs and go off welfare within two years of going on it, and to be quite successful with their children. For the younger women, especially those who were never married, all the statistical profiles offered a bleaker prospect.

Indeed, our research turned up a group of about four million Americans between the ages of eighteen and thirty whose most serious problem was "dependency" rather than "poverty." We gave the term "dependency" a fairly precise meaning: young and healthy adults who are dependent upon the public purse; and, second, unable to fulfill their obligation toward others in their family, younger and older, who would normally be dependent upon them. In other words, they were not acting, perhaps through no fault of their own, as independent, self-sustaining citizens, on whom their own children could depend.

In addition to this, studies revealed a pronounced tendency for such persons to be caught in a *cycle of dependency*; that is, although they might be off welfare for a year or two, they tended to have frequent bouts of dependency on the public purse and, their children also tended to be dependent upon the public purse. This pattern flew against the American expectation of upward mobility. It showed that a substantial number of persons—about four million, plus their children—were not seizing the opportunity to rise out of poverty; on the contrary, they seemed to be stuck in it. This indicated something seriously wrong in the social order.

Meanwhile, millions of new immigrants who arrived on American shores poorer than the American poor, often without the knowledge of English, tended to seize opportunities and move out of poverty within four or five years. By contrast, the healthy young Americans trapped in dependency had considerably more spending money (from the public purse) and considerably less prospect of moving out of dependency. They seemed to be caught in what Hilaire Belloc and Friedrich Hayek, from quite different points of view, had described as a kind of "serfdom."

The legions of the dependent were especially concentrated in the poverty districts of the nation's one hundred largest cities. They seemed impervious to the efforts of the War on Poverty to improve their conditions; indeed, their appearance in social history seemed to coincide with the War on Poverty. To be perfectly clear about this, we found little evidence that the War on Poverty caused the new dependency among so many. But there was a great deal of evidence for the judgment that the War on Poverty was not making much headway in reducing their numbers. Their lot seemed to be getting worse. They were, as social theorist Charles Murray put it, "losing ground."

Perhaps the most interesting part of our study consisted of the seventy or so positive recommendations for action on which we agreed. Many of these are now the subjects of social experiments in the fifty states, and some by the federal government. Indeed, the national Welfare Reform Act of 1996 went into effect in the autumn of 1997. Since its passage, welfare roles have shrunken voluntarily (before sanctions were phased in) by significant percentages in every state—as much as 30 to 40 percent. This means far more welfare funding is now available for further experiments and new initiatives. Although much heartened by initial indications, we are, of course, waiting to see the full results, well aware that even the best intended reforms have unintended consequences.

5. From State to Civil Society

The great guiding theme of the twentieth century was provided by Hegel: The state as the embodiment of human desire and human action; the state imagined as beneficent, compassionate, and noble.

Yet the state, obviously, is neither the only nor the best instrument of the common good. Not only the totalitarian state, but also the welfare state, falls far short of the dreams that millions vested in the state during this century. To their credit, the welfare states of the Atlantic community have greatly eased the burdens of the impoverished peoples who emerged from the Depression of the

1930s and the ruins of World War II, and introduced them to unprecedented levels of prosperity, a significant gain in quality of life and increase in longevity for the elderly, and a broad array of liberties and rights. Nonetheless, its moral and financial costs, there is wide recognition, are unsustainable. Its aims and methods must be radically renegotiated.

Although Tony Blair of Britain has recognized the problem, it is not clear as yet what he will imagine as the way out, or what goal he will present as the new and better conception. It is not clear that other European social democrats yet recognize the problem.

In such an axial period as ours, it is of the first importance to go back to first principles. A return to first principles is a kind of revolution—*re* + *volvere*—and in this case it seems to be the only kind that has a hope of working. This involves a review of many seeming simplicities.

For instance, the first fundamental question is this: What is a free society worthy of free men and women? Can it be agreed that a free society is first of all a project in self-government, in which self-starting and provident citizens, in order to secure their own rights to liberty and to promote the common good, come together to form a government through their own consent? Since the main idea of an experiment in self-government is that people ought to be free to do for themselves all that they can do for themselves, in their own associations and communities, independently of the state, they must keep the government strictly limited. "Conservatives" will tend to stress the limits; social democrats will favor generous interpretations of the necessities. Both tendencies, each checked by the other, contribute to the common good.

This is no place for a further discourse on government, but at least a few sentences are necessary if we are to develop a common view about the character of the free citizen. A *citizen* is quite different from a *subject* (as in "subject of the Austro-Hungarian Empire," like my grandparents). The citizen belongs to the class of sovereigns, the possessors of ultimate power. In the free society, the principal repository of power is the personal responsibility of citizens. If things are not going well, it is up to the citizen to organize an association or a movement that tries to get them back on the right track.

The virtue of *social justice*, in this context, is the habit of forming associations to improve the good of the city. The virtue of social justice, then, is "social" in two senses. Its aim is the improvement in some respect of the city—the whole nation or a locality within it. Second, its practice entails learning skills such as association, cooperation, and how to inspire and organize others; clearly, *social* skills.

As Tocqueville pointed out, the habit of forming associations is the first law of democracy. No free associations, no genuine democracy. Forming associations is the first task of social justice. Self-government is exercised through the associations formed by free persons. The exercise of this habit is one of the primary political responsibilities of the citizen. It is wrong to identify social justice solely or even principally with the state, as some activists seem to do; social justice is the virtue that energizes the free associations of civil society.

The citizen also has serious economic responsibilities. Since human capital is the primary form of capital, the human person is the chief economic resource of every nation. In the economy of free societies, the acting person is the principal dynamo. From the imagination, creativity and initiative of acting persons, economic associations are put together and corporations are formed. The inventiveness and enterprise of acting persons generate both new goods and services, and new ways to deliver them.

The political economy of the free society, therefore, depends to an unprecedented degree on the personal responsibility and associational skills (political and economic) of its citizens. This is the heart of any experiment in self-government.

Public policies that obstruct, weaken, or remove personal responsibility are oppressive to citizens; they are also destructive of the experiment in self-government.[12] Unintended as it may be, it is impossible to doubt that the welfare state has begun to have this effect. Further, isn't it the case that social democrats for some years concentrated more energy on helping the needy than on generating growth and opportunity? Valued equality higher than liberty? Gave higher priority to redistribution than to incentives that reward achievement? In recent years, fortunately, it appears that the social democratic ideal is being adjusted to take greater account of personal initiative and personal responsibility.

Thus, social democrats now have a chance to take a large step forward, and make the project of a self-government their own. If this is what Tony Blair intends, his progress will be well worth studying. Whether or not he intends it—or achieves it—this is a project that, for the sake of the future of the free society in Europe, someone must undertake to lead.

The main outline of this project is simple enough to state: What the free world needs, rapidly, is a devolution of significant responsibilities from centralized bureaucracies to citizens, alone and in their multiple associations. *Devolution* is the key word: Devolution from the state to civil society. Devolution, also, from central governments to the regions and localities. Devolution to centers of responsibility closer to the immediate practical knowledge that separates realism from irrational bureaucratic edict. The main theme is devolution from state to civil society—from bureaucrats to citizens and their civic associations in every sphere, including the family and religious associations, economic associations and political associations, and artistic and scientific associations and other social groups of various types and purposes. (I am not denying that there is a simultaneous reorganization of larger international structures, both regional and global, only insisting that these not become oblivious to energies from below.)

Obviously, the state cannot and should not simply "wither away." Obviously, too, some elements of the welfare state will continue to be necessary, especially in continental-sized, highly mobile, flexible economies. Nonetheless, it was always a mistake to think that the chief or even sole way of fulfilling the social nature of man is through the state and its collectivist activities. The state constitutes only one small slice of an authentic human social life, an important one, but far from being either the heart or the whole of the matter. Moreover, it is wrong to allow the state to seize primacy over civil society. The state is not the master but the servant. The welfare state must be kept in due perspective and tight limits.

Through which public policies can this devolution be carried out over the next generation? With all these points—some, perhaps, painfully obvious—social democrats may well be in rough agreement. Can they walk a few more steps? First some general principles; then three practical policies.

6. Seven Principles of Devolution

General Principles: It is wise and useful to refocus the goals we are trying to reach.

First, the overarching aim is to carry through the historic project of self-government. To achieve this aim, we need to raise up large numbers of strong, independent, creative, civic-minded and above all responsible citizens, without whom this project is dead. A negative way of stating this aim is that we must reduce the dependency, passivity, and irresponsibility now widespread in our societies.

Second, it is most efficient to nourish strong families, for the family is the formative institution of strong personalities. Nearly all individuals can be reached through public policies that strengthen the independence of families and heighten their incentives for responsible behavior.

Third, it is crucial to nourish in all spheres of life—and not to oppress (as most governments do)—personal habits of initiative, creativity, and enterprise. This is the path of human vitality. It is also the path that most closely conforms human beings to the image of their Creator.

Fourth, a necessary instrument of creativity is a capital fund, and so it ought to be the goal of public policy to help every family accumulate a capital fund to transfer across the generations. For more than a hundred years, social reformers have concentrated attention on income maintenance. Henceforward, that may be not nearly so creative a focus as emphasis on family capital formation.

Fifth, the path of family capital formation is a useful route out of poverty and other vulnerabilities for individuals; but it also relieves the state treasury of insupportable burdens.

Sixth, after decades of centralization, it is necessary to devolve as many decisions as practical from national bureaucracies to individuals, or at least to local centers.

A more creative balance between national and local must be restored. (This "balance" implies that, in some matters, intervention from above is highly useful for the common good.)

And, seventh, it is necessary to simplify government rules and regulations, especially regarding taxation and the conduct of economic activities. Every complexity in the tax and regulatory code is both a veil blocking transparency and an occasion of corruption. What you want more of (growth, for example), do not heavily tax.

Once these seven principles are firm and clear in the mind, many citizens will have many practical ideas about how to proceed. Here are three recommendations of my own. I state them in general terms, without the specifics by which to adapt them to different national situations and practical circumstances.

7. Three Policy Proposals

1. Pension reform. Chile has shown that the traditional method of paying the pensions of elderly citizens can be altered peacefully and quickly, in fulfillment of all the general principles mentioned above. An entire bureaucracy was made to disappear, government involvement in pensions was simplified; individual persons and families accrued an unprecedented degree of independence and wealth; and Chile's national savings rate has become one of the highest in the world.

What I like best about Chile's new system is that the funds in a family head's pension fund that he may not exhaust in his lifetime are inherited by his family. Thus, pensions become a capital asset for the entire family, not solely an income maintenance scheme valid only for as long as the pensioner lives. This heightens the incentive to invest more of your lifetime earnings in your pension fund, for your family's sake.

Essentially, Chilean pension law is now simple: Every wage earner is obliged to invest a stated fraction of his income in a tax-exempt pension plan in one of a government-approved list of mutual investment funds. That fund is vested in his person and follows him from job to job, wherever he goes. Both freedom and creativity are enhanced; personal incentives are improved; families are strengthened; and the prosperity of the whole nation benefits by a huge jump in the national savings rate.

Senator Daniel Patrick Moynihan, a Democrat, has recently proposed a highly limited but important step in this direction;[13] he has had a long career as reformer of the U.S. public pension system.

2. *Medical savings accounts*: Here, too, in an effort to fulfill the seven general principles listed above, every citizen ought to be required by law to establish a medical savings fund, in which an obligatory proportion of his earnings would by law be invested in a private account. This account would be tax-exempt, personally vested and portable—it would belong to the citizen and his (or her) family. A portion of the fund would be deducted each month to purchase catastrophic insurance, at a relatively "high deductible" (say, in the U.S., about $1,500). The remainder would be withdrawn as needed for routine medical expenses. Whatever the individual or family does not spend during their lives remains as an inheritance, a capital fund, for the next generation.

What I like best about this policy is that it greatly reduces the government health bureaucracy, replaces it with personal responsibility, and dramatically alters the incentives of citizens and the location of decision-making power in the health profession. Most of the burden of medical costs on national budgets is removed. Responsibility is restored to individual citizens. Instead of a zero-sum game, medical insurance becomes another way of accumulating a family inheritance. If, God forbid, the family's medical accounts are exhausted by accidents or illnesses, their catastrophic insurance covers their needs.

3. *A simplified proportional income tax*: Just as Chile has demonstrated that the old-age pension bureaucracy can be disbanded, to the benefit of the common good; and just as medical savings accounts offer a way of dramatically reducing if not eliminating the health care bureaucracy; so also it is possible to simplify national income taxes so as to virtually eliminate another bureaucracy—and certainly to eliminate its arbitrariness, arrogance, obscurantism, favoritism and corruption. The instrument for doing so is to simplify the tax code in a radical way.

It is well known that tax revenues, the actual money governments take in, are by no means identical to tax rates, the percentage to be contributed to government. If rates are very high, citizens alter their behavior so as to pay less than predicted. There are many strategies for doing this, some legitimate, others illegal and/or immoral. A government can set rates lower and, nonetheless, bring in revenues that are higher. And, of course, rates set too high have been known to reduce revenues substantially.

Therefore, let the government establish one fixed rate for all income from whatever source—at, say, 20 percent. Next, exempt from income taxes all families in the bottom half of the income distribution, by the following method. To each parent in the family, allow a substantial exemption, and to each child (dependent) allow one half of that exemption.

In the United States, for example, an exemption of $12,000 for each parent and $6,000 for each of two children would exempt from income the first $36,000 earned by families of four. Since the median income of all U.S. families is approximately $36,000, that means that half of all families would be exempt from income taxes. That in itself would be an enormous simplification.

In this respect, such a reform is family-friendly. It would apply to all families, and protect family income for the cost of childrearing. Grandparents who live in the household as dependents might also bring with them another exemption. This would make them a financial asset or at least much lighten the burden of caring for them, while enabling families to benefit by their presence.

I also like the fact that, while exempting the poor, the tax is strictly proportional to income. The poor and most of the working class are exempted from income taxes altogether. As for the middle class and the rich, the more they earn, the more taxes they pay. The rate remains the same, but the actual tax payment on an additional $10,000 of income ($2,000) is far lower than the actual tax payment on an additional $100,000 of income ($20,000). Holding the same rates for all is highly likely to increase compliance and transparency, and to reduce evasion and corruption.

The flat tax—I prefer to call it the proportional tax, to emphasize that everyone pays taxes in proportion to their income and according to the same proportion (the quintessence of fairness)—is, of course controversial.[14] The American Enterprise Institute has mounted a long series of debates on the flat tax and its chief rivals (the national sales tax, Minority Leader Gephardt's reformed set of five "progressive" levels, and others).[15]

One of the main objections to the proportional or flat tax, suggested above, is that it is not "progressive." This is the main objection Minority Leader Gephardt articulates on behalf of his five-rate alternative. Why does he insist on progressive rates? "No arguments," he says, "just a gut feeling" that the rich and the poor should pay at different rates; somehow that seems more fair.[16] He boasts that, in his plan, 70 percent of all taxpayers would pay a maximum rate of only 10 percent.

Two rebuttals are offered to Gephardt. First, under the flat tax, half of all taxpayers (those earning $36,000 or lower for a family of four), would pay no income tax at all; those below $55,000 would pay at rates of 5.6 percent (or lower) [see chart, p. 115]. This is better for low income households than Gephardt's 10 percent rate. Even taxpayers with annual incomes up to $100,000— more that 90 percent of all taxpayers—would pay only 12.8 percent (or lower), barely higher than Gephardt's 10 percent. For those who want "progressivity," the flat tax offers more of it than Gephardt, even if progressivity is not its main intention.

The second argument is this: since the lower 50 percent of income earners pay no income tax at all, any redistributive effects on who pays how much in taxes are confined within the top 50 percent. In the U.S., as we have seen, 50 percent of all household income begins at about $36,000. Moreover, households earning up to $55,000 are still paying only a small amount of income tax (5.6 percent or less). The rationale for progressivity is supposed to be to relieve the poor. Is it worth it to fight over which portion of the income earners in the top 40 percent pay a slightly higher (or lower) proportion than others? Does $55,000 per annum count as poor?

A newer argument is also relevant. My colleague Kevin Hassett is working on a paper that puts a number—a cost—on the preference for the current system over the flat tax. Even its opponents admit that the efficiencies of the flat tax would result in a 5 percent gain in GDP. (More realistic estimates are twice that or more.) On a $9 trillion GDP, a 5 percent gain is equivalent to about $450 billion. Thus, to resist the flat tax in order to keep the current complicated scheme comes at a cost of $450 billion. (The real cost, of course, could be significantly higher, as much as a trillion dollars per year or more.) Do those who value progressivity value it highly enough to renounce $450 billion or more in annual economic growth? Any progressivity that they do achieve will consist solely in rearranging the proportions of tax paid by the top 40 percent of income earners. Do they really care that much whether the top 5 percent, or the next 15 percent, pay a slight proportion less (or more) than they are now paying? After all, under the proportional or flat tax, the bottom 50 percent pay no income tax at all.

For completeness, I should also examine various proposals for a national sales tax or consumption tax, as a replacement for the current income tax and as an alternative to the proportional or flat tax. But that would excessively complicate an already long paper.

8. Conclusion

These three modest public policy initiatives will not inaugurate the kingdom of God among men, but they will be at least small steps on the way to reducing the role of big government in our lives and to empowering individual citizens, their families, and their associations in civil society.

They are modest steps in the devolution from state to civil society that is likely to characterize the political and social history of the twenty-first century.

A friend of mine has christened this set of ideas "universal family capitalism." However, his proposal for naming this set of ideas might rub against the prejudices of Europe. Europe has spent more than 150 years denigrating capital. Too bad. Ordinary families are much helped by having it. Making a capital stock universal among families is a worthy aim.

Appendix: "Progressivity" of a Flat Tax for a Family of Four at Various Income Levels (Flat Tax = 20%)

Average Gross Income	Taxable Income	Actual Tax	Tax Rate
$ 36,000 & below	0	0	0.0%
$ 50,000	$ 14,000	$ 2,800	5.6%
$ 100,000	$ 64,000	$ 12,800	12.8%
$ 200,000	$164,000	$ 32,800	16.4%
$ 500,000	$464,000	$ 92,800	18.56%
$1,000,000	$964,000	$192,800	19.28%

As income rises, the value of the $36,000 exemption proportionally shrinks, and the effective tax rate climbs.

· 6 ·

In Praise of Bourgeois Virtues

The White House Conference on Families, after a five-year labor, finally brought forth a monster. Its history is instructive. In 1975, Jimmy Carter, virtually unknown outside Georgia, listened to an idea for a White House conference to honor the traditional family.[1] Some months later, the nominee of his party, Carter designated Joseph Califano to begin planning a program on the family for the new administration and still later, in September 1976, he opened his campaign with a Labor Day speech on the family.

Almost at once the infighting started. Frank Butler, a bright young organizer from the U.S Catholic Conference, was slotted to be the director of the White House Conference, but the social science establishment in the Department of Health, Education, and Welfare, with feminist assistance, blocked his appointment. The professionals insisted that the name of the conference be changed to the White House Conference on Families—plural, not singular, any hint of a normative ideal carefully excised.

This essay, an early intervention on the plight of the family and its centrality to the future of the free society, was published in *Society*, January/February 1981.

Sensing the political passion aroused by this norma-tive ideal—85 percent of all Americans, according to Gallup, count the family "the most" or "one of the most" important elements in their lives—President Car-ter pushed the White House Conference away from the White House out into the states. Local constituencies began to elect delegates who believed in the family. Alarmed, the planning staff began to "balance" the dele-gations with handpicked appointees so that at least 40 percent were professionals "in family-related fields" and of approved politics.

Members of the White House Conference planning staff spoke openly of "the nostalgic family," by which they meant the heterosexual couple united in matrimony and bringing up children. They included as "families" any household somehow involved in "nurture" or "ful-filling one another's basic needs"—homosexual liaisons, childless and unmarried couples living together, com-munes, and similar affinity groups. They did not seem anxious to exclude any arrangement. This bias is star-tling if one considers the demographics.

The latest figures from the U.S. Department of Com-merce indicate that there are today 95,324,000 hus-bands and wives in the United States. (By contrast, there are 2,692,000 men and women living as unmarried cou-ples and 17,202,000 adults living alone.) There are 50,847,000 children living with two parents and 11,542,000 children living with one parent. What the staff members of the White House Conference on Fami-lies are pleased to call "the nostalgic family" actually includes, then, a solid two thirds of the nation's popula-tion. In addition, single parents with children constitute families in a quite traditional sense; in the past, disease or accident often brought early death to one or both spouses. Of those adults in childless households, most are over forty-five; though their children have left home, few may be assumed to regard the traditional family with contempt. Finally, millions of widows and widowers living alone invest emotion in the families of their children. The "nostalgic family" seems to include as a living reality all but a vocal minority of Americans.

No doubt high divorce rates and other statistics of family breakup indicate that not all is well with the family in America. It never was. A free society encourages such great mobility that grandparents today poignantly boast to all who will listen that their children are scattered across the world, not a one "close to home." Such mobility (not only geographic but emotional as well) is partly a source of pride; but it also places strains upon families comparable to those of the great migrations, wars, and dispersals of the past.

So the ideal lives; and no wonder, since nature must of necessity constantly reinvent it. Human offspring require some twenty years of nurture. Three thousand years of civilization must be passed on to children during those years; without that, progress would halt. An elementary stability is essential for this process; more than nature, culture demands it. The original intention of the White House Conference was to give some small honor and moral support to those who accomplish this noble work. Why were the professionals so hostile to this simple idea? What were the antifamily professionals up to?

Although there is much vocal contempt for "the nostalgic family," few such critics seem ready to propose that having one parent is superior to having two; that prodigal separation, divorce, and infidelity have only good effects; that coupling without marriage and marriage without children best serve the common good; and that the best of all societies would encourage an impermanent, childless, sexual free-for-all (and will the last one out please turn off the lights?). The hostile critics of the family are shockingly vague about what they plan to put in its place, beyond "liberation" and "openness."

Attacks on the family take three forms, derogating its economic, political, and moral-cultural accomplishments. The family is called "bourgeois," "repressive," and "narrow." In it are discerned the roots of this nation's political economy, such that radicals who would destroy the latter believe they must extirpate the former. In a way they do not intend, they appear to be correct. It seems impossible to imagine democratic governance, a free economy, and a liberal culture apart from the much disdained bourgeois family.

To be sure, classic theoreticians of "the new order of the world" did not write at length, profoundly, or with unmitigated admiration of the family. Some later scholars think they took it for granted as a given of nature and good sense. But the truth is that the great intellectual breakthroughs of the modern era occurred, rather, around the polar concepts of the *individual* and the *state*. Rousseau wrote eloquently, if with a certain detached romanticism, about the family and about childhood, and nearly all the scholars of the Anglo-Scottish Enlightenment, from John Locke through Adam Smith to John Stuart Mill, wrote at least briefly of the family. Yet one must recall the order they wrote *against*.

The feudal world was fixated on inherited status. No newborn child chose the family he was born into, yet birth fixed class, station, religion, and occupation forever. In the feudal order, concepts of family were half submerged in less than rational materials like blood, habit, custom, tradition, ethnicity, and religion. Original minds concerned with a central role for intellect, liberty, and the flowering of talent wherever it is found were obliged to look beyond the family for the dynamism of a new order. Thus, the discoverers of "the natural system of liberty" stressed the distinctive, aspiring individual and the self-limiting state that would liberate his energies. For generations, political theory, economic theory, and moral theory, preoccupied with the individual and the state, have systematically neglected the social vitality of the family.

In our day, when such genuine freedoms are available that anything may be tried, we are driven to face directly what our forebears neglected or took for granted. It is useful to reflect on our own common experiences in the three areas in which the traditional family is under relentless attack: in the economic order, the political order, and the moral-cultural order.

Even today libertarian scholars, like David Friedman in *The Machinery of Freedom*, place at the center of their analysis the rational will of the free individual, and so do most textbooks in economics. But is this analytic assumption fair to our actual experience? David Friedman dedicates his book to his father, Milton Friedman, and pays prefatory homage to his wife and children; one suspects that whole regions of ordinary experience lie, unanalyzed, behind these brief hints of familial reality. According to libertarian theory, the economic motivation of individuals arises from rational self-interest. Yet, according to the same theory, individual self-interest includes far more than a merely self-absorbed, self-regarding solipsism. When Adam Smith writes that it is not to the benevolence of the butcher or the baker, but to their self-love, that we look for provision of our dinners, it is entirely consistent with the tenor of his thought to recognize that most butchers and bakers endure the blood and the heat of their labors not for themselves alone but for the benefit of their families. The "self-love" Smith writes of is to be taken in a large rather than a narrow sense, so as to include forms of natural benevolence, duty, sympathy, and other-centered ambition. Above all, economic self-interest includes the family. This is an important qualification. Too much economic analysis seems to ignore it.

Economic Order

In our ordinary experience, our own economic starting place in life is given us by our families. Nearly all have multiple reasons to be grateful to the families that gave us birth, nourished us, instructed us, prepared us, and made an endless series of sacrifices in our behalf, long before we were capable of economic or educational choices of our own. We did not suddenly invent ourselves out of whole cloth. When at last we began to attain self-consciousness and self-direction, we had already been *thrown*, we were already in motion. Impulses which did not originate with us moved us forward with a kind of imparted gravity. Thus, it is analytically improper to take the individual alone as the sufficient unit of economic analysis. Individual human beings are social animals. More exactly than that, each of us is a familial animal. Our families enter into our very constitution, not only genetically but also psychologically, educationally, and morally.

In many of our family traditions, high priority was attached to education. As Thomas Sowell demonstrates in *Race and Economics* and in *American Ethnic Groups*, family culture is a critical variable in economic performance. It is through no choice of their own, or at least only in a diminished sense, that some 70 percent of all Jewish youngsters in America find themselves between the ages of eighteen and twenty-two in colleges or universities, and in so many diverse ways directed toward a high use of intelligence.

Inherited, cherished culture impels their family life. Put another way, the family is the major carrier of culture, transmitting ancient values and lessons in ways that escape full rational articulation, carrying forward motivations and standards of judgment, and shaping the distribution of energy and emotion, preferences and inclinations. To ask, "Who am I?" is always, in part, to ask "Who are we—my family, my people, my fellows?"

In many families in America, the economic welfare of each individual depended in very large part not only upon the immediate family (father, mother, and siblings) but also upon an extended network of others (grandparents, uncles, aunts, cousins, and in-laws). To some extent, various family members supplied economic role models. On occasion, especially during hard times, one family took another in. Older generations sometimes provided at least a little capital, so that one generation might begin at a higher financial level than the preceding. But the family network also provided countless exchanges of goods and services, which individual families could not have afforded otherwise. One brother in one business helped out another brother in another business, and each received benefits outside normal markets. A successful family member was a source of jobs, information, or assistance to others; perhaps even the discreet use of his or her name might open doors. Finally, family networks have been sources of invaluable economic lore about techniques for advancement, mistakes to avoid, opportunities to seize. Economic skills rarely develop in a vacuum. Every family, particularly through its brightest and most intelligent members, transmits economic advantages to its entire network, without which individuals would begin life far more ignorant and helpless than they do.

It follows, then, that families defy simple and abstract schemes of equality. Families with an intelligent and effective economic tradition are not equal to families with less developed traditions. Their individual members, unless they choose to neglect the acquired family wisdom, do not begin at the same "starting line" as other individuals of less highly developed family traditions. It is in the interests of a healthy and dynamic society, of course, to upgrade the economic traditions of every family for the sake of every individual. But every family network that becomes a center of intelligent economic activity and a repository of hard-won economic habits is an immeasurable resource for the nation of which it is a part.

Furthermore, it seems obvious that, each individual life being short, the most profound of economic motives is almost always—and must necessarily be—family oriented. Economic laborers seldom work only for themselves. It is no doubt true that those who do not have families of their own do work rather more for themselves; but even in such cases one often observes the help generously given by such persons to the elderly, sick, or very young members of their extended families of birth. For those men and women who have chosen to establish families of their own, there can be no doubt that much of their economic conduct makes no sense apart from the benefits they are trying to accrue for their children. Far more than economists commonly suggest, the fundamental motive of all economic activity seems clearly to be concern for family. It is for the family's welfare that so much gratification is deferred; that so many excruciating medical, educational, and emotional struggles are engaged in; that so much saving is attempted; and that investments which regard the future so much more than the present are undertaken. One does meet parents who say, "You only live once, and I intend to enjoy it, leaving my children to fend, as I did, for themselves." This is not always, other things being equal, an immoral or even a necessarily harmful choice so far as the children are concerned. But it does not appear to be the common sentiment.

Insofar as democratic capitalism depends for its economic vitality upon deferred gratification, savings, and long-term investment, no motive for such behavior is the equivalent of regard for the future welfare of one's own progeny. Self-interest is not a felicitous name for this regard for the welfare of one's children and one's children's children. Yet it is just this extended motivation which cuts to the quick. This is the motivation that adequately explains herculean economic activities. This is the only rational motivation for long-range economic decisions. For, in the long run, the individual economic agent is dead. Only his progeny survive to enjoy the fruits of his labors, intelligence, and concern.

This regard for family might, indeed, be designated "familial socialism." Through it, the isolated individual escapes mere self-interest or self-regardingness. Through it, "charity begins at home." Through it, human sociality achieves its normal full development, in the very territory closest to the knowledge and wise concern of the individual agent. Indeed, until the collectivist state began to take over more and more of its economic functions, it was through familial socialism that most highly developed cultures cared for the poor, the sick, the retarded, the needy, the very young, and the very old in their midst. Their religious traditions, meanwhile, taught them also to care for those most unfortunate of all, the widows and orphans and those who were "homeless."

But if the family is a form of socialism which corrects

the exaggerated individualism of capitalist economists, it is also a form of liberty which corrects the exaggerated collectivism of statists. Although most writers seem to employ the word "bourgeois" as a term of faint contempt, detached observation suggests that bourgeois institutions nourish surprising moral qualities. In the first place, a bourgeois has economic independence, perhaps as a shopkeeper in his or her own enterprise. A bourgeois owns property. A bourgeois (normally) shares the cultural life of the city rather than that of the rural countryside. These are not trivial matters for the life of the spirit. Not until Europe began to break free from the fixed status of the feudal order did the bourgeoisie attain sufficient critical mass to define a significant new social class. The bourgeoisie, defined negatively, were not aristocrats; they were not serfs or peasants; and finally, they were not the landed gentry of the countryside. A new politics, a new economics, a new culture, and a new morality were generated by their coming center stage. Much that we hold dear was won by the bourgeoisie.

To some extent, the bourgeoisie violated significant taboos of feudalism. Their growing competence, ambition, wealth, and power constituted a threat to the authority of the aristocratic class. They upset feudal conceptions of status and place. Their "new morality" gave higher value to the economic order—to industry, savings, acquisition of wealth, upward mobility, and economic rationality—than the "old morality" of aristocrats, churchmen, monks, and humanists. As the bourgeoisie gained in influence and power, aristocrats (first the less well off, and gradually even the best off) began a long descent. With the aristocrats, many humanist scholars and artists also suffered a relative loss in status. By contrast, peasants and yeomen, who could never aspire to noble birth or the privileges of aristocracy, *could* aspire to "better their condition" by entering the bourgeois class. The bourgeois class was, in a sense, the most open, dynamic, and expansive class. Aristocrats who chose to play by the new economic rules could joint it, and so could former serfs, peasants, and the urban or rural poor. Karl Marx imagined that the "class war" of the nineteenth century would pit the bourgeoisie—as the new owners of the new instruments of production— against the growing urban proletariat. The reality appears to have been that most proletarians aspired to, and succeeded in embodying, *embourgeoisement*. The new middle class turned out to have political, economic, and moral attractions which many intellectuals have overlooked.

What were these attractions? A measure of economic independence and well-being is certainly one. Compared to the mud floors, glassless windows, inadequate sanitation, crowding, lack of warmth, and other inadequacies of the medieval farm hut, common all through Europe during the eighteenth and nineteenth centuries (and still seen today in rural areas of Eastern Europe), the increasingly sturdy and independent dwellings of the bourgeois class seemed attractive indeed. Moreover, the philosophical and legal basis of *the freehold or private property* saw to it that not even the king had the right of entry and search, and thus made the independently owned home of the bourgeois as well defended as a castle. The law provided a kind of spiritual moat around the home. Independence and liberty have attractions above and beyond the material order. The bourgeoisie may have lacked the high status of noble birth; but, as historical carriers of the dream of personal independence and liberty, they struggled for rights formerly reserved to royalty and the aristocracy. To the free man a home became a castle: the very phrase signifies rights wrested from nobler estates. But these reflections lead us to politics.

Political Order

As for the economic order, so for the political order of republican governance and democratic institutions, it appears that the family is rather less dispensable than political scientists commonly emphasize. First and foremost, the relative economic independence of the family and the right of the freehold set the most effective barrier upon the state. A state which controls all the means of production, all the terms of employment, and every aspect of exchange controls the daily reality of its citizens in every sphere. Political revolt under such circumstances is virtually impossible. So many citizens are in the direct employ of the state that spying upon every small beginning of dissent serves the self-interest of the forces of control. State ownership of the printing presses and other media might be thought to be sufficient for total political control; but total public control over every economic activity extends political control into every material activity from food to housing, from production to consumption, from savings and credit to every act of exchange.

The right of a family to transmit property to its progeny is not the sole contribution of the bourgeois family to political liberty. Republican government is preeminently self-government, and it is in the family that the habits of mind and will indispensable to the conception and practice of self-government are best taught—can alone be taught. If individuals have no space protecting them from the state, they have no "self" for self-government. The family provides such space. The family is the seat of the primary right in education. The state may require certain areas and levels of competency in the education of its citizens; but it may not usurp the right of parents to direct the education of their own children. As the limited state may not infringe upon personal conscience, so it may not infringe upon the intellectual and moral traditions of the family. Human children differ from the young of all other animals in requiring a very long period of physical, emotional, intellectual, and moral nurture before they attain adulthood. The primary agency of such nurture is the family. The family, in that sphere, has inalienable rights. Between the omnipotent state and the naked individual looms the first line of resistance against totalitarianism: the economically and politically independent family, protecting the space within which free and independent individuals may receive the necessary years of nurture.

No self-government can stand where individuals choose to live as slaves and wards. Just as tyrannies may on occasion be benevolent, the powerful modern state may also be paternalistic, providing for the material welfare of its citizens in exchange for the surrender of self-government. Thus nearly every utopian vision of a paternal paradise on earth begins by undermining the sanctity of the bourgeois family. The more the state invades the family, the less likely the prospect of self-government. It was not by accident that the apparently mad Jim Jones of Jonestown, in launching his explicitly socialist utopian experiment, concentrated first on breaking down the family rights of every family in his community. When each person of each sex was reduced to dependence upon the community alone (it is relatively insignificant that Jones sought their total dependence upon himself), the effective resistance of individuals was also broken. It is an obscure but important truth of political economy that the self is primarily familial, and only secondarily independent as an individual. When the primary familial self is effectively destroyed, the independence of the individual also disintegrates and nothing is left of the self but the will of the community. The practice of totalitarian societies supplies universal verification of this principle. For those who seek totalitarian state control, it is always evident that the independent bourgeois family must be destroyed.

This is so because the individual bound by responsibilities and loyalties to spouse and children is bound, as well, to traditions welling up from the past and extending into the future. In human life, the family is the ordinary institution of self-transcendence. Through it, the sociality of the self is realized in flesh and blood, gains perspective on past and future, and is made to belong not to the self alone, not to the present alone, and not to the regime of the moment alone, but to the ages. In this light, the pretensions of the totalitarian state wither. The totalitarian spirit, nourished by abstractions, is inevitably utopian. It impresses the majority through effective, although perhaps disguised, terror. Its appeal to the idealistic (at least to those outside its effective grip) consists in an abstract vision of a society that never yet has been, is not now, and never will be. Family ties lead individuals to count concrete costs. Watching their children, taking thought about their daily family circumstances, husband and wife have concrete evidence about the realities of their brief lifetime. Family reality has a shorter and more realistic lifespan than that required for the realization of utopian dreams. The family is the human race's natural defense against utopianism. For that reason, every form of totalitarianism must first destroy the bourgeois family.

Moral Order

Our reflections about morality are still colored dispro-
portionately by the values of the ancient, aristocratic
order. When, in a famous essay intended to put everyone
in his place, Matthew Arnold distinguished the "barbarians" (the "nobility") from the "philistines" (the commercial class), he celebrated the moral imperative of
high culture to draw all citizens, from every walk of life,
into a higher order of sensibility. Yet there are overtones
in that essay of far greater sympathy for "barbarians"
than for "philistines" (not to mention "populace").
Many of our terms of approbation, moral and aesthetic—
like *graceful, princely, regal,* and the like—are colored
by lenses of class and romantic memory. We somehow
assume that the aristocracy sets the highest standard of
excellence. But is that true? Aristocrats may have paid
for excellence and been its patrons; less frequently, it appears, did they achieve it in person.

It was, rather, the bourgeoisie which from earliest feudal times furnished the artisans and builders who imagined and constructed the works we so admire. While the
dukes and counts seldom dirtied their hands, the bourgeoisie, by their own industry and competitive habits,
slowly replaced the aristocracy as the bearers of cultural
excellence. France, to return a compliment, is today the
most bourgeois of nations, "the nation of shopkeepers."
The privately owned, family-centered enterprises of
France still set worldwide standards for the arts of daily
living. Good wine, delicious bread, inimitable cheese,
lace of the finest workmanship, elegant hats, imaginative
sartorial arts, sophisticated cuisine—France has long
supplied such excellent products through the small family-centered enterprises of the bourgeoisie. Scholars and

artists who recall with nostalgia the high status of aristocratic patronage may continue to have contempt for the
bourgeoisie. But they are dramatically wrong about the
sources of excellence in the arts, crafts, and workmanship on which the aristocracy drew for their palaces,
monuments, and salons. These things were virtually
never developed or supplied by aristocrats. They were
produced by competitive bourgeois enterprises.

Terminologically, then, the denigration of the bourgeois class is not plausible in the arena of practicality;
but it is not even fair in the arena of aesthetics and morals. Its source appears to lie in the resentment of an aristocracy experiencing downward mobility. Aristocrats of
inherited status experienced cultural defeat at the hands
of persons of lower birth but higher passion for excellence. In one of the choice ironies of intellectual history,
many great scholars and artists of the first rank, themselves children of the middle class, celebrated the virtues
of aristocracy in preference to their own heritage. The
cultural ideals of the aristocracy, no doubt, provided the
most accessible metaphors for describing new forms of
excellence. European royalty continued to commission
works of art and scholarship. Eminent thinkers supported themselves, more often than not, by tutoring the
children of aristocrats. Great humanists and inventive
scientists found income as ornaments of the court and
noble families. The European aristocracy won the spiritual allegiance of the intellectuals, even as the meritoc-
racy of the bourgeoisie produced a disproportionate
share of their numbers.

As in the economic order and the political order, so
also in the moral order; the bourgeois family is the primary institution of realism. The schemes of utopians
customarily exclude the family, as they must, for the

family is a most un-utopian institution. What it teaches spouses with each other and parents with their children is humble acceptance of human frailty. Those who seek moral perfection, full self-fulfillment, high happiness, and other manifestations of the utopian imagination can scarcely abide the constraints of matrimony and child-rearing. No man is god, no woman a goddess; each has feet of clay. Moreover, the prolonged exposure of each to each, day after day, year after year, is bound to instruct them in ways they did not expect, both in the manifold faults of the other and—still more dispiriting—in their own faults.

Honesty and sincerity are said to be the most highly praised ideals of sophisticated, sensitive Americans. Yet in matrimony man or wife is bound for life to a spouse who appears to be sworn to discerning all those truths about the other which the other never wanted to know. Hardly a gesture escapes the criticism of a much-practiced, observant, self-defending eye. Matrimony induces realism precisely where the immaturity of each of us least desires it: in the destruction of our illusions about our own goodness, virtue, and attractiveness. The other cannot afford to be deceived by our self-illusions. If you do not admire unrelenting honesty, avoid matrimony.

From the Declaration of Independence through *The Federalist*, and in every wise document of our realist revolutionary tradition, it is confidently asserted that the possibility of self-government rests upon the virtue of its citizens. Were the citizens of a republic to seek to remain teenagers forever, "one of the kids," such virtue could never come to maturity, and self-government would fall. Such citizens would, in increasing numbers, find matrimony intolerable, except serially, and childrearing far too burdensome for one short life. The flight into illusions about their own virtue would trap them in insatiable hypocrisies, by which they would endlessly boast of their superior morality, liberation, and sensitivity, while manifesting in their lives a noteworthy self-absorption. For such citizens, virtue would less and less entail personal suffering, self-discipline, and hard personal choice (that is, self-denial), and would more and more consist in identifying themselves with enlightened opinion. They would count themselves virtuous, not by the quality of their personal lives, but by the number of enlightened causes for which they issued public statements. It is not "the decline of public man" they would embody but the decline of personal man. Their virtue would consist in the public face. This is the inner meaning of the widespread hypocrisy of our era. In the name of "independent thinking," the saints ally themselves with every new turn of conventional consciousness-raising. They resist nothing that "advanced thinking" tells them they should think. Self dissolves, only the welfare state remains. It is scarcely a matter for wonderment that advanced thinking should come to this: The state must do more! (Except in self-defense against states more collectivist than ours.)

Nature's own school for virtue—and, hence, that of any political economy based upon self-government—is primarily the family. In the family, one encounters the limitations of one's own sex, vocation, and station in life. In this respect, today, the limitations of sex are most telling, since conventional ideologies about sex would have us think only properly enlightened thoughts, however far they might be from reality. A father neither bears nor nurses children; his maleness confines him at crucial moments to a helplessness for which nothing prepares him. A wife suffers constraints of biological time with respect to childbearing not shared by her husband. In many ways, time plays a quite different role in the life of a wife than in the life of her husband. Ideology to the contrary, whole realms of tenderness, nurturing instinct, and mysterious feelings of fatherhood are today, as they have been since time began, tutors of male sensitivity. The current myth of the unfeeling male, cold and impersonal and locked out of his full "personhood" by an inability to be as sensitive, caring, tender, and intimate as a woman, seems to be more a deliverance of feminist imperialism that of actual experience. Do men and women, even apart from feminist consciousness-raising, share different ranges of feeling? Do men need to be liberated from some "masculine mystique" through indoctrination by feminists? Such matters may be left to personal experience.

Suffice it to say that the project of living daily with a person of the opposite sex teaches one a great deal about the unknown mysteries of one's own sex, as well as about those of the other. These mysteries are not easily brought into consciousness, let alone into words, but they are marvelously instructive. They are also laden with requirements of self-discipline. Anyone who would wish to live with another had better begin acquiring ancient and constantly required virtues. The other person will insist upon it. Indeed, it is precisely in order to obtain such insistence that one submits to the school of matrimony. The act of love, signifying perfect union of the spouses in body and soul, does not accomplish at once what it signifies. As a symbol, it promises a more perfect union to be attained by the disciplining of intelligence, passion, and will over a lifetime. Ten years into a marriage, and twenty, and thirty, this symbolic act should be more truthful than it was in its beginnings. Marriage, too, teaches a realistic rather than a utopian discipline.

Childrearing is also instructive in a kind of ordinary heroism. A typical mother or father, without thinking twice about it, would willingly die—in fire or accident, say—in order to save one of their children. While in most circumstances this human act would be regarded as heroic, for parents it is only ordinary. Thus nature, and perhaps the Creator, has shaped family life to teach as a matter of course the role of heroic virtue. This admittedly extreme example suggests that family life is not so mundane and empty of transcendence as some of its cultural despisers would suggest. There are many acts of self-denial short of death which parents, hardly taking thought of, willingly perform for children.

Finally, childrearing teaches one lessons about self-governance. The deferral of gratification is one such lesson. Furthermore, the lessons one learns as a child about independence, the rule of law, liberty, and obedience teach one only half the requirements which a self-governing republic imposes upon its citizens. On the parental side of that generational divide, problems of liberty and authority wear a different aspect. A parent cannot avoid the exercise of authority, although our civilization is particularly fertile in suggesting innumerable systems for such avoidance. If one cares at all, one simply must learn to say no. One must also learn to accept the consequences of saying yes and no at precisely the wrong times. The application of discipline to a young child—let alone a teenager—is an enormously demanding act. It cannot be faked by permissiveness. Self-government is not possible without self-discipline. Nor is it possible, men and women being what they are, without the whip of the law. The childrearing practices of families either strengthen or undermine the habits of mind and soul— the moral skills, so to speak—of the republic itself.

At the heart of the bourgeois family lies judgment based on reason. Above everything else, the bourgeois family is built on critical judgment. Critical judgment is more than calculation, or logic, or analytic reason, or positivism. The bourgeois family is quite well known for being practical, religious, and, at times, sentimental and romantic. Under the sway of "middle-class Christianity," for example, great international religious communities went out to the far corners of the earth, to the slums of the cities, to islands where lepers needed care, to the sick and the insane and the homeless. These religious communities, like the bourgeoisie generally, are known for their practicality more than for their mysticism. Practical wisdom characterizes their charity. Thus, in attributing to the bourgeois family a special regard for critical judgment, I intend to attribute no narrow rationalism, but rather the capacity of practical peoples to reflect clearly upon the world of their experience, to make practical judgments about it, and to act.

To make critical judgment the center of family life is to live under a high form of discipline, for human beings do not rise easily or often to that height of their own powers required for critical judgment. Whole populations sometimes seem to be asleep, passive, inert, accepting. Thus, as the Declaration of Independence notes, tyranny, although almost universal, does not always lead to revolution. For those families whose views the Declaration of Independence expressed, the consent of the governed springs from reasoned judgment, not from sleepy acquiescence or unreflective passion: "Prudence indeed will dictate that governments long established should not be changed for light and transient causes; and accordingly all experience hath shewn that mankind are more disposed to suffer while evils are sufferable than to right themselves by abolishing the form to which they are accustomed."

Judgment and Passion

The bourgeois family is, then, to be distinguished from the sorts of family that have preceded it and have recently begun to follow it. It is different from the aristocratic family because its sense of self-worth comes not from noble birth but from self-directed accomplishment; not from attributed status but from status earned through excellence. The children of the successful middle class begin life with inherited advantages, but it does not follow that, like the aristocracy, they can maintain title to these till death; from riches to rags is the story of many of the downwardly mobile. The bourgeois family is different, as well, from the peasant family, chiefly by reason of its affinity for the values of an urban rather than a rural civilization, with its consequent emphasis upon those habits of mind and soul suited to a pluralistic, rapidly changing environment. Finally, the bourgeois family is different from the traditional ethnic family (of many different cultures) not only through the experience of transcultural migration but also, and especially, through its emphasis upon the nuclear family and the individual rather than upon the entire family network, the clan, and the ethnic group. Many of us who have experienced in our own lives the tension between the traditional ethnic family and the bourgeois family recognize full well the contrasting values of each, even as we make our own choice.

Finally, in the startling and historically untypical explosion of affluence which followed upon World War II, an entire generation of bourgeois families in the United States experienced a wave of what at first appeared as liberation, but lately has come to seem like moral confusion and even decadence. Children born in the meanness of the Depression were not prepared, as parents, to bring up children under heretofore never experienced conditions of affluence. Wanting to spare their children their own remembered deprivations, they indulged them more than they themselves had ever been indulged. Learning a new cosmopolitanism and experiencing, perhaps, a form of culture shock, they abandoned the forms of authority under which they had been reared. Much influenced by new psychological theories linking discipline to repression and repression to fascism, the parents who fought the war against Hitler—and, even more, their children—tried desperately not to appear to be authoritarian. One aspect of this immense cultural repression of the natural instinct of parental authority was the sustained effort not to be "judgmental."

Thus, the best-selling writer of pornographic books for children tells a radio talk show host, who pretends to be admiring, that she "tries very hard not to be judgmental, not to make my readers feel bad about things they might do, like the characters in my book." This flight from critical judgment runs precisely against the grain of the bourgeois family. The bourgeois family does make judgments. It does so not only in codes of ethical conduct and in schemes of self-improvement, but also in terms of practical achievement. The code of the bourgeois family is to measure—to measure in order to compete against oneself, to inspire self-improvement, to "better oneself." By contrast, the family of the new class (the postbourgeois family) fears measurement, disdains competition with the self, and prefers to "find" rather than to "better" the self. The heart of the difference lies in the respect of the bourgeois family for critical judgment, and of the family of the new class for being nonjudgmental.

From this radical difference there follow two quite different approaches to the ancient contest between reasoned judgment and the passions. There can scarcely be any doubt that the family of the new class gives greater play to the passions and esteems reasoned judgment less than does the bourgeois family. Indeed, the family of the new class is praised by its champions for its moral superiority—for being "liberated"—in precisely these respects.

In personal life, rule by one's passions and liberation from the disciplines of reasoned judgment are the opposite of what is meant by self-government. While the self may freely choose to follow its passions where they list—to let it all hang out—it would be claiming too much to describe that process as government. Rebellion, dissidence, dissonance, and "letting go" are closer to the mark. Government itself is a bourgeois word, self-government even more so. The new class prefers a rebellious "nontraditional lifestyle," and treats the self less as an object of government than as an object of search.

Where self-government is not possible in personal life, it remains to be seen whether it is possible in the public. Every prognosis based upon history would suggest that lack of self-government in the individual citizenry will lead to lack of restraint in the government of the republic. Personal prodigality will be paralleled by public prodigality. As individuals live beyond their means, so will the state. As individuals liberate themselves from costs, responsibilities, and a prudent concern for the future, so will their political leaders. When self-government is no longer an ideal for individuals, it cannot be credible for the republic. Unwilling to be judgmental, one cannot make up one's mind about reality. One drifts as in a pleasant dream. Since only the judgmental are capable of resolute, long-term action, a republic whose citizens have abandoned critical judgment is rudderless among its enemies, adrift on shifting seas.

Because the bourgeois family's sole reason for being is

to nourish critical judgment, how can we not mourn its passing, and hope that its demise has been exaggerated? Without the bourgeois family and the virtues it nourishes, democratic self-government does not seem possible. In that case, the American experiment, like a meteor flashing briefly through history, has commenced an accelerating descent.

· II ·

LIBERTY:
THE TRADITION
AND
SOME OF ITS HEROES

· 7 ·

THE CATHOLIC WHIG
REVISITED

In his famous postscript to *The Constitution of Liberty*
Friedrich von Hayek identified Thomas Aquinas as
"the first Whig," and has several times since noted how
important it is to distinguish the Whig tradition from
that of many exponents of the classical liberal tradition.
Among Hayek's favorite exemplars of the Whig tradition
are Alexis de Tocqueville and Lord Acton. It is noteworthy that all three of Hayek's models are Catholic, and to
his list other names can readily be added: Jacques Maritain, Yves R. Simon, and John Courtney Murray.

In important ways, all these thinkers go beyond the
usual positions of "liberals." For example, they have a
respect for language, law, liturgy, and tradition that, in
some senses, marks them as "conservative." Still, they
believe in some human progress, and they emphasize
human capacities for reflection on alternatives and free
choice—characteristics that mark them as realistic progressives. With the liberals, they locate human dignity in
liberty, but *ordered* liberty (just as, for Aquinas, practical wisdom is *recta ratio*). The Catholic Whigs, then,

First published in *First Things*, March 1990.

present a distinctive mix: conservative, progressive, liberal, and realistic.

One of the best ways of seeing the richness of the Catholic Whig point of view is to examine its concept of community—or, rather, its codefinition of community and person. The present purpose is to present thereof a brief exposition.

In the Catholic Whig tradition, a true community respects free persons; an inadequate or false community does not. Correlatively, a fully developed person is capable of knowing and loving; but these are exactly the two human capacities that are inherently communitarian. Note again the codefinition: To be a free person is to know and to love others in community. A community is true when, in the ordinary circumstances of daily life, its institutions and practices enable persons to multiply the frequency of their acts of knowing and loving. False community represses capacities for reflection and choice. True community enlarges them. These are the lessons that guided the new human experiment in the Americas, in the city aptly named for the love of brothers, Philadelphia.

I

The primal experience of the two continents of the Americas has been the struggle to build new communities. When the first pilgrims departed from Holland to set sail across the great Atlantic for what they would call New England, they knew what they would not find waiting for them. They would not find warm inns with cheerful fires in fireplaces already built. They would not find fields ripe with grain, already protected by soundly built fences. On the contrary, they were pursuing an errand into a wilderness. The work of building up homes and cities loomed before them as a formidable task. Nearly everything they were to have they would have to create themselves. Climate and environment might well be more hostile than they could withstand; certainly no one person alone could survive. The future depended on their ability to build communities, and to build them in such fashion as would take root and eventually prosper.

While they were very conscious, indeed, of building a *new* world, and even then were beginning to imagine a *new order*, our ancestors were far from being indifferent to tradition. They brought books, ideas, artifacts, tools, and goods that they could not at first hope to provide for themselves. Even on shipboard, their faces were turned toward the immense tasks of building cities, churches, civic buildings, markets, and even facilities for carpenters, metalworkers, brickmakers, ironworkers, glassblowers, and for all the other crafts and trades indispensable for the fairly high levels of common life to which they had been accustomed.

Our ancestors also brought with them a complex heritage of ideas. Some historians of the American experience emphasize the radical break between the ancient, classical tradition of the "liberal" arts and the modern liberal tradition. The first springs from Plato and Aristotle, the second from Hobbes. The first roots itself in natural law, the second in natural rights. The first holds that humans are by nature social animals; the second holds that in "the state of nature" human is to human as wolf to wolf. By its harshness, the second injected perhaps sufficient realism and an ardent desire for checks and balances, so as to make a new experiment more likely of success. The first grounded better, perhaps, the hope of genuine human progress and success, as proper to the social constitution of the human heart and mind.

Nevertheless, the conflict between these two visions—that of the ancients and that of the moderns—should not be exaggerated. The formal light under which the ancients looked at nature was different from the formal light under which, e.g., Hobbes looked at the "state of nature." The ancients noted the ideal form of human nature, the human capacity for knowing and loving. These capacities are inherently social. Therefore, for the ancients, humans are (in their capacities, even if not always in their actual practice) social animals. Not all the ancients were idealists, however. There have not been many shrewder realists than Aristotle, who said that in politics we must be satisfied to see "some tincture of virtue."

And this, precisely, was Hobbes's starting place. He argued that, apart from civilization, humans showed barely a tincture of virtue. In the precivilized state, "nature" displays a barbaric "war of all against all." The formal light through which Hobbes inspects experience is not historical. He does not mean that once upon a time there was a Garden of Evil ("the state of nature"), the experience of which taught humans at a specific date to value civilization. Rather, his formal light was conceptual, and consisted in stressing the antisocial capacities of those human beings who lack all civilizing virtues. Hobbes thought that in our common life we are never very far from the state of nature, and indeed the experiences of our century have taught us to respect a certain Hobbesian pessimism.

Still, it is much more difficult than Hobbes thinks for humans to be purely evil in all respects. If the horrors of the modern age suggest that human evil is perhaps even more awful in its reach than he imagined, it is also the case that there is a broadly shared human revulsion against such evil. It is not "unnatural" for humans to be moved by the torture, pain, and death of others far away. Thus today, the human rights revolution is slowly affecting nearly all of humankind. In any case, the very scholars who insist upon the sharp divide between the world of Aristotle and the world of Hobbes prize mightily "the better angels of our nature" represented by higher standards of human rights performance.

It is precisely here that the Catholic Whig tradition has a crucial philosophical role to play in bridging the best of the ancient tradition with the best of the modern tradition. In a general way—to state my thesis baldly—the modern "liberal" tradition excelled in devising practical institutional protections for human rights. By contrast, the Great Tradition of the *philosophia perennis* excelled in casting a more accurate light upon those basic philosophical conceptions that undergird liberal institutions. Put another way, the philosophies of Hobbes, Locke, and others among the moderns are less than adequate *as philosophies*. Meanwhile, the philosophies of Aristotle, St. Thomas Aquinas, and others are less than adequate with regard to the practical institutions that would incarnate their conceptions in social structures. The present task of the Catholic Whig tradition is to form a new synthesis of philosophical conceptions and practical institutions that do justice, together, to "private rights" and "public happiness." This synthesis must join together the full actualization of both the human person and the human community.

II

It is obvious that the key conceptions here are "person" and "community." Here the Catholic intellectual tradition, in particular, is able to offer special light. As the German historian of philosophy Wilhelm Windel-brand has pointed out, the concept of "person" is richer than the concept of "individual," and arose historically from the efforts of Catholic theologians to do justice to the theological statement that *Jesus Christ is one person sharing two natures*, human and divine. Beyond Jesus' human individuality, theologians had to tangle with the concept of his personhood. Therefore, they thought long and hard about the difference between the two concepts, the individual and the person. "Individual" will serve for material things—one snowflake is unlike another. "Person" points to something that exceeds the capacities of material things, and may be used of nonmaterial agents of understanding and love such as angels (if there are such) and God. For human beings, "person" is better than "individual."

The human person, precisely *qua* person, is a founda-tional source of insight and love: autonomous, autarkic, whole, inviolable, inalienable, an end and not only a means. The human person is called directly to union with God, as even philosophers ignorant of the Bible (long ago) figured out. The person, therefore, can never be treated, even by the community, as a means rather than as an end. Conversely, it is in the nature of the human person—an originating source of knowing and of loving—to be in communion with others, who share in his or her knowing and loving. Knowing and loving are inherently acts of communion.

Thus the classical view, brought in Aquinas to a full-ness that was less developed in Aristotle, holds simulta-neously that, in one sense, the inherent end of person-hood is communion and, in a reciprocal sense, that the inherent end of a true community is full respect for the personhood of each of its members. A human commu-nity, therefore, is *sui generis*. It is not like a hive, or a herd, or a mere collective. Each of its members is not merely a member, a part of the whole. On the contrary, each is a whole, wholly worthy of respect in herself or himself. Each must be treated as an end, not solely as a means. Each has an autonomous life of his or her own, worthy of infinite respect as a participant in God's own originating power of knowing and of loving. Each is an agent of reflection and choice. Unless he or she is injuring others, the only way in which a genuine community can approach a rational person is by way of knowing and of loving; that is to say, through rational and civil persuasion, not through coercion, force, or systematic oppression.

Just the same, the classic Catholic tradition, even while working out wonderfully balanced accounts of person and community, tended to tip the balance toward community. Why is this? Perhaps it was because the social, familial, political, and economic institutions that would in later times enlarge the scope of liberty open to the human person remained for many long centuries unknown. Perhaps it was because existing communities were small and their survival was often threatened. (This fact is still visible to us in the thick battlements by which the walled cities of ancient and medieval Europe vainly tried to repel generations of hostile invaders.)

In any case, at least sixty times in his many works St. Thomas Aquinas articulates one variant or another of a classic dictum that goes back as far as Aristotle: "The good of the many is more godlike than the good of the individual." The example that made this observation cogent to the Great Tradition is the willingness of individuals to die to defend the common good of the city. It is easy to see why the sacrifice of self for the community seemed godlike. But there is also a danger in this formulation. It may suggest to the unwary that the individual is but a means to the survival of the community. Only in extraordinary circumstances, and for a full set of sound reasons, can a community justly ask so much of its citizens. Otherwise, it is wrong to imagine that the individual is always expendable if only the social whole chooses that expedient. Aquinas did not himself accept this dangerously broad implication. He could not, because of his concept of the human person.

Civilization, Thomas Aquinas liked to say, is constituted by reasoned discourse. The difference between barbarism and civilization consists in this: barbaric regimes coerce their citizens, civilized regimes approach citizens through their own autonomous capacities for full consent. Persons are treated as persons only when approached through knowing and loving. For free persons, the legitimacy of government lies in the consent of the governed.

The "consent of the governed" is a nonpartisan principle, clearly articulated in the American Declaration of Independence of 1776. This principle flows from the reality of the human person, an autonomous creature whose essential nature consists in a capacity for reflection and choice. The only appropriate approach to such agents is through reasoned consent. That truth, declared to be self-evident in 1776, was not then self-evident to all human beings. But historical experience worldwide, under tyranny and torture, has made that truth increasingly self-evident in our era. All the world recognizes today that any approach through tyranny, torture, or coercion—any attempt to treat human beings as part of a mere collective, as ants in an anthill, bees in a hive, sheep in a herd, or animals on an "animal farm"—distorts and oppresses the true capacities of human persons. Any such regime is bound to be as oppressive, uncreative, and unproductive as it is illegitimate. From many sad experiences, the world has learned that the source of human creativity is the human capacity for reflective choice.

It is therefore a mark of modern thought that it offers sharper and more sustained attention to the nature and the rights of the human person than did ancient thought. Where ancient and medieval societies tipped the balance toward the common good, modern societies have placed compensating weights—and sometimes more than compensating weights—on the side of the person. Modern institutions make this new emphasis practical, concrete, and consequential.

But where should one draw the line? How should one strike a balance? This debate is more than academic. Push too far in the direction of solidarity, and the outcome is the totalitarian collective. Push too far in the direction of the individual, and the outcome is egotism, moral relativism (subjectivism), and a war of all against all. Even among thinkers determined to avoid both extremes, how exactly to do due justice both to person and to community is not easily discernible—not in daily family life, not in the institutions of religion, not in political action, and not in the business corporation. Thinkers of a moderate bent wish to honor both the person and the community, both the needs of individuals and the needs of social harmony. But how, where, and in what degree?

My aim here is not to answer that question in the abstract. Instead, I take a hint from Tocqueville in *Democracy in America*. Tocqueville suggests that the terms of the ancient debate between the person and the community (between *personalism* and *solidarism*, as certain Europeans put it in the 1930s) have been changed by the American experience. The New World is different from the Old World. What we mean by "person" is different here, as well as what we mean by "community." And the

Novus Ordo has accordingly suggested a fresh historical solution to an ancient conundrum.

III

Alexis de Tocqueville was not only an astute observer: he was also a social scientist of the first rank. And he formulated from what he observed among those he took to be the first people to embody the "new order of the ages" the first "law" of the "new science of politics." His purpose was to alert Europe to a new tide in human history, a tide deep and wide and directed by Providence, that would soon, or eventually, sweep the whole world. He meant the tide of a new kind of democracy, a democratic republic with an effective respect for the singular human person. A new kind of political-economic-moral order was rising—under the hand of Providence, he thought—and perhaps the most striking thing about this new order was that in it "men have in our time carried to the highest perfection the art of pursuing in common the object of common desires, and have applied this new technique to the greatest number of purposes." Here Tocqueville called attention to a new reality, one which can fairly be described neither as individualistic nor, quite, as constituting a full community. This new reality is a new form of social life: the voluntary association.

In America, Tocqueville observed, when citizens discerned new needs or purposes, they voluntarily formed committees or other informal organizations to meet them. What in France citizens turned to the state to do for them, Tocqueville exclaimed, and what in Great Britain they turned to the aristocracy to do, in America they formed their own associations to accomplish. Thus they built great universities, museums, and art galleries; sent missionaries to the Antipodes; raised funds for the disabled; put up public monuments; fed and clothed victims of natural disasters, and the like. This new form of social life—never total enough to constitute a fully defined community, but far beyond the power of individuals alone—called for a new "knowledge of association."

> This new "knowledge of association" [Tocqueville explains] is the mother of all other forms of knowledge; on its progress depends that of all the others. . . . Among laws controlling human societies there is one more precise and clearer, it seems to me, than all the others. If men are to remain civilized or to become civilized, the art of association must develop and improve among them at the same speed as equality of conditions spreads.

Why association? Because inherent in respect for the human person is respect for the reflectively chosen forms of association that persons create in order to pursue their common interests. In order to constitute a people out of mere masses or mere mobs, such freely, rationally chosen associations are indispensable.

In an important sense (not only an historical sense, as actually happened in the United States), such freely chosen associations are prior to the state—prior philosophically and practically. Philosophically, because they ground the social nature of the human person in reflective and voluntary social life, duly proportioned to the human need of proximity, voice, and active participation. Practically, because human beings need immediate participation in the forming of social consent and they also need social protection, lest in their solitary individual selves they stand naked before the power of an omnipotent state.

In short, "mediating associations" or "mediating institutions," as these voluntarily formed local structures are technically called, are crucial forms of human sociality, and they are prior to the formation of a national society. They are defenses against the state. They are also natural expressions of concrete, fleshly human sociality. Before humans are citizens of states, they are active participants in society.

As Jacques Maritain has stressed, "society" is a far larger and more vital reality than "state." Only a densely active society with many vital civic associations is sufficiently defended against the state, whose tendencies have historically been tyrannous. Only a society with many vital associations fully expresses the social nature of the person. The new science of association, therefore, meets two basic needs of human nature, one positive, one negative. The social nature of humans gives rise to associations not only because individuals need protection from abuse, but also because they have a positive need for participation and self-expression. In addition, in a way entirely appropriate to the human person, associations come into being through personal consent.

Tocqueville is surely correct: the principle of association is, in fact, the first law of democracy. Without vital mediating institutions, intermediate between the lone individual and the state, democracy has no muscular social fiber: it is a void within which a mere mob is blown about by demagoguery. The strength of a people, as distinguished from a mob, lies in its capacity for voluntarily forming multiple associations of self-government and social purpose on its own. The social life of a people is rich, complex, and strong even before the question of a national state arises.

It is sometimes charged that the Anglo-American liberal tradition is excessive in its emphasis upon the individual and deficient in its philosophy of community.

That charge is not quite accurate; still, for the sake of argument, let me accept its burden. Suppose that it is true that the philosophy of the liberal society is inferior to, say, Catholic social thought on these two points. From that it does not follow that the institutional praxis of the liberal society is inferior to the institutional praxis of existing Catholic social orders. It is at least conceivable that liberal societies such as West Germany, Great Britain, France, and the United States pay a more just respect to the rights of persons on the one hand and, on the other hand, to the building up of intermediate social bodies through reflection and choice than do some existing Catholic countries. Explicit philosophy and institutional practice do not always coincide. Indeed, practice may often be better than philosophy. This was the judgment of Jacques Maritain in his *Reflections on America*: American practices are better, deeper, and richer, he concluded, than American ideology.

Let me further propose the Novak rule of philosophical interpretation. Philosophers (and theologians) often stress in their writings exactly what their cultures lack, and are silent about solid habits readily taken for granted. Thus in Great Britain, where social conformity has long been in fashion, where individuals are supremely sensitive to others around them and have a sort of social conscience internalized within their hearts, philosophers speak incessantly about the individual. By contrast, in Italy philosophers speak incessantly about community—while practicing an almost medieval and princely self-assertion and exhibiting a fiercely proud individualism that borders on anarchy. Compare in those two countries the social practice of boarding a bus. In London, citizens patiently and respectfully queue up in orderly fashion. In Rome, boarding a bus is one of the world's wildest adventures in laissez-faire as well as one of its most sensuous experiences. In London, where philosophers praise individualism, individuals defer to others; in Rome, where philosophers praise community, it's every man for himself. The Novak rule anticipates this turn.

IV

In sum, those who in the long run trust realism and the lessons of vivid human experience—and who hold to first principles such as the "self-evident truth" that human persons are appropriately respected solely when their native capacities for reflection and choice are permitted free play—seem to have been vindicated by human history. "The God who gave us life gave us liberty," Thomas Jefferson exclaimed, the same point he made in the text of the Declaration of Independence when declaiming on men's equal and inalienable rights. None of the rights he had in mind are American rights; they are human rights. They inhere in persons—they are the properties proper to human persons—because they were conferred on each directly by the Creator, who made all human persons in His image. Catholic thought adds further that as the proper life of God is insight and love, so also is the life proper to human persons. As God is a person, so are humans.

It is the distinctive achievement of the modern Catholic Whig tradition to have added to the classical perception of the primacy (in certain respects) of the community the modern perception of the primacy (in other respects) of the person. This achievement permits an unparalleled degree of societal concern for the rights, liberties, and dignity of human persons qua persons (i.e., not because of their opinions, beliefs, religion, ethnicity, or race). But it also nourishes the achievement of a vastly larger number of voluntary associations, a higher degree of voluntary social cooperation, a broader base of love and gratitude for the commonwealth, and a more explicitly consensual national community than was known in ancient or medieval times.

It is more than a theoretical possibility that we can create new social systems—or reconstitute old ones—so that historically unparalleled respect is shown both for individual persons and for the common good. Some three dozen societies on this planet (none of them, of course, saintly or likely to be mistaken for the Kingdom of God) have actually shown such respect, in their institutions and in their daily practice. Though far from perfection, and with each manifesting much to be done before liberty and justice for all are fully served, such societies afford protections for basic rights more broadly and efficaciously than was ever accomplished in any traditional, premodern, precapitalist, or prerepublican society.

To my way of thinking, the Whig tradition—and particularly the Catholic Whig tradition—offers the world's best statement of philosophical principles and practical guidelines concerning how and why free citizens should shape new societies worthy of their human rights and ordered liberties. Such societies, to secure these rights, must give primacy to community. But to build true and authentic communities, these societies must give primacy to persons. Both forms of primacy are important. Each is necessary for the other's definition—and for the other's flourishing.

To secure the rights of the person, give primacy to community. To build a genuinely human community, give primacy to the person. Such is the Catholic Whig tradition, tutored by the experience of the Americas and shocked by the terrors of the twentieth century. And such, now is most of the world's agenda.

· 8 ·

THOMAS AQUINAS V. HERETICS

Not long ago, I gave a paper on St. Thomas as the first Whig; that is, one of the founders of "the party of liberty."[1] One clue to this judgment came from the essays of Lord Acton on the origins of the idea of liberty.[2] The antecedents of my argument are clear enough in the political writings of Jacques Maritain, Thomas Gilby, O.P., and John Courtney Murray, S.J.[3] Basic concepts sharpened by St. Thomas—on the human person, conscience, liberty, the source of political power in the people, and the twin principles of the consent of the governed and the "mixed regime"—provided rich soil for the free institutions that were to arise much later in history.

To all this, however, there is one exception, although a very large one. Among serious thinkers in America who are hostile to Catholicism, article 3 of question 11 in the *Secunda Secundae* has probably been more frequently cited than any other paragraph in the entire collected works of St. Thomas Aquinas. His subject is, *Are heretics*

Based on a lecture delivered at the Center for Thomistic Studies, University of St. Thomas, Houston, Texas, February 15–16, 1996; first published in *First Things*, December 1995.

to be tolerated? A short summary of the answer of Aquinas is, No. How on earth did Aquinas justify such a shocking judgment?

1. The Context: The Great Heretic

The answer Thomas gave did not, of course, shock his contemporaries. That fact does not exonerate him. On the contrary, it reinforces the views of those who believe that Catholic teaching is inherently intolerant, by handing them evidence that the Catholic culture of the thirteenth century was narrow-minded, cold-blooded, and cruel. And, indeed, it is true that the world of the thirteenth century was cruel (although perhaps not more so than the world of the twentieth century). In the thirteenth century the Christian peoples of Italy, Germany, and France frightened one another by telling stories at night of the savageries of the peoples to the east, both Mongols and Saracens.

Within Christendom, codes of knighthood were established to curb, channel, and even civilize the passions of warriors. Just the same, acts of horror and terror were committed by Christian knights, and much feared by civilian populations. For Christian rulers or knights to inflict acts of terror on other Christians was thought to be heinous. That did not prevent the heinous from sometimes being done. Giving vent to passions of vengeance, cruelty, and bloodlust was held to be sinful. But some men of that time thought the Church was being unrealistic.

When Thomas Aquinas was a mere lad of thirteen or so, the Benedictine Monastery of Monte Cassino where he was a boarding student and oblate, was put to fire and sword by determined cavalry of Frederick II, the proud and defiant German emperor. Eleven monks were run through and burned to death. This was the monastery over which the Aquino family—and even the pope—had realistic hopes of making Thomas abbot. The young Thomas was sent home for a year, and later enrolled at the new University of Naples, where he met the newly founded Order of Preachers.

A few years later, Frederick II was excommunicated by the Council of Lyons, purportedly for the reign of massacre and terror that he had inflicted upon cities throughout Italy. At a whim, Frederick was capable of ordering an entire city razed, its men butchered or sold into slavery, its women sent eastward to become slaves of his Saracen friends. Frederick considered himself duty-bound to protect and to extend the patrimony of his family, the Hohenstaufen. He was in almost constant conflict with the popes, mostly for territorial and worldly reasons, although his personal habits and deeds also made him vulnerable to censure on spiritual grounds. His most recent biographer, David Abulafia of Cambridge University, shows considerable evidence that Frederick II—despite being condemned by some (and praised by others) for being the scourge of the papacy and even the anti-Christ—wished to remain by his own lights an orthodox, if rather eccentric, Catholic.[4] Frederick II remains an ambiguous figure who has haunted the German imagination even into our own century.[5]

After his excommunication at Lyons, the two older brothers of Thomas Aquinas who had served in Frederick's court for decades joined in a rebellion against Frederick at Parma that eventually failed, but not without coming close to success. When the rebellion's leader, the elderly Baron San Severino, was finally captured, Frederick ordered the seventy-year-old's nose cut off, tongue cut out, and one leg hacked off, and then commanded that he be carted in rags from village to village, so that Italians could see for themselves the price of rebellion. San Severino was the father-in-law of St. Thomas's beautiful younger sister, Theodora. The two brothers of Aquinas, former courtiers of Frederick, were tortured, made to languish in prison for years, and at last executed.

Frederick II was held by many to be the Great Heretic of the epoch who, for nearly thirty years, waged constant warfare throughout Italy, leaving a train of ruin, slaughter, humiliation, and misery. Just as St. Thomas was fortunate to know personally one king who was widely regarded as a saint, Louis IX of France, and at least two who were, on the whole, "good" kings, Edward Plantagenet of England and Charles of Anjou, so he knew at first hand, through bloody experience, one who was—and rejoiced in being—an on-again, off-again foe of the popes. In short, when the term "heretic" was used, it was not for Thomas Aquinas or his contemporaries an abstraction.

On the other hand, Frederick II was himself the foe of heresy. In his own legal code promulgated at Melfi in 1231, Frederick followed the legal precedents of the era, including those of the IV Lateran Council of 1215, in condemning heresy, sacrilege, treason, usury, and counterfeiting (in that order) as structural crimes against the state. Professor Abulafia, himself no friend of the Church of that time, explains the rationale of the Melfi code as follows:

Heresy, indeed, is presented as treason. Those who deny the articles of the Catholic faith implicitly deny the claims of rulers to derive their authority from God. They are enemies not merely of God and of the souls of individuals, but of the social fabric. Their questioning of religious truth involves a questioning of the monarch's command over the law; as enemies of the law, they are its legitimate targets, and the position of primacy accorded to legislation against heretics is thus entirely proper.[6]

The growing preoccupation with heresy in the thirteenth century, such as became apparent at the IV Lateran Council, seems to have been partly due to the scandals that accompanied the wealth and political power of the medieval papacy. The vivid contrast between the evangelical witness to poverty and charity and the grandiosity of the papal court stirred many popular passions. The constant warfare, heavy taxation, and depredations of battle that the poor were obliged to endure for generation after generation threw scores of thousands into misery and discontent.

Meanwhile, the ways of thinking of ordinary peoples (as well as of many of the learned) in the Mediterranean basin remained as they had been for centuries, tinged with Platonism and Manicheanism. In a pre-Christian manner, people tended to believe that the essential conflict in the human soul is the battle between the flesh and the spirit. Sometimes they inflated this battle to such grand dimensions that for them the world was divided between two cosmic forces, good and evil. From this it was a short step to declaring that everything connected with the human body is evil, and that in a "higher," purely spiritual state of consciousness lay the only human good. Such views had been common in gnostic circles for centuries. (One still encounters them in the novels of Nikos Kazantzakis.)

Corollaries to these fundamental principles were that embodied human beings are intrinsically evil, and must undertake severe ascetical practices to "free" the soul from its carnal prison; that marriage and the getting of children is evil; and that the Catholic Church, with its bodily sacraments and its doctrines of "the resurrection of the flesh," not to mention its rich and worldly ways, is a principle of evil. Holding such beliefs, a significant body of citizens in northern Italy and southern France "cut" themselves off (*sectare*) from the Catholic consensus, and began to form churches, even dioceses, of their own. These "sects" came to be called *Cathari* (the Pure Ones) or Albigensians, and came to be seen as radical threats not only to the moral and religious order but even to the political order of the time. Against them popes and kings launched local crusades, just as they had against the distant Saracen occupiers of the Holy Lands.

It is likely that the term "heretics" in the writings of St. Thomas conjured up images of these sectarians most of all.[7] Indeed, the founding of the Order of Preachers in Toulouse in southern France immediately involved St. Dominic and his colleagues in preaching against the *Cathari* throughout the region. At a time when the doctrines of Joachim of Fiore (1135–1202) were rapidly spreading, the poor were especially vulnerable to the millennarianism of the *Cathari*, their attacks on the riches of the church and the worldliness of kings, and their evocations of poverty and contempt for the body. By assuming themselves a life of evangelical poverty, combined with orthodox preaching about the goodness of creation and the human body, the Dominicans undercut the preaching of the *Cathari*. The Dominicans and the Franciscans sponsored the first *creches*, which were becoming popular at this time, offering tender scenes of the birth of Jesus in the crib at Bethlehem. They wished to bring out the human, fleshly side of Christianity.

The *Cathari*, in effect, forced the Catholic community to distinguish itself far more sharply than before against Platonism and Manicheanism. The body-affirming, incarnate side of Christian teaching, combined with a re-awakening of the aspiration toward a life of evangelical poverty, also came to vivid life in the preaching both of St. Dominic and St. Francis of Assisi (1182–1226), nota-bly in his hymns to the goodness of birds, animals, and all the earth.

At the same time, the philosophy of Aristotle was also beginning to reach the Christian world of the thirteenth century, correcting the philosophy of Plato on the place of the body, earth, empiricism, time, and contingency in human life. Even here, however, the clarity of Aristotle was clouded by the Platonic preferences of the Islamic Commentators, especially Avicenna and Averroes, through whom the newly discovered texts of Aristotle—missing from the West for a millennium—were becoming known. In universities from Naples and Bologna to Paris and Oxford, secular masters opposed to the religious or-ders and to the constraints of the existing Christian order gladly embraced these Arabian glosses on Aristotle.

These glosses called into question the creation of the world in time, the role of the senses and the imagination in human knowing, the individuality (and personal re-sponsibility) of the human intellect and will, the immor-tality of the human composite of body and soul, the role of divine Providence, the single standard of one truth governing both theology and philosophy, and other foundations of both Catholic faith and empirical (as dis-tinct from gnostic) reason. Among Scholastic philoso-phers themselves, Platonists and Averroists such as the brilliant Siger of Brabant championed these doctrines, sometimes in full appreciation for the devastation they wrought in Christian teaching, sometimes blindly.

Thus, in the thirteenth century, within the bosom of Christianity and in the heart of the Christian universities themselves, the intellectual stakes were very high. Small mistakes in philosophy (concerning the role of the senses in cognition, for example) led inexorably to the denial of basic foundations of the Christian faith. In such heady, fertile, creative times, moreover, pride in one's own intellectual originality was an ever-present intoxicant. Truth often intermixed with falsehood, good with evil. The art of discernment was a vital necessity, both in the arena of theory and in the arena of practice; discernment was a good much to be prized. The Catholic world felt in these new times an urgent need for a *sensus Christi*, a way of thinking in, through, and with the revelation of Jesus Christ, the *Logos* "through Whom and with Whom and in Whom were made all the things that are made."

Such was the context within which St. Albert the Great discovered in his pupil, Thomas of Aquino, a rare equanimity of spirit and a fearless intellect, and saw in this tall, large-framed lad, regarded by his fellow students as a speechless ox, "An ox whose bellows will be heard around the world." Aquinas took to the insights of Aristotle into the relations of body and spirit as a fish to water. He seized upon these (not least in his tractatus *Against the Averroists: On There Being Only One Intellect*)[8] as a key for shedding crucial light on aspects of Christian doctrine much threatened by the *Cathari*, on the one hand, and by the Averroists, on the other.

Of course, Aquinas saw that Aristotle was not always right, and did not hesitate to correct him, to push his thought further (to original notions of the conscience and the will, for instance), and above all to build an entirely new context—that of the revelation of love in Jesus Christ—for understanding even the things Aristotle got right. In brief, Albert the Great, the most learned man of his time, saw in his pupil the new master of the Christian inheritance to that time. That brief era itself, of course, had its own faults, and the Thomistic synthesis, like everything human, would itself contain damaging weaknesses.

Some of these weaknesses are clearly revealed in Thomas's response to the famous question 11, article 3, which is our present subject.

2. The Text Itself

Thomas begins question 11, article 3, by citing three traditional texts. The first of these texts urges forbearance and gentleness; the second, the necessity of factions in the Church in order that "those who are genuine among you may be recognized"; and the third, the parable that the servant should suffer the tares to grow along with the wheat until the end of time. After repeating these traditional texts, St. Thomas turns his face sharply against the heretic. Let me quote in full what he writes, because the text runs so directly against contemporary sensibilities, understandings, and social institutions:

> I reply: With regard to heretics there are two points to be observed, one on their side, the other on the side of the Church. As for heretics their sin deserves banishment, not only from the Church by excommunication, but also from this world by death. To corrupt the faith, whereby the soul lives, is much graver than to counterfeit money, which supports temporal life. Since forgers and other malefactors are summarily condemned to death by the civil authorities, with much more reason may heretics as soon as they are convicted of heresy be not only excommunicated, but also justly be put to death.
>
> But on the side of the Church is mercy which seeks the conversion of the wanderer, and she condemns not at once, but after the first and second admonition, as the Apostle directs.[9] Afterwards, however, if he is yet stub-

born, the Church no longer confident about his conversion, takes care of the salvation of others by separating him from the Church by excommunication, and furthermore delivers him to the secular court to be removed from this world by death. The *Decretum* repeats Jerome's comment, *Cut off the decayed flesh, expel the mangy sheep from the fold, lest the whole house, the whole paste, the whole body, the whole flock burn, perish, rot, die. Arius was but a single spark in Alexandria, but as it was not at once put out, the whole world was laid waste by his flame.*[10]

In reading this repugnant text, the first requirement is to clarify what Aquinas means by *heretic*. He does not mean a Moslem or a Jew, an unbeliever or an infidel. He means a Catholic who has chosen to deny his faith, in whole or in part.

For Jews and Moslems, Aquinas argues for toleration, not only of their persons but also of their public rites. It is true that from his viewpoint their faiths are incomplete and to that extent erroneous. It is also true that for Thomas toleration is a means for gaining respect for the true faith, rather than an end in itself, a duty simply owed to the conscience of others. But he does argue for toleration for Jews and Moslems in an emphatic way, as he does not for heretics. About the Jews, for example, he writes: "Among unbelievers there are some who have never received the faith, such as heathens and Jews. These are by no means to be compelled, for belief is voluntary."[11] And about the religious rites of Jews and Muslims, he adds:

Thus from the fact that the Jews keep their ceremonies, which once foreshadowed the truth of the faith we now hold, there follows this good, that our very enemies bear witness to our faith, and that what we believe is set forth

as in a figure. The rites of other infidels, which bear no
truth or profit, are not to be tolerated in the same way,
except perhaps to avoid some evil, for instance the scandal or disturbance that might result, or the hindrance to
the salvation of those who, were they unmolested, might
gradually be converted to the faith.[12]

Similarly, Aquinas shows a great deal more respect for
unbelievers, such as his beloved Aristotle, who knew
nothing whatever about Christ and his revelation, than
he does for heretics. He admires in unbelievers how
much of the truth about man revealed by Christ they had
come to, simply by studying the laws of their own
being.[13] (For Aquinas, it is inconceivable that there are
two truths, one learned from the things that are, the
other learned from faith. For him, the one God, the Creator, is the one source of truth.) For that he respects
them, acknowledging that by fidelity to truth they served
the God they did not know, and so are dear to God.

Moreover, the student of Aquinas already familiar
with his teachings on individual personal responsibility,
conscience, and the role of reason and will in free choice
is likely to be surprised by his unremitting hostility to
heretics. Did Thomas not write many such passages as
this one:

> Every judgment of conscience, be it right or wrong, be it
> about things evil in themselves or morally indifferent, is
> obligatory, in such wise that he who acts against his con-
> science always sins. (*III Quodlibet, 27*)

Or again, this passage from the *Summa Theologica* (*1a-
2ae, xix, 5*):

> Since conscience is the dictate of reason, the application
> of theory to practice, the inquiry, *whether a will that dis-*

obeys an erroneous conscience is right, is the same as, *whether a man is obliged to follow a mistaken conscience*.

Now because the object of a volition is that which is proposed by the reason, if the will chooses to do what the reason considers to be wrong, then the will goes out to it in the guise of evil. Therefore it must be said flatly that the will which disobeys the reason, whether true or mistaken, is always in the wrong.

Given such teachings as these, why could not Thomas respect the conscience of heretics?

By heretic, Aquinas meant a person of Catholic faith who deliberately and resolutely, even after having been called to reflect on the matter, has *chosen* to renounce that faith in some important particular. Aquinas points out that the word *heresy* comes from the Greek word for *choice*. Heresy for him is not a mistake of the intellect but a choice of the will. It is a choice of adherence to a proposition, or set of propositions, known by the chooser to contradict the Catholic faith. It is a choice to cut oneself off from communion in the Catholic faith (to put oneself in a *sect*—a thing cut off).

But suppose, we Americans might say today, a contemporary of Aquinas had honestly come to believe that the Church of Innocent III, Gregory IX, inquisitors, torturers, benefice-rich monks, and conniving clerics of the thirteenth century no longer represented the evangelical *ecclesia* founded by Christ? Suppose someone thought that only a reform that overthrew centuries of accretion could save Christian truth? That, of course, would be a most grave sin against the unity that Christ willed for his Church.

But what about the thousands throughout France and Italy and Spain falsely accused of heresy, or wrongly caught up in the machinery of heresy-hunting, such as

Paul Johnson describes in his *History of Christianity*?[14] One such man, Johnson reports, was burned at the flaming stake simply for refusing to accept trial by ordeal, unless his inquisitors could prove to him that by exposing himself to ordeal he was not improperly testing God and thus putting his soul in jeopardy. Cloistered Aquinas might be, but he could hardly have helped knowing at least a little about the role that some Dominicans of his day were playing in the inquisition of heretics.

In the thirteenth century, all sorts of cruelties were common. The popes themselves committed ten of nineteen descendants of Frederick II to prison, one of his daughters for forty-eight years, and saw to the deaths of others in battle or capture. When Frederick II's chief advisor, Taddeo da Suessy, was taken prisoner at Parma, his hands were immediately cut off by those loyal to the pope and he was thrown into a dungeon. For suspicion of stealing from him, Frederick seized his other chief advisor (later celebrated by Dante) the poet della Vigna, had his eyes burned out, and threw him into a dungeon. There the poet killed himself by pounding his head against the damp stone walls. In southern France, men and women alike were accused of being heretics, given no way to defend themselves except by enduring torture, and if found guilty covered with pitch and set aflame. Swords aloft, soldiers were set free upon entire settlements of heretics, which they torched. During the lifetime of Aquinas, all of Provence was swept by violence against heretics—some of whom were living according to their own lights admirable evangelical lives.

Yet the cold words of Aquinas stand there, approving of the use of the secular arm, describing heresy as a pestilence to be blotted out, diseased cells to be cut away. And Aquinas concludes with the terrible ruthlessness of the words of St. Jerome: Arius and the sons of Arius should be extinguished before their contagion spreads.

In 1215, the IV Lateran Council itself had commended the sentence of death for heretics, and popes and bishops were urging the secular arm to be more active in uprooting heresy. As we have seen in the case of Frederick II, the reasons why kings and emperors, even those at war with the papacy, listed heresy first among the crimes against the state were several and profound. For one thing, kings claimed power from God according to the Christian faith and, often enough, especially in that age of exaggerated papal claims to universal worldly power, their power was tangibly and visibly legitimated directly through coronation by the pope of Rome. (Well after the founding of the United States, Napoleon still sought such a coronation.) Heresy directly undercut kingly power.

For another thing, thirteenth-century societies were highly fragile. Most people, even many nobles, were illiterate. Beyond ties of kinship, many had little to bind them to others. "The many" were subjects of "the few"—and one ruling aristocrat was often overturned by another. Sharing in the local horizons of small cities or villages might bond people in intimate memories, and participating in guilds or trades might offer some association outside of family or neighborhood life. But geographical isolation was often intense, and shifting patterns of warfare, baronial allegiance, and foreign occupation awakened acute local insecurity. Under political anarchy, the common people and the poor suffered much. Under all these uncertainties, the chief consensual bond among peoples was Catholic faith and Catholic ritual. Virtually all unifying conceptions of relationship and social weight, meaning and order, came from that faith.

Neither the rich nor the nobility (increasingly, as trade

and commerce grew, these were not necessarily the same) could trust one another. Barons and counts were obliged to protect themselves against each other by dwelling within heavily armed fortresses. (Even the Aquino family had three castles, with knights sufficient to defend them; the novelist Louis de Wohl imagines that the Aquinos could bring one hundred knights to the service of the emperor.)[15] The vendetta was the most reliable and common form of justice. The politics even of princes was first and chiefly about naked power, and princes were thrown back upon shifting alliances based upon self-interest. The struggle to build even national, let alone international, systems of justice, reason, and legality was still in its infancy. Such systems were more clearly articulated on parchment than available in reality.

On the other hand, in the no-man's-land between warring barons and ordinary people, lay confraternities were beginning to spring up to fill the looming social vacuum by undertaking needed civic projects. A new class of lay professionals led by trailblazers such as Albertanus of Brescia[16] was laying the foundations of a civic order. But the emergence of a true civil society lay still far in the future. In the thirteenth century, there still seemed to be something like the war of all against all. Emperors, kings, barons, counts, and even bishops and popes seemed to be in perpetual strife with one another.

The time was not yet ripe for the impulses of modernity, nor even for the reformation of the Church. The precariousness of *life*, under threat from famine and plague as well as from war, was signalled in the apocalyptic feelings and expressions of the time. The still greater precariousness of *civilization*, now barely exiting from centuries of illiterate tribal barbarism, was widely felt. Monastery schools and libraries, professional schools and universities, were still relatively new institutions frequented only by a few.

"Civilization" itself was in those days more a matter of ideas and symbols in the mind, an interior conversation across centuries, so to speak, than a set of integrating public institutions and laws. Civic institutions were still far from catching up to vaguely felt aspirations and ideals. Practically the only international organization—even to speak of "nations" in the modern sense is premature—was the Catholic Church, which itself was stronger in its network of faith and symbols grasped by minds and imaginations than in its institutional effectiveness. There was more in common in the life of souls than in public organization. Even the idea of one common (and holy!) European empire was more a dream of emperors than a feat mastered by those who tried to realize it. Europe consisted of divided, sometimes isolated, and nearly always warring fiefdoms, not yet institutionally united.

This was the context within which, no matter how horrendous the measures being practiced to keep it in check, heresy was perceived as the primal threat to social order, both by ecclesiastics and by secular rulers (even those at war with the papacy, as most at one time or another were). What Thomas Aquinas argued in that repugnant question 11, article 3, had already been codified in both civil and ecclesiastical law for at least two generations. One might have hoped that many of Thomas's own principles about the human person, liberty, conscience, and the indispensable freedom of faith would have led him to oppose the widespread legal consensus. Perhaps, though, an even greater moral and civic anarchy would have resulted than people were then already experiencing. Perhaps their sense of precariousness was already stretched beyond human tolerance.

Narrow and constricted as it was, the order supplied

to the European peoples by primitive Christendom, that premature construction of a supposed City of God on earth, may have seemed better than the chaos of a war of all against all. Bad as it was, an enforced consensus in the faith, at least among those who had once accepted it (and only they could be defined as heretics), seemed to most at the time better than the alternative.

These preceding paragraphs are the best I can do in trying to understand how good minds in the thirteenth century could have accepted the consensus reflected in question 11, article 3.

It would not always be so. The Protestant Reformation was lurking only two centuries ahead. But by then civic institutions, commerce, prosperity, literacy, and many other fundamentals of a new order would be much farther advanced.

Still, we ought not to leave question 11, article 3, without asking ourselves what sort of institutions, and what sort of social understandings, are preconditions, if the basic principles of personhood, liberty, and conscience ("the Whig principles") elsewhere articulated by Aquinas are to be applied to heresy. No theologian today would hold the doctrine of question 11, article 3. Vatican Council II certainly did not.[17] What steps in theological reflection were necessary to take us from the reply of the *Secunda Secundae* to Vatican II? We should not allow so long a step as that to be taken in silence and darkness.

3. A Theology of the Open Society

It has often been said that the Christian faith must work in human history like yeast in dough. It is not designed to bring about miraculous results, as if the Son of Man had come with legions of angels and archangels and transformed the face of the earth. On the contrary, life on earth was to remain a vale of tears, and the human race was to expect, like Jesus, to have to pick up the cross and follow him. Thus, although an outline of the noble possibilities that God had in mind for human beings could be discerned in the words and life of Jesus, the institutions that might routinize the flowering of those possibilities did not yet exist in the time of the Roman Empire nor its fall—nor yet in the thirteenth century, and not yet today.

The social problem of the thirteenth century had three aspects. First, torture and tyranny ran amok; there were far too few protections of the dignity and freedom of individuals and minorities, and for that matter even of majorities. Second, poverty was often grinding and bitter, and there were few institutions for creating new wealth and, on that basis, steady improvement in the lives of the poor. Third, the spiritual center and moral core of the entire political, economic, and cultural order was improperly (although at that time perhaps necessarily) invested in the Catholic Church. It is this third aspect of the social problem of the thirteenth century that is brought into relief by the answer of Aquinas to question 11, article 3.

It is easy to see how many Christians might have thought that the "City of God" imagined by St. Augustine required a system in which cult would be the center of culture. It is not even too hard to understand how the primacy of the spiritual power revealed by Jesus Christ, by comparison with the secular power, might be thought to require official, public recognition of the primacy of the Church. From that, it would have been a small step to the claims of Innocent III, that the secular power was subordinate to the spiritual power, so that the pope deserved primacy over all merely secular powers. The *logic* of how such ideas would have developed is clear.

But the unintended consequences of such conceptions are many—and very damaging both to human societies and to the Church. As I say, perhaps in the actual flow of history it was obligatory and even useful for the Church, and especially the papacy, to step into the vacuum left by the collapse of the Roman Empire in Europe and the Middle East. In any case, that is what happened. Unless it had happened, it is hard to see what other institution would have inspired and actually accomplished the building of the libraries, universities, and schools that preserved, collected, and sponsored the study of the great treasures of Greece and Rome, and the new discoveries of later centuries. Apart from the guardianship of the Church over many centuries, it is hard to see whence would have derived the resources that later gave birth to the rise of modern science, the Renaissance, and the Enlightenment. The fundamental conceptions of progress, truth, compassion, the dignity of the individual, and the centrality of personal liberty on which modern progress rests are rooted in Jewish and Christian beliefs about human nature and destiny.[18]

Nonetheless, from what happened in fact, as a matter of historical contingency, it is a mistake to conclude that what happened was ideal. On the contrary, by placing the guardianship of the consensual ideals of worldly civilization in the hands of the institutions of the Christian Church, the Christian West was highly likely to end up violating consciences and putting heretics to death in abominable ways. However divinely protected the human institutions of the Church may be, they are bound to be weighed down in daily practice by human frailty and sin. And many protests against frailty and sin—against corruptions and abuses—are likely to be interpreted as heresy. Since the integrity of the social fabric has been made to rest on key Christian beliefs (and the power of legitimate rulers on ecclesiastical approbation), criticisms of Christian practice that spill over into criticism of underlying interpretations of the gospels are highly likely to be taken as acts of treason against the state.

In short, by allowing Christian faith to be the consensual foundation of the political and social order, as it were the *form* of political life, the shaping spiritual life of the state, Christendom confounded the things of Caesar with the things of God. In modern times, such a vision, at least in analogous if not precisely the same thirteenth-century form, has been called "integrism." Integrism is a premature uniting of the institutions of faith and the institutions of the state. (I do not say the institutions of *church* and state, but those of *faith* and state, since the latter is a more profound temptation, even, than the former. One might imagine a pope, say, filling in through some contingency as the head of a great state—as perhaps the greatest available talent in some dire secular emergency—without thereby committing that state to taking as its inner form the Christian faith. It is the latter that is the greater danger.)

The Christendom of the thirteenth century understood itself as having as its foundational *form* the integrity of Christian faith. For this reason, it was bound to reject heresy as treason to the state. The state could tolerate those who did not pretend to be Christian, for Christian teachings themselves commended such toleration (and actually more than that, a genuine respect for good-faith differences of conscience). What it could not tolerate was those of *counterfeit* faith, those who said they were Christians while choosing to deny important aspects of Christian faith. This was far too severe a monism. Its most highly probable consequence was a regime of terror, trying to ferret out false consciences from true, trampling on the inner forum of the soul that belongs most properly to God. For the likelihood of many persons at once launching diverse interpretations of the gospels, and organizing themselves in rival organizations, and thus undermining the foundations of the monistic state was extremely high, as Europe was to experience in the centuries after the thirteenth.

At the close of the twentieth century, it cannot be said that we have yet solved the problem of how to imagine the proper relation between the Christian faith and the state. (The Jewish state Israel and the Muslim states have not solved this problem either; nor have the forces of secular humanism proven any more adept at addressing the moral and cultural crisis of modern societies.) As the great French social philosopher Pierre Manent has pointed out in his brilliant essay, "Christianity and Democracy,"[19] the modern secular nation state is itself in a crisis of transition; and the Catholic Church, having made its peace with and given its support to democratic experiments, is necessarily concerned with the "privatizing" and relativizing of conscience that seems to be growing like a corrosive infection within secular democracies.

It is obvious that the interests of Thomas Aquinas were, above all, metaphysical and theological, far more than social or political. His treatment of questions regarding the former sparkle with originality and limpid brilliance; his treatments of the latter are, for the most part, perfunctory. But for those whose vocations lie in the area of political and social philosophy (and theology), a great question remains: What is the proper ideal for the relation of Christian faith to the open society? It is clear enough that a relation that entails the persecution of heretics is repugnant to Christian faith. The special circumstances of the thirteenth century remain a vivid case study in what *not* to do. But if the profession of Christian faith is *not* to be constitutionally required, as certainly it should not be, just *how* can Christian faith escape from being merely privatized and relativized? And how can open societies themselves be saved from giving a posthumous victory to such relativists as Hitler and Mussolini, who began by stating that nothing in politics is right or wrong, only power matters?

Such problems have not received resolution even in our own time. Perhaps they can never be resolved with finality, but only by trial and error, and on an always tentative basis.

· 9 ·

THE ACHIEVEMENT OF
JACQUES MARITAIN

Although the twentieth century was often proclaimed by the church to be the "Age of the Laity," it remains true that most Catholic discourse is still taken up with the words of popes, bishops, priests, and sisters. Nonetheless, as in the nineteenth century so in the twentieth, a number of lay men and women have made intellectual contributions to religious discourse of such magnitude as to place not just Roman Catholics but the entire body of Christians in their debt. Of these, no one has been so influential in so many different spheres as Jacques Maritain (1882–1973), a man who, in addition to his intellectual stature, was widely esteemed for his holiness of life.

His range was truly catholic. Perhaps no one in any tradition has written more beautifully of the subject he addressed in his book *Creative Intuition in Art and Poetry*. (So lovely is that book that often, while reading it as an undergraduate, I had to put it down and go for a long walk, my heart burning with more than it could bear.) In political and social thought, no Christian has ever written a more profound defense of the democratic

First published in *First Things*, December 1990.

idea and its component parts, such as the dignity of the person, the sharp distinction between society and the state, the role of practical wisdom, the common good, the transcendent anchoring of human rights, transcendent judgment upon societies, and the interplay of goodness and evil in human individuals and institutions. Indeed, in the thrust that this body of thought gave to Christian Democratic parties after World War II, Maritain gained the right to be thought of as one of the architects of Christian Democratic politics both in Europe and Latin America.

Nonetheless, it is perhaps in his profound grasp of the metaphysics of the *philosophia perennis* that one must seek the essence of Maritain's achievement. More clearly and subtly than anyone else in modern times, and over a larger body of materials, Maritain grasped the "intuition of being" that animates the deepest stratum of Catholic intellectual life. For him, this was at once an intuition of charity as well as of being. He chose most often to express this intuition philosophically—philosophy, not theology, was his vocation—but his vision of *caritas*, "the Love that moves the sun and all the stars," broke through over and over again.

A number of critics have pointed out that of all Maritain's books no doubt the most seminal, like a pebble plunked in a quiet pool and rippling outward in ever-expanding circles, is his tiny *Existence and the Existent*. This "Essay on Christian Existentialism," a difficult and dense but immensely poignant book, lies at the heart of his work. Its brief 142 pages were penned in Rome from January through April of 1947, as much of Europe still lay in the ruins of war and as the terribly disappointing Cold War of the subsequent era was just beginning. Its five compact chapters, it is safe to predict, will echo in the world's thinking for generations to come. Indeed, their full meaning is likely to become more apparent in the future than at the time of the book's first appearance, as thinkers from other world traditions engage its arguments.

I would not suggest that there are no faults or limits in Maritain's achievement. Concerned as much as he was for the poor (or, as he usually expressed it in the vulgar Marxism current at the time, the "workers"), it is surprising how little sustained attention Maritain gave to the most significant new discipline of postmedieval times, political economy, with the accent on economy. Maritain came to the problems of politics and society rather late in his reflections and then, having achieved much, never took up a study of the great economic classics, especially those of the Austrian and Anglo-American worlds. Further, much as he admired the United States—a civilization, he felt, full of reverberations of the realities to which he was trying to point in *Integral Humanism*—Maritain never fully grappled with such classics of American political economy as *The Federalist*, his fellow Frenchman Alexis de Tocqueville's *Democracy in America*, or the writings of Abraham Lincoln.

On the whole, Maritain wrote a beautiful prose, a prose that reaches the heart and the imagination more than that of most philosophers, even while manifesting a Thomist love of exquisite clarity, particularly in the making of distinctions. To read him on any subject is to be forced to look, through such distinctions, from many angles of vision at once. And all for the sake of unity: "To distinguish in order to unite" was a most suitable motto for his life's work. He had a passion for clear and precise ideas, distinguished sharply from their nearest neighbors, as well as for the relations that tie each idea to every other. Sometimes, indeed, he tried to capture too much at once, piling up within a single sentence distinctions within distinctions or introducing an analogous aside, all the while trying to encapsulate an entire argument. Many of his sentences require rereading. But the effort is almost always worthwhile, for Maritain's true conversation partners were less his contemporary critics than the classics, whose intricate treasures he did not wish to muffle, encrust, or belittle by oversimplification.

I

In the autumn of 1960, in one of my first conversations with a full professor in Harvard's philosophy department, a teacher of metaphysics and ethics who confessed cheerily that he deeply admired Hume's happy atheism, mentioned how nonetheless deeply impressed he had been with Jacques Maritain during the latter's presence on campus. "He was perhaps the most saintly philosopher I have ever known," he said, "gentle, kind, honest, almost childlike. Of course, I didn't agree with a single position he took. But I did come to admire him a great deal." This was meant to be a warning to me, of course; I, also a Catholic, should not expect an easy time at Harvard. Yet it was also meant as a token of esteem for a significant tradition and a remarkable thinker: no small tribute considering its source.

That professor's tribute to Maritain's saintliness, his gentleness, his childlike manner has remained with me, especially the unusual word (for Harvard), "childlike." This is, I think, the key to Maritain's intuition of being, a way of seeing in which so many other philosophers simply could not follow him. Maritain approached each day with a certain wonder—at the color of the sky, the scent of the grass, the feel of the breeze. He marveled that such a world could have come to be. There was, he understood, no necessity in its coming to be. It had happened. Here it was. He could sense it, his every sensible organ alive to its active solicitations of color, sound, scent, taste, and feel. More than that, his intellect would wonder at it, knowing that it did not have to be as it was on that particular day, or on any other day. And it could also cease to be.

Well before the cloudburst of the first atomic bomb, long before a perceived "ecological crisis," Maritain perceived the fragility of life on earth—not only in his personal mortality, nor even in the fragility of planet earth. Rather, Maritain sensed, in the obscure way of the human intellect at its most childlike and most profound, that all changeable created things—all things short of an Existent necessarily and fully existing in Itself—are fragile and dependent.

My professors at Harvard found this intuition difficult to grasp or, rather, even at the edge of comprehension, profoundly resisted it. I remember a seminar on the Existence of God taught by Professor Rogers Albritton, a student of Wittgenstein who imported many of Wittgenstein's legendary mannerisms into our classroom. Professor Albritton was diagramming on the blackboard Aquinas's Way to the Existence of God from Contingency and Necessity. The good professor, an honest man as far as he could go, kept pointing to the major and minor premises, one after the other, and then confessed that he could find no notion of "necessity" that made the argument flow into Aquinas's conclusion. He tried to supply all the definitions of "necessity" known to him. None would work. I remember summoning up my courage and raising my hand. It was about twenty minutes before class was to adjourn.

Nervously, I reminded him (Professor Albritton also taught Aristotle) that, based upon a rudimentary (and now recognized to be false) empirical observation, Aristotle and Aquinas thought that the stars in the firmament were unchangeable, permanent, and, thus in a special sense, "necessary beings," different from all other changeable substances they had observed. Suppose, I hesitantly said, this gave them a warrant for speaking empirically of "necessary beings." And suppose, further, that they postulated still other necessary beings, in a different class, not composed of material properties at all, yet nonetheless not contingent, not changeable, but beings-in-themselves, which, once existing, never cease to exist. Suppose, further, that such necessary beings could cause the coming into existence of the contingent beings of whose existence we had no doubt. All these suppositions might be false, I remember saying. Still, if Aristotle and Aquinas held them (and clearly the texts make plain that they did), then, looking again at the premises on the board, doesn't the conclusion suddenly flow? Professor Albritton rubbed his chin Wittgenstein-style and looked again at the board. "Hmmm," he said. "Good point." He looked at his watch. "Well, let's think about that until next time." The class adjourned early. We never went back to the Argument from Contingency.

Young as I was, I had no illusions that suddenly Harvard would reach the conclusion that, indeed, mysterious and terrifying as it may be, there is (or even could be) a necessary Existent that explains how this fragile world of change and contingency could come to be and, perhaps, to perish. No one had any problem contemplating some Big Bang of "happening to come to be" nor, at least in later years, does anyone have severe doubts that, whether with bang or whimper, this fragile world of ours could cease to be. The *hard* thing to accept, it seems, is that there is an Existent not doomed to our changeability, on whom our existence depends. (Why should that be so hard, I wondered, since so many millions of human beings have always believed it? Life for Harvard philosophers, it seems, is more difficult than for others.)

A childlike adult, however, aware of no special need to see the world as a Harvard philosopher does, could not help being struck by the marvel that no one denies: that things marvelously are and then are not. The fragility of all beings that we encounter is all too obvious to the sensitive intellect. This sharp taste of fragile existence is "the intuition of being"—or, to be more precise, since the one word *being* is sometimes used of more than one aspect of reality, "the intuition of existing."

Let us consider for a moment the difference between the existing of things and their essential characteristics. The air outside as I write is a cool, fresh October air, blown in from Canada, whereas yesterday's air, blown in from the Caribbean, was muggy and moist. It is at moments not their *coolness* and their *mugginess* that so much attract my attention as the fact that one is and the other was but is not; and the sure knowledge that the one that today is will also pass away. So it is also with the pen so comfortable now in my fingers; and with this narrow-lined paper on which I write and soon (once the typescript is prepared) to be thrown away; and with my very fingers themselves. All will return to dust. Yet today they gloriously *are*, and the taste of that existing is so keen that it sometimes makes one wish to exult and to break into glories.

I do not wish to confuse this insight into existing with the further inference (although it seems to be almost instantaneous) that I should thank Someone, Something, Some Glory for the good fortune of existing. These are two separate movements of the soul. Yet the most salient one, surely, if only because for us it is the first, is the intuition of the sheer existing of fragile, unnecessary things. (Had I died on the numerous occasions when I am aware of almost having done so, the particular existents mentioned above would never have been; had my parents never given me birth, or their parents them . . . so easily would the world never have experienced these fragile existents.)

Nonetheless, I am emboldened by the recent testimony of my second-favorite atheist humanist, Sidney Hook—Albert Camus still being my first—who just before his death confided to the American Jewish Committee Archives that there were many times in his life, at the height of his powers, that he often felt well up within him the desire to say thanks that things, which might have gone badly, worked out in existence as they had. This barely conscious, intuitive inference seems to me wholly natural. It seems to me also a bit of data about the human intellect that ought never to be lost to the attention of philosophers. Sidney Hook was a supremely honest man, willing to put on the record evidence that went against his own philosophy. True, Hook never understood that bit of data as Maritain did, or accepted the interpretation of human life that went with it, but his experience of the movement of human intellect to utter thanks remains a phenomenon to be explained.

II

It is not my intention, however, to spell out the implications that Maritain derived from his intuition of the existent, not at least in the direction of metaphysics, the philosophy of God, or even Jewish and Christian faith. (Maritain was deeply involved through his wife Raissa in questions of Jewish as well as Christian faith; in fact, he may have done as much as any Christian in our time to lay the intellectual groundwork for a special instinct of fraternity among Christians and Jews.) I would prefer here to carry the intuition of the existent into Maritain's further reflections on politics and society.

For if all of human existence is fragile, even more fragile is human action, above all in the political sphere. Maritain writes in *Existence and the Existent* that the end of practical wisdom is "not to know that which exists but to cause to exist what is not yet." Between the cup and the lip, many a slip. It is easier to intend results in ethical or in political action than to achieve those results. Politics, in a language more favored by Reinhold Neibuhr than by Maritain but by no means in conflict with the latter's, is the realm of the contingent, the ironic, and the tragic.

We might pause here to observe the sharp difference between a Thomist view of politics, such as that of Maritain, and that of classical conservatives such as Russell Kirk. Struck by the contingency and organic relatedness of social institutions, practices, and actions, and dismayed by the utopian ideologies to which so many modern minds are prone, paleoconservatives (as they now style themselves) such as Kirk are opposed to "ideological infatuation" or even to imagining social projects for the future at all. Considering the projection of social notions into the future to be signs of the disease of "ideology," such conservatives prefer to let things continue, to move along "organically," to be. They resist "thinking for the future," for fear of contamination by ideology.

Maritain had a significantly different view. For him (as for Thomas Aquinas), practical intellect is aimed by its very nature not at knowing that which already exists, but at causing to exist what is not yet. Practical intellect is oriented toward the future, more precisely, to changing the future, to making the future different, "to cause to exist what does not yet exist." For this reason, Maritain did not hesitate in *Integral Humanism* (1936) to imagine possible futures or to suggest new courses of action that would alter the awful European present in the direction of a better—a more humane, more Christian—proximate future.

Maritain took considerable care not to think in a merely utopian fashion. But he did not hesitate to try to imagine proximate, achievable next steps, which might in turn lead to yet further achievable steps, toward building up a more humane and more Christian civilization than the world had yet known. In brief, Maritain shared with those who are currently known as neoconservatives a willingness to project a future at once more attractive and more plausible than socialists or others could imagine, a future thoroughly realizable within the bounds of proximate probable developments. Unlike Kirk, Maritain was not willing to embrace social *laissez-faire* in the political realm, and he was resolutely opposed to mere nostalgia about some supposedly more human premodern era. Maritain claimed the future. Indeed, insofar as the Christian Democratic parties of Don Luigi Sturzo, de Gasperi, Schuman, and Adenauer drew crucial inspiration from his work, Maritain may be said to have in fact caused to exist much that had not existed before him.

In this sense, Aquinas is properly called the "first Whig" because his ethics and his politics did lay claims upon the future, did inspire, down the ages, a search for political institutions worthy of the rational, consensual dignity of humans. This is the sense in which Maritain was able in *Christianity and Democracy, Man and the State*, and other works to claim for a specific idea of democracy the support of the main spine of the Christian intellectual tradition. For this tradition nourished over the centuries the slow emergence of the ideal of a civilized politics, a politics of civil conversation, of noncoercion, of the consent of the governed, of pluralism, of religious liberty, of respect for the inalienable dignity of every human person, of voluntary cooperation in pursuit of the common good, and of checks and balances against the wayward tendencies of sinful men and women. As we shall see presently, Maritain did not claim too much for the historical efficacy of the Christian intellectual tradition; he chastised its failures severely and gave credit to nonbelievers for crucial advances. But neither did he wish to claim too little.

Here it is necessary to see how profound was Maritain's understanding of the hold that the ideal of *caritas* had upon the political thinking of Thomas Aquinas. Maritain held that action in the world—whether ethical action among individuals or political action among systems, institutions, and groups—is always action among *existents*, among real sinners and saints and all those in between, not among purely "rational agents." For him, realistic thinking about ethics and politics could not be conducted wholly within the boundaries of philosophy; theology was necessarily required.

Why? Because ethics and politics are about the real, existing world, and in this existing world humans are not purely rational agents but rather fallen creatures redeemed by grace on the condition that they are willing to accept God's action within them. To proceed in purely philosophical categories about ethics and politics would be utopian; one must deal with real, existing creatures locked in the actual historical drama of sin and grace.

That is why, in explicating "the fundamentally existential character of Thomist ethics," Maritain stresses two points, one regarding charity, the other regarding practical wisdom or prudence. Concerning the first, he writes:

> St. Thomas teaches that perfection consists in charity, and that each of us is bound to tend towards the perfection of love according to his condition and in so far as it is in his power. All morality thus hangs upon that which is most existential in the world. For love (this is another Thomist theme) does not deal with possibles or pure essences, it deals with existents. We do not love possibles, we love that which exists or is destined to exist.

Regarding practical wisdom, Maritain makes two extremely subtle points whose fullness I will not be able to reproduce. The first is that, at the heart of concrete existence, when an actual person is confronted with a set of particulars among which to decide to act, that person's appetite—that person's will or secret and deepest loves—enters into the quality of his or her perception of alternatives. More than that, for Aquinas, the rectitude of an existing person's intellect depends upon the rectitude of his existing loves. This is a powerfully realistic doctrine. Intellect follows love, and if the love is errant so also will be the judgment of practical intellect or "conscience." Although, for Maritain as for Aquinas, practical intellect still exerts a major discipline over the soul (over its loves, for example), nonetheless, *here and now*, under the immediate pressure of choice, the predispositions of one's loves are highly likely to bend the intellect to their purposes. (Were not David Hume and Adam Smith, under different background assumptions but with the same Augustinian sense for real experience, to make an analogous point?)

Hence, for Aquinas, there is necessary in one's ethical formation in advance of such choices a deep and pro-

found habit of disciplining and directing one's loves, se-
ducing them so to speak, so that in every case they will
love the good, the true, and the just, and be habituated
to being restless with anything less. Absent a right will,
a right practical intelligence will also be absent. In doing
what they think is best, those whose loves are disordered
will distort even their own intellects. As they love, so will
they perceive. "Love is blind," we say, meaning that,
disordered, it is more powerful than light, obscures the
light, and darkens the eye of intelligence itself.

The second subtle point that Maritain makes about
practical intellect begins again with the fact that ethical
and political action are always about existents. This time
he points out that such action always faces two wholly
singular, unrepeatable realities: first, the singular character, here and now, of this particular agent; and, second, the singular, never-to-be-repeated circumstances of
the here and now. For these reasons, practical wisdom is
utterly different from science. Whereas scientific judgment depends upon regularities, moral judgment must
cope with singulars. "The same moral case never appears twice in the world. To speak absolutely strictly,
precedent does not exist." Practical wisdom concerns
unprecedented singulars ("Useless to thumb through the
dictionary of cases of conscience!") At the same time,
however, its point is "not to know that which exists, but
to cause that to exist which is not yet," and so it is moved
by the appetite of will or love that thrusts us toward creating something new, whether of evil or of good.

III

From this discussion of the sheer existing of ethical
and political action—here and now, singular, unprece-

dented, unrepeatable—it follows that building a humane, Christian society is an uncertain business. It cannot be built upon any institutional framework at all; it has preconditions; many things can go wrong. Thus, to be faithful to the full measure of Christian intellectual conviction about the dignity (and fallibility) of the human person, about civilization as a state of society characterized by uncoerced decisions arrived at through civil discourse, and about the pull upon human love of God's own command of love, new forms of social institutions will have to be labored toward in history, and not without setbacks. For reasons Maritain articulates at some length, a certain kind of democracy, guarded against the diseases to which "pure" democracies are prey, best represents the full flowering of human practical wisdom about the sorts of institutions worthy of Jewish and Christian thought. This particular kind of democratic reality gives the broken world some hope for a better future.

Maritain is not unsophisticated about democracy. He knows, writing in 1944 in the depths of destruction, that "the very name democracy has a different ring in America and in Europe." And before proceeding very far on this subject in *Christianity and Democracy*, Maritain makes three important distinctions, each of which he discusses at more length than we can here duplicate. "First, the word democracy, as used by modern peoples, has a wider meaning than in the classical treatises on the science of government. It designates first and foremost a general philosophy of human and political life." Its inner dynamism, although consistent with a monarchic regime and even other classic "regimes" or "forms of government," leads "in the words of Abraham Lincoln," to "government of the people, by the people, for the people." Democratic regimes are not the only good regimes, but all good regimes will have to embody the dynamism of respect for free persons and their consent.

Second, Maritain argues that democracy after the war will certainly have to be ordered democracy, based on constitutions that have at least three characteristics: formation through the consent of the governed; protection of "the essential bases of common life, respect for human dignity and the rights of the person"; and grounding in a "long process of education." This long process of education will be necessary to lead peoples away from habits of dictatorship, nationalistic impulses, and the mental sloth of unfree and coercively minded peoples. It will have to lead them toward the "slow and difficult construction" of new habits in the temporal life of nations, supportive of "the soul of democracy," that is, "the law of brotherly love and the spiritual dignity of the person."

By these first two distinctions, Maritain shows that he intends what in the United States we mean by a democratic republic, protective of the rights of the person. He means no totalitarian or merely majoritarian democracy, but limited government, grounded in a tradition of sound habits, associations, and institutions. Moreover, he means a set of principles not exhausted by any one form of regime, and yet capable of distinguishing false from true ideas of democracy.

Then, by his third distinction, Maritain makes clear both that Christian faith cannot be made subservient to democracy as a philosophy of life and that democracy cannot claim to be the only form of regime demanded by Christian belief. He intends "by no means to pretend that Christianity is linked to democracy and that a Christian faith compels every Christian to be a democrat." To so argue would be to mix the things of Caesar and the things of God. Nonetheless, Maritain does affirm "that democracy is linked to Christianity and that the democratic impulse has arisen in human history as a temporal manifestation of the inspiration of the Gospel."

Maritain does not believe that Christianity exists in the world solely as the Church of the body of believers. Rather, he sees Christianity "as historical energy at work in the world. It is not in the heights of theology, it is in the depths of the secular conscience and secular existence that Christianity works in this fashion." Maritain is equally far from asserting that Christians brought modern democratic institutions into existence: "It was not given to believers in Catholic dogma but to rationalists to proclaim in France the rights of man and of the citizen, to Puritans to strike the last blow at slavery in America." He knows full well the many non-Christian sources of the democratic impulse: "Neither Locke nor Jean-Jacques Rousseau nor the Encyclopedists can pass as thinkers faithful to the integrity of the Christian trust."

Once again, Maritain is interested in existents, not essences. In the existing world of 1944, "The chances of religion, conscience, and civilization coincide with those of freedom; freedom's chances coincide with those of the evangelical message." The terrors of war have obliged the democracies to rethink their spiritual foundations so as to recover their spiritual energies and humanizing mission. They dare not go back to what they were before. The demands of the human spirit for that time include authentic understandings, many of them rooted in the Gospels and in the deepest Christian intellectual traditions, about the nature of human existents. But these have not always been best expressed, or best developed in practical life, by believers.

It is clear that Maritain considers the Christian message about the cry of the poor for justice to be a motor of human temporal improvements. He holds simultaneously that existing democratic ideas, traditions, and institutions were often championed in actual history by those who were non-Christians or even anti-Christian; and yet that, in building better than they knew, such persons were often generating in human temporal life constructs whose foundations were not only consistent with Jewish and Christian convictions about the realities of ethical and political life, but in a sense dependent on them. Pull out from under democratic principles the beliefs of Judaism and Christianity about the transcendent dignity of the person and the human propensity to sin, and the existing edifice of democratic thought is exposed to radical doubt.

Thus, Maritain argued, existing democratic institutions need to be grounded on a deeper, sounder foundation of intellectual conviction and moral habits than had been achieved in previous history. He urged Christians to take up this work both in intellect and in active practice. He saw a great deal to be done, both intellectually and morally, in the "slow and difficult construction" of a more humane world, whether considered from a Christian or a humanistic viewpoint.

IV

I have said enough, I hope, to show why so many of us feel so immensely indebted to this layman, perhaps the greatest exemplar of the Catholic laity in the last two centuries—a master of many wisdoms, a metaphysician, a philosopher at once humane and Christian, an ethicist and philosopher of history, a political philosopher, a saintly and childlike man.

Jacques Maritain, we salute you. And with the thanks that Sidney Hook often felt the impulse to utter, we thank the Creator of all existents for your brief presence among us. May you and Sidney, and all the just and righteous philosophers, enjoy that endless pursuit of Truth, face to face, that you conducted so lovingly on this fragile earth.

· 10 ·

REINHOLD NIEBUHR, FATHER OF NEOCONSERVATIVES

Why do so many conservatives, especially neoconservatives, regard Reinhold Niebuhr as their
teacher? Consider these words of Will Herberg, written
in 1956 about a time in the later 1930s: "I was then at
a most crucial moment in my life . . . left literally without
any ground to stand on, deprived of the commitment and
understanding that alone had made life livable." At this
point, Herberg came upon *Moral Man and Immoral Society* and promptly read everything else of Niebuhr's he
could get hold of. In 1956, having forgotten precise details, Herberg testified:

> What I do know is that the "meeting" with Niebuhr's
> thought—I did not yet know him personally—quite liter-
> ally changed my mind and life. Humanly speaking, it
> "converted" me, for in some manner I cannot describe, I
> felt my whole being, and not merely my thinking, shifted
> to a new center.[1]

An excerpt from this essay was first published in *National
Review*, May 11, 1992.

Many were affected by Niebuhr in this way, far below the level of partisan politics.

Not nearly so dramatic, but on a similar level, was my own first encounter with Niebuhr's work, in my case, *Beyond Tragedy*, in about 1956. I was at the time an undergraduate studying Thomistic philosophy, in preparation for ordination to the Roman Catholic priesthood. Niebuhr's book struck classical Aristotelian chords in me; his sense of contingency and irony rang true. That was pre-Vatican II; the Age of Ecumenism had not dawned. Nonetheless, about three years later I wrote one of the most favorable reviews a Niebuhr book ever received from a Catholic author; it was of a collection of essays on social ethics put together by D. B. Robertson (later my colleague at Syracuse University). I had already determined that Niebuhr, together with Jacques Maritain and Bernard Lonergan, were to be my mentors and lifelong companions.

Still, let us be clear about one thing. Reinhold Niebuhr always was and wanted to be a man of the left. In the years of his vigor, indeed, it would have been hard to imagine what "an intellectual giant of the Republican Party" would even have looked like; the very sound of the phrase would have sounded oxymoronic. So it must be one of the ironies of history in which he took pleasure that so many who read him not only became conservatives or neoconservatives but attributed their conversions in this direction to him. They had been Marxists or liberals or social democrats, until his criticisms of sentimental, idealistic, and rational liberalism liberated them. More than that. Niebuhr also taught them how to be conservative in a new way—fresh, future-oriented, alert, alive to factors of power and interest, and concerned with social justice in a way countercultural even to Niebuhr's own intellectual culture. It seemed to some of them that Niebuhr never followed the full logic of all his own insights. Hear again Will Herberg's testimony:

> As far back as 1944, in *The Children of Light and the Children of Darkness*, signs of the essentially "conservative" cast of mind of this leading "liberal" could be discerned, for what is *The Children of Light* but a truly "conservative" defense of American democracy? Niebuhr's recent writings combine a more conscious and explicit formulation of this "conservatism" with an embarrassed repudiation of the term. Yet the fact itself cannot be denied. . . . Nor should we be surprised to see his earlier "prophetic" radicalism culminate in the "new conservatism"; there is an *inner connection* between the two, and no real reversal is involved. For the "prophetic" radicalism implied a radical relativization of all political programs, institutions, and movements, and therefore a thoroughgoing rejection of *every* form of political rationalism. Add to this a renewed emphasis on the historic continuities of social life, and Niebuhr's brand of "conservatism" emerges. It is manifestly not the conservatism of those who are called conservatives in American public life [in 1956], but it is enough apparently to establish a kinship with Burke and to give Niebuhr a prominent place in all recent histories and anthologies of the "new conservatism." [Italics added] (42–43)

That there is an "inner connection" between Niebuhr's foundational ideas (as distinct from his own contingent applications of them) and "the new conservatism" seems much truer in 1992 than it did in 1956. Yet even today it seems to be a difficult connection for "Niebuhrians of the left" to grasp.

Quite naturally, Niebuhrians of the left want to keep Niebuhr pristinely "theirs." They are quite correct to do so, insofar as an historical account of Niebuhr's own public commitments demands it; consider, for example, his highly visible commitment to the left wing of the Democratic party through Americans for Democratic Action. What leftwing Niebuhrians fail to dwell on, however, are two further considerations. First, many new conservatives of the 1950s, neoconservatives of a later generation, and assorted Aristotelians, Burkeans, Churchillians, Reaganauts, and Thatcherites broke with the left in some measure because of *the arguments* they learned from Niebuhr. (It has apparently not occurred to some leftwing Niebuhrians that Niebuhr's arguments are often tailor-made for use against *them*.)

Second, and perhaps most important, many on the left do not recognize the tremendous shift in the balance of cultural power that has occurred in the years since Niebuhr completed his major work, and even more so since his death in 1971.

Whereas in 1960 the media were for the most part on the right, and even in the universities those on the left felt themselves to be a *pusillus grex*, from at least the time of Richard Nixon onward both journalism and the universities have moved overwhelmingly to the moderate left. In those circles today it takes little "prophetic" courage to stand with the left, whereas opposing the left does take stamina. Indeed, today's left—sometimes its center, even—is far to the left of Niebuhr and unusually abusive in its style of argument. The extreme left asserts that Niebuhr was only a conservative in disguise. His much vaunted "realism," they say, was but a thin cover for the status quo. Today, in fact, many moderate Niebuhrians who once felt like a minority on the left find themselves under attack (like Niebuhr himself) from whole hordes to *their* left. They know in their own experience how far the pendulum has swung.

Indeed, Ronald Preston, in an interesting essay "Reinhold Niebuhr and the New Right,"[2] takes it as a "fact that relative justice is likely to be with the radical Left because the Right has more power, as well as the force of inertia, on its side." But Preston fails to distinguish cultural power from political and economic power. In recent years the left has been humbled in the political and economic spheres. Leftwing ideas of political economy are in public decline. Nonetheless, in the cultural sphere the left is still today the regnant power and on the campuses leftwing extremists have gained unprecedented power. In an age of communications, meanwhile, power over ideas, symbols, and perceptions is sometimes greater than inert political or economic power. This basic shift in the balance of cultural power gives to the more conservative Niebuhrians the sweet elixir of practicing the "prophetic" role in the sphere of culture, against what David Halberstam in his book on the media some years ago called *The Powers That Be*.[3]

Niebuhr himself, of course, was accustomed to doing battle with the left. Like a theological Stonewall Jackson, he led many a punishing cavalry charge against sentimental and idealistic liberalism, hard and soft utopians, Marxists, pacifists, and unthinking anti-Americans. In return, he took heavy fire from his left. Thus, it is easy to understand why leftwing Niebuhrians so dislike being attacked, *in Niebuhr's name*, from their *right*. Ronald Preston's way of getting round this, is to call the views of the New Right, "unnuanced," a criticism he borrows from John Bennett. One looks eagerly, therefore, to Ronald Preston for nuance.

Alas, since their hearts are not involved in leftwing sectarian divisions (all of which they consider to be wrongheaded), many on the right do lump together everyone to their left, without differentiation. And many on the left manifest the same indifference regarding the right. Thus, Professor Preston makes the drastic error of listing Russell Kirk as a "neoconservative," having no idea how much heartburn that will cause in Mecosta, Michigan. He demonstrates no instinct whatever for the many ways in which neoconservatives distinguish themselves both from conservatives and from libertarians. He doesn't even faintly suggest the enormous differences between the New Right in Britain (which is itself a movement of many important intellectual differences) and the cultural conservatives in the United States. Nor does he detect the other amazing and often hotly contested divisions on the American right. Nuance indeed.

Moreover, considerably more nuance would be needed than Professor Preston offers to use the word "capitalism" intelligently today. Under that heading, Preston lumps together Adam Smith, social Darwinism, "possessive individualism," libertarianism, and laissez-faire. He allows to the New Right little more than unthinking stupidity and moral backwardness. As confidently as a man who doesn't see how thin the ice is under his feet, Preston asserts that "the economic views of the new Right contain nothing new. They are the resurrection of notions which were current in the 1920s, and falsified following the years of the Wall Street crash of 1929. Since we know what Niebuhr said of them before, it is not hard to see what he would say of them now." One averts one's eyes in pity from this ignorance of massive changes in fact and theory that have affected the rebirth of capitalist conviction in this century.

To cite but one example, since about 1960 evidence has been pouring in for an important *empirical* proposition; viz., that capitalism is a necessary but not sufficient condition for democracy. As a good empirical sociologist, Peter Berger has put in place all the necessary "nuances" of that proposition in *The Capitalist Revolution* (1987)[4]. The essential points had already been sketched in my

The Spirit of Democratic Capitalism (1982), and indeed by Niebuhr himself, who wrote:

> There are elements of truth in classical economics which remain a permanent treasure of a free society, since some forms of a "free market" are essential to democracy. The alternative is the regulation of economic process through bureaucratic political decisions. Such regulation, too consistently applied, involves the final peril of combining political and economic power.[5]

In interpreting this sentence, Preston singles out the phrase *"some forms of the free market,"* claiming that this phrase "hides all the problems at issue in the struggle to find in the area of social democracy and democratic socialism an economic order which is both efficient and humane." But in my mind an entirely different phrase lit up like neon; viz., *"the final peril of combining political and economic power."* That phrase flashed a red warning light about the root danger inherent in social democracy and democratic socialism, and diagnosed the reason why neither is likely to lead to a society at once humane and efficient. On Niebuhr's own radical suspicion of unchecked power, the fateful combination of political and economic power in the hands of a new administrative class could not but be inhumane. Then, social democracy by its very inner constitution is bound to empower the educated and highly organized middle class, at the expense of the disorganized poor. This is exactly what is happening in all social democracies today, as the more astute social democrats (especially in Britain) are beginning to concede.

Here again, Niebuhr—living in a different time, amid a different constellation of powers—did not follow the logic of his own insight. This is not surprising, since Niebuhr did not give much attention to economic issues; as Preston writes: "his interests were more focussed politically than economically." Precisely in Niebuhr's neglect, I found my own vocation. Surely, I thought, the next generation of Niebuhrians ought to push some of the deeper insights of Niebuhr into the one major area he neglected, economics. Moreover, since most of the Niebuhrians were, and are, by temperament and tradition tilted toward the left, the Niebuhrian principle of countervailing intellectual power demands that some of his students, at least, should push inquiry in directions that Niebuhr himself never quite took, even though he had peered down their valleys. It seemed to me further (and as the germ of an idea) that the deepest insights of Niebuhr concerning social order demand a threefold division of systems and powers.

Thus, as the passage above indicates, Niebuhr thought it utterly essential to separate political and economic power and to prevent their unchecked combination. But Niebuhr's sustained criticism of economic liberalism shed light on the need to identify yet a third system to divide from political and economic power, viz., the moral and cultural system. This third factor becomes particularly clear in the maturing Niebuhr's dissatisfactions with both the liberalism and the conservatism of his time, as he set them forth in Chapter 5 of *Christian Realism and Political Problems*, "The Foreign Policy of American Conservatives and Liberals." Such discussions set me on the search for the three-sided system of countervailing powers that became the backbone of *The Spirit of Democratic Capitalism*. Indeed, one passage in Niebuhr's chapter defines the need for such a system quite clearly. It also helps to explain why former businessmen such as former Secretary of State James A. Baker find themselves baffled by ethnicity, nationalism,

Islamic fundamentalism and other such moral and cultural realities:

> Unfortunately the businessman, as a man of affairs, fails us in the complexities of politics, because his experience is limited to a type of fairly simple collective endeavor in which the economic motive is isolated from other lusts and ambitions of men. He therefore gains a rather too simple view of human nature. . . . These facts dispose the commercial classes to that puzzling alternation between a pacifism, which obscures the factors of power [as in the 1930s, which Niebuhr never forgot], and an assertion of power, which is heedless of all the moral and cultural factors in an international situation.[6]

Here we see all three systems suggested in one passage: the economic system, plus the political system, and the moral/cultural system, all three of which are necessary for the whole.

Note, too, in this passage that if Niebuhr here lampoons the blindness of businessmen to two of these systems, his students may on the same ground lampoon the blindness of political activists to the two other systems, and the blindness of clergymen, academics, and journalists, as well. "In God we trust" meant to Niebuhr "No one else."

From Niebuhr, in any case, neoconservatives in the United States have taken a great many lessons. Like him, most of us are biblical in our vision of human nature and destiny. Most of us, as it happens, are Catholics and Jews, although not a few (and the numbers keep growing as people learn the "nuances") are Protestant, both mainline and evangelical. Like Niebuhr, we see the essential need of "some form of market system" as "a permanent treasure of the free society," in order to prevent "the perilous combination of political and economic power" in the hands of the political class. Like Niebuhr, we reject social Darwinism, "possessive individualism," the abstraction "economic man," and the conceptual purity of libertarianism. We accept the need for the welfare state, although we have many powerful criticisms concerning its current destructive practices, and many future proposals for its reform.[7] Like him, we are forward-looking, not backward-looking. We contest with the left the future direction in which true social progress lies.

Like Niebuhr, neoconservatives hold to the priority of politics over economics in some particular realms, real but limited. We do not accept "the market" as a universal tool for every human need. For that matter, we do not accept "democracy," either, as a universal tool for every human need; like the American framers, we are aware of the "diseases to which democracies have ever been prey." Like Niebuhr, we hold that both capitalism and the democratic republic depend on the primacy of certain claims of the Creator and Judge, to Whom we owe our rights and all we are.

The necessity of the free market, the limited priority of politics over economics, and the primacy of the spirit—that is a fairly good summary of the neoconservative position, as outlined in Irving Kristol's *Reflections of a Neoconservative* (1984).[8] We think that this vision, or something like it, is better fitted to the *Imago Dei* in humans, *simul iusti et peccatores*, than are its current rivals. Corrected for its inherent tendency to tilt in the direction of freedom's hereditary enemy, the state, we think that social democracy is an acceptable variant of democratic capitalism. Otherwise, without this corrective, social democracy is quite dangerous, because of its class bias and its concentrations of power. In particular, we fear that social democracy rushes the world toward that "new soft despotism" which Tocqueville glimpsed as the terminus of egalitarian democracy. Nonetheless, in the name of countervailing powers, we welcome social democrats to the always useful debate concerning which path to take in particular circumstances.

In sum, conservative Niebuhrians offer a necessary corrective to leftwing Niebuhrians. For the last decade or so, for instance, conservative Niebuhrians have read "the signs of the times" with considerably greater accuracy than their leftwing counterparts, though given our convictions about human nature we don't expect the latter to admit it. Nonetheless, the left has done far better than the right on one thing. Since about 1968, it has swung to its side most of the *literati*, professors of humanities and social science, higher clergy, editors and publishers, reporters, rock stars and filmmakers—that is, most of the cultured despisers of conservatism in all its forms. Since these dominate the media, the seminaries, and the universities, leftwing Niebuhrians like to think that they control the mainstream. It is to the advantage of conservative Niebuhrians that they continue to believe this.

· 11 ·

TWICE CHOSEN: IRVING
KRISTOL AS AMERICAN

> I really cannot believe that Americans are a histor-
> ically unique and chosen people. I am myself a Jew
> and an American, and with all due respect to the
> Deity, I think the odds are prohibitive that He
> would have gone out of His way to choose me
> twice over.
>
> —"American Historians and the American Idea"

When he wrote these words, Irving Kristol was modest to a fault. He had been, in fact, twice blessed:
first blessed by being born Jewish, twice blessed by being
born American. Not that, from a Catholic point of view,
these two blessings are on the same level. Those of us
who are Catholic (including Tocqueville and the Third
Plenary Council of Baltimore) do see the founding of the
democratic experiment in America as an act of Providence. But the first blessing appertains to the City of
God; the latter, only to the City of Man.

One of Irving Kristol's quiet contributions is to have

This tribute to the "Godfather of neoconservatism" first appeared in *The Neoconservative Imagination: Essays in Honor
of Irving Kristol*, ed. W. Kristol and C. DeMuth (Washington:
AEI Press, 1995).

restored to many on the American left a profound—
almost a biblical—understanding of the American idea,
which most of us had left behind in moving leftward.
The comprehension of the American idea most common
among journalists, intellectuals, and public officials, he
prodded us, is quite unworthy of the sober political philosophy worked out by this nation's founding generation,
and embodied in its institutions.

1.

Two or three times, when I was young, I wrote a note
of appreciation to a writer who had done something
really good. I remember writing such a letter to Irving
Kristol in about 1972, upon reading his little book—I
still think it is his best—*On the Democratic Idea in
America* (Harper & Row, 1972). Like his other books,
this was a collection of essays, the first of which had been
published in 1967. Those were the years, 1967 to 1972,
of student riots, antiwar protests, the assassinations of
Robert F. Kennedy and Martin Luther King, Jr., and
Watergate. A new utopianism was bursting out everywhere, paired (of course) with a rapidly spreading cynicism. Some intellectuals were beginning to lose faith in
socialism, and even in European social democracy. I was
one such.

The questions we were asking ourselves had this central core: If I am not a Socialist, or a Social Democrat,
what am I? In the dark clouds and electrical energy that
were gathering in my mind at that time, Kristol's reflections on America broke like a long and brilliant lightning
flash. Once you reject socialism, his book suggested to
me, one place to look is the American experience—the

most neglected experience of political economy in modern intellectual life.

2.

Since my own interests and biases are religious, I was most interested at that time in writers who, while not necessarily hostile to religion, wrote from a point of view that could be read without discomfort by agnostics or atheists. I liked, as it were, the abstinence and self-denial implicit in Kristol's prose. In his essays of that period, he for the most part kept his serious religious inquiries to himself; for all I knew, he could have been an agnostic. When he happened to corroborate my views, therefore, his was an especially valuable corroboration. When he contradicted them, he raised an especially demanding challenge.

I also liked Kristol's dry sense of irony and tragedy. This is what had attracted me to Reinhold Niebuhr during the preceding decade. Moreover, Kristol wrote with the sort of skeptical attitude that especially pleased me, in part because it ran against my own tendencies. I tend to look for the good sides of things. Irving is always looking for the things to be questioned, the things that are suspect, the things that might go wrong. For me, this was a wonderful balancing mechanism. I resolved to read everything of Irving Kristol's I could lay my hands upon (a pledge that some twenty years later I am happy to have kept).

There is another aspect of Irving Kristol's thinking that greatly attracted me. One always feels in reading him that he has kept his worldly eyes open. He listens to what people say, reads carefully what they write, and watches for those small significant events that shed light on whether words have purchase on reality—or not. He is an empiricist, not in the sense that he counts up numbers, but rather in the sense that he watches for those concrete occurrences that jut out where they're not supposed to; he has a sharp eye for events that falsify grand theories. He practices the falsifiability principle, a favorite of Karl Popper's. This habit somehow seems very American. To me it represents, as well, a habit of rabbinic Judaism, the habit of looking for sharp counterexamples, based upon a highly refined version of common sense. Instead of keeping one's eyes on the heaven of theory, in other words, one makes better progress by watching the ground carefully.

Let me just run through the titles of the eight chapters of *On The Democratic Idea in America*. Even the titles convey an impression of the mental landscape I am trying to describe. Savor them: Urban Civilization and Its Discontents; The Shaking of the Foundations; Pornography, Obscenity, and the Case for Censorship; American Historians and the Democratic Idea; American Intellectuals and Foreign Policy; "When Virtue Loses All Her Loveliness"—Some Reflections on Capitalism and "The Free Society"; Toward a Restructuring of the University; Utopianism and American Politics. There is a mixture of both hope and realistic expectations in these titles. They aim at a better future. But a large part of what we may expect to be better, they suggest, is that we will have abandoned illusory expectations. A sane, hopeful realism will have replaced the cynicism that follows from extravagant utopian hopes.

In some respects, Kristol's point of view reminded me of G. K. Chesterton's, especially the latter's *Outline of Sanity*. Kristol is far less the fantasist, of course, far less the romantic; and he is hardly tempted to be so playful with words. (He does share Chesterton's love for mystery stories—as a reader who devours hundreds of them, though, rather than as an author.) The Chesterton-Kristol commitment to common sense, their war against the intellectual illusions of the age, and their love for the literary essay bear a curious resemblance.

3.

In order to remind myself why Irving's essays had such a big effect on me, I recently returned to *On the Democratic Idea in America*, and especially to its fourth chapter, "American Historians and the Democratic Idea." Irving says that he had intended to write a book on this subject. But of course he did not. The irony his mind is suited to works best in shorter essays. While his method needs the grist of concrete persons and concrete events, his mind is not really an historian's mind, committed to patient searches through historical detail. It is, rather, the mind of the social philosopher. It is not so much that Irving concentrates on big ideas; about these he is properly skeptical. But he does like to examine those ideas that shape the mind, those that operate perhaps as frameworks, or in that recent expression, as "paradigms." There are certain ideas that structure the imagination, and it is these that fascinate Kristol. They are always the subject of his best essays.

The first thing that Irving Kristol noticed in the chapter in question, based on an address to the Organization of American Historians at Philadelphia in April, 1969, is that the democratic idea in America, remarkably clear in the minds of the founders of this nation, became quite confused within a generation. The second thing he had noticed is that American historians have themselves been thoroughly confused about the idea of democracy. Kristol cites an example: Almost invariably, American historians regard the increasing frequency of the popular referendum as a progressive step forward, for both democracy and liberal purposes. But is it really? For one thing, the popular referendum is often used by a conservative population in rebellion against a liberal legislature. For another, it is an expression of the direct popular will, which the framers of the Constitution feared as a type of majoritarian tyranny. Historians don't seem troubled by such facts. For them, democracy is always progressive, no matter what.

In this fashion, historians have developed a way of thinking that has become, by now, "an ideology so powerful as to represent a kind of religious faith." This "democratic faith" places much more emphasis on men's good intentions than on the way their actions actually work out. Many historians tend to believe such propositions as Al Smith's, "the cure for democracy is more democracy." Thus, they displace evil from inside the democratic faith to outside it: if there is evil, it must come from a conspiracy of wicked vested interests or from ideals alien to the democratic faith. By contrast, Kristol points out, the founders of this nation had a clear-headed political philosophy, not a quasi-religious faith:

The difference between a democratic faith and a democratic political philosophy is basically this: whereas a faith may be attentive to the problems of democracy, it has great difficulty perceiving or thinking about the problematics of democracy. By "problematics" I mean those kinds of problems that flow from, that are inherent in, that are generated by democracy itself. . . . It really is quite extraordinary how the majority of American historians have, until quite recently, determinedly refused to pay attention to any thinker, or any book, that treated democracy as problematic.

As of 1969, no American historian, Kristol noted, had yet written a book on *The Federalist*. Among prominent historians were plenty of Turnerites and Beardites and even Marxists, portraying a course of unproblematic, irresistible progress—but few Madisonians or Hamiltonians. None were disciples of the greatest historian of democracy, Henry Adams, whose vision of democracy was dark and complex. Although many historians quoted from Tocqueville, one could find among them no Tocquevillians.

By contrast with most historians, the founders of this country held that democracy is quite capable of bringing evil into the world. With considerable forethought, they designed a system to frustrate its evil tendencies, and provided it with spurs toward self-correction. The American founders thought hard about the systemic remedies that might correct deficiencies inherent in democracy.

> In short, the founding fathers sought to establish a "popular government" that could be stable, just, free; where there was security of person and property; and whose public leaders would claim legitimacy not only because they were elected officials but also because their character and behavior approximated some accepted models of excellence.

Kristol was always sensitive to the moral dimension of the good society. Whether men judge their society to be moral, just, and even noble is important to them—not least when they are asked (as Kristol's generation was) to lay down their lives for it. It is important, Kristol believed, for a democratic society to work hard to establish high moral standards for its citizens to aspire to—

critically important, since democracies do not tend naturally to do this on their own.

> They thought that political institutions had something to do with the shaping of common men, and they took the question, *"What kind of common man does our popular government produce?"* to be as crucial a consideration as any other.

Kristol quotes Matthew Arnold's warning: "The difficulty for democracy is, how to find and keep high ideals." In aristocracies, this function was supplied by aristocrats. What can a society without aristocrats do? He quotes Arnold again:

> Nations are not truly great solely because the individuals composing them are numerous, free, and active; but they are great when these numbers, this freedom, and this activity are employed in the service of an ideal higher than that of an ordinary man, taken by himself.

In this respect, democracies depend on moral ideas even more than nondemocratic societies, because they depend on the free choices of their citizens. For their very survival, they must shape ordinary people into an extraordinary moral force. If they depend upon a democratic faith which supposes that within democracy there are no evils to be combatted, they err disastrously. They require a realistic philosophy, alert to the systemic weaknesses of democratic institutions, as well as to the fallibility and evil in the human heart.

4.

Kristol then turns to the nation's first major historian, George Bancroft. Barely fifty years after the Constitutional Convention, Bancroft was already ignoring *The Federalist* and claiming that the men who framed the Constitution "followed the lead of no theoretical writer of their own or preceding times." Bancroft replaced the authority of the founders with an exaltation of the common man, as if the common man were a supreme arbiter of the beautiful and the ugly, good and evil, progress and decline. From within a religion of the common man, Bancroft treated the founders as if they had been aristocratic interlopers, temporarily standing in the common man's way.

Three generations later, such supremely influential historians as Frederick Turner and Charles A. Beard were explicitly repudiating the political philosophy of the founding fathers. Whereas the framers had taken care to supply remedies for the dangerous tendencies of democracy, the historians now meant by "democracy" a Jacksonian-egalitarian-populist faith in the common man. Further, they held that this new faith "was something different from, and antithetical to, the kind of democratic political philosophy that the founding fathers believed in." They were ready to supplant the nation's original founders.

In his reading of the historians, Kristol had come upon an essay by E. L. Godkin, entitled "Aristocratic Opinions of Democracy," published in 1865, but hardly ever read or cited by other historians. Unlike Bancroft, Turner, and Beard, Godkin held that egalitarianism is a problem for democracy. He was dismayed by "the aggressive, self-seeking individualism, the public disorderliness, the philistine materialism of the American frontier that prevented American democracy from achieving a more splendid destiny." Godkin believed that certain high republican ideals, once protected by the American aristocracy, remain crucial to the high degree of civilization aimed at by American democracy, but are often thwarted by its vulgarity, under the malign influence of egalitarianism. That is to say, Godkin identified another difficult *problematic* in the American democratic idea.

By contrast, Charles A. Beard "ended up with the aggressive assertion that the founding fathers were not Jacksonian democrats." To which Kristol comments: "He was right, of course. The really interesting question is *why* they were not." Perhaps they had good reason for being, as Beard called them, "men of only partial democratic faith." Maybe they had thought more deeply about evils that lie in the heart of common men than Beard had.

Kristol recognizes that later "revisionists" have exposed the shallowness of the progressives' accounts of reality. But even among the historians who thrived after World War II, he finds an unwillingness to come to grips with a serious political philosophy. Take Louis Hartz. Hartz, in particular, interprets the American idea as "compounded of a few Lockean dogmas." These Hartz describes as involving certain mechanisms of self-interest, such as "group coercion, crowd psychology, and economic power," out of whose push and pull there emerges a kind of gross public interest. Hartz himself points out that there is no mind in this mechanism, only blind political forces, locked in checks and balances, pulleys and gears. Here is Kristol's succinct comment: "Only in America . . . could a historian of ideas . . . end up with the assertion that political mind has no dominion over political matter."

Reflecting on how badly American historians have understood the realistic political philosophy of the founding generation, Kristol is struck by the fact "that America has been a very lucky country." But luck does not prove that America has a good form of government. Kristol finds it impossible to believe that Hartz—or any of his predecessors—actually lived by the shallow idea that the mind has no dominion over political matter.

> I honestly don't see how any intelligent man with even the slightest bit of worldly experience could entertain this belief. The political ideas that men have always help to shape the political reality they live in—and this is so whether these be habitual opinions, tacit convictions, or explicit ideologies. It is ideas that establish and define in men's minds the categories of the politically possible and the politically impossible, the desirable and the undesirable, the tolerable and the intolerable. And what is more ultimately real, politically, than the structure of man's political imagination?

5.

There we have it. *"What is more ultimately real, politically, than the structure of man's political imagination?"* Irving Kristol is, preeminently, a social philosopher of the political imagination, especially the American political imagination. The ideas that most interest him are those that intersect with the imagination of active human beings. What such human beings will find tolerable and intolerable varies enormously across history. It depends very much on the ideas they carry in their heads, and the shape of the drama in which they see themselves playing a part.

It is the impoverishment of the American political imagination, the failure of later generations to come up to the measure of the political philosophy of the founding generation, that is our gravest national danger. "Is it not possible that many of the ills of our democracy can be traced to this democracy itself," he asks, "or, more exactly, to this democracy's conception of itself?"

All those historians who attempt to glorify the common man seem to have forgotten the dangers inherent in "the tyranny of the majority," that tyranny which the founders so much feared. Whether it appeared as an essentially mindless, self-seeking majority or simply as a rancorous, divisive coalition, they feared it. And took practical steps to block its unchecked action.

Democracy as a form of progress-on-automatic-pilot, a sort of mindless movement forward of the common man in history, does not seem to Kristol an especially attractive religious faith. "I do not see that the condition of American democracy is such as automatically to call forth my love and honor."

Kristol has a number of important questions to raise, which have scarcely even today been addressed:

> To begin with, one would like to know *why* the political philosophy of the founding fathers was so ruthlessly unmanned by American history. Was it the result of inherent flaws in that political philosophy itself? Was it a failure of statesmanship? Was it a consequence of external developments that were unpredictable and uncontrollable? These questions have hardly been asked, let alone answered.

6.

Not many years ago, the fifth grade daughter of one of my philosopher friends at the university where I taught took an exam in a history class. The question read "Socrates was—" and she filled in the blank space with "The philosopher who taught by asking questions." The examiner marked her wrong. The correct answer, he said, should have been "a Greek philosopher." When this was reported to him, my philosopher friend was ready to tear out his hair, except that he was already bald.

Like that earlier Greek philosopher, Irving Kristol's way of teaching is often by asking questions—questions that we have all been avoiding. He does not do this out of laziness. It takes quite a lot of effort to fight one's way through many mazes and false turns, only then to discern what the truly useful questions are. Irving Kristol seems to have unerring instinct in his pursuit of such questions. Why did the political philosophy of the founding fathers meet such an early and unmourned death? And why have so many impostors been allowed to speak in their name?

Twenty-five years after he raised such questions in his essay, they still remain urgent questions for this Republic. They may be even more important. More than two-thirds of the public in recent polls believe that the nation has "gone off the track." Irving Kristol suggests some of the basic reasons why that might have happened, and his essay still urges us to get the conversation going that will put us back on track. That will require a more realistic brand of thinking than we typically encounter in current discourse. It has been Irving Kristol's vocation to call us back to such discourse and to deepen and enrich our public life.

· 12 ·

ALEKSANDR
SOLZHENITSYN:
OF GOD AND MAN

The text of Aleksandr Solzhenitsyn's address at Harvard is, in my view, the most important religious document of our time, more shattering than *Pacem in Terris*, more sharply analytical of the human condition in our century than any word from the World Council of Churches. Out of the long grayness of his own despair, out of the years in which surrender must have seemed attractive and hopelessness realistic, Solzhenitsyn was saved by faith in the power of simple truth. His was not solely a salvation for his soul through faith in Jesus Christ; it was also a ray of light for the entire race of men. He kept his eye upon the need to tell the truth, come what may.

The spiritual center of Solzhenitsyn's analysis of Western society occurs in section five of the speech and again

On June 8, 1978, Aleksandr Solzhenitsyn delivered his now-famous Harvard Address, "A World Split Apart." This essay, drawn from the collection *Solzhenitsyn at Harvard: The Address, Twelve Early Responses and Six Later Reflections* (Washington, D.C.: Ethics and Public Policy Center, 1981), was written before Novak had published his ground-breaking *The Spirit of Democratic Capitalism*.

in section fourteen. He says that "the decline of courage is perhaps the most striking feature of the Western world today. . . . This loss of courage is more evident among the ruling and intellectual elites, thus creating an impression that the entire society suffers this decline of courage. . . . Need I remind you that from ancient times a decline in courage has been considered the first symptom of the end?" He then examines the ways in which this loss of courage has occurred. In section fourteen, he returns to the fundamental theme of the inner loss of will: "To defend oneself, one must also be ready to die; but there is little such readiness in a society raised in the cult of affluence. There is then nothing left but concessions, procrastinations, and betrayals." And again: "Western thinking has become conservative: the world situation must stay as it is at any cost. There must be no changes. . . . *How is it possible to lose the will to defend yourself to such an extent?*" (italics added). The remainder of Solzhenitsyn's analysis constitutes a profound investigation into the soul and intellectual roots of the West, in search of an answer to that painful question.

Thus Solzhenitsyn observes the malady: loss of courage, lack of will even to defend oneself. He offers two diagnoses of the malady's origin, one centering on the institutions of Western society (notably the law and the press), the other on the vision of man fashioned at the very beginning of the modern era. The mistake "must be at the root," he argues, "at the very foundation of thought in modern times. I refer to the prevailing Western view of the world which was born during the Renaissance and which since the Age of Enlightenment has cast the political mold."

It is at this point that Solzhenitsyn most alarms Western humanists, particularly those who do not believe in God and hold no allegiance to Jewish or Christian thought. Solzhenitsyn seems to be blaming them for the impending catastrophe. If we are to hear him at all, we must deal seriously with this accusation.

The first thing to be said is that Solzhenitsyn's analysis seems classically Catholic. Its general line is that a wrong turn was taken in Western history. Even some of Solzhenitsyn's terms (such as "anthropocentrism") resemble those used by the Catholic philosopher Jacques Maritain in *Integral Humanism*, and join a tradition that encompasses many other Christian and Jewish humanists (Paul Tillich, Reinhold Niebuhr, Will Herberg, T. S. Eliot, Christopher Dawson, Emil Fackenheim).

One objection to this interpretation may be that, apart from the "rationalistic humanism" or "humanistic autonomy" that Solzhenitsyn rejects, neither Western liberties nor the creative spirit of productivity and technological invention would have emerged in history. The various theocracies, whether medieval Catholic or later Protestant, or even the theocracies of Russian Orthodoxy better known to Solzhenitsyn, did not always assist the birth of liberty and creativity; on the contrary, they often represented obscurantism, repression, and even the power to halt the course of liberty. In brief, the response to Solzhenitsyn is: We poor secular humanists, with all our faults, have precious little to learn from theocrats or those who (history has taught us) have often enough been forces of reaction. Why should we surrender what we have, problematic as it is, for what appears to be worse?

When Solzhenitsyn speaks of "the disaster of humanistic, autonomous, irreligious consciousness," the unbeliever might, in good conscience, ask for evidence that religious consciousness is not an even more profound calamity. Solzhenitsyn asserts that irreligion "has made man the measure of all things on earth—imperfect man, who is never free of pride, greed, envy, vanity, and dozens of other sins." The unbeliever replies that, on the basis of the evidence, religion seems to do no better. Solzhenitsyn asserts: "We are now being avenged for the mistakes that were not properly appraised at the beginning of the journey. On the way from the Renaissance to our time we have enriched our experience, but we have lost the concept of a Supreme Complete Entity, which once placed a limit on our passions and our irresponsibility. We have placed too much hope in political and social transformations, only to find out that we were being deprived of our most precious possession: our inner life. A party mob attacks it in the East, and the commercial marketplace does the same in the West." Again, the unbeliever replies that a man without God may be just as moral as a believer and have just as profound a spiritual life, perhaps even more profound.

It will seem, then, that Solzhenitsyn is merely being chauvinistic, attempting to impose upon those who think religion is evil the entire blame for the cataclysm that is about to descend upon all, and trying rhetorically to coerce them into accepting his own religious commitments—that is, practicing a kind of spiritual imperialism. Besides, they may think, let him experience some of the more muddleheaded religious spokesmen of the West and then see whether he remains so confident of the power of religion.

Yet all this is, in a way, to miss the point. I do not believe that any honest thinker in the twentieth century can fail to see that there are singularly heroic individuals who, though atheistic or agnostic, have been worthy guides of the human spirit in the midst of despair: men of courage who against fascism, Stalinism, or whatever other massive evil exhibited no lack of courage, suffered no loss of will. Solzhenitsyn is not, I think, impugning the heroism of spirit possible to the individual atheist or agnostic. He cannot be doing so from a religious point of view, in any case, for as he well recognizes, faith is a gift; without it, before it, a man must do his utmost alone.

Solzhenitsyn is, by contrast, performing a social analysis, examining the spiritual life of that large middle band of human life, in which in any society the vast majority, even of its intellectual elite, must live. Solzhenitsyn is observing the malady, not in rare individuals, whom he specifically exempts, but in the typical citizen under typical institutional and symbolic influences. Here, I believe, he makes a stunning observation. There is one major difference—for the more or less middling persons, neither the most heroic nor the most vicious—between a society that is anthropocentric and a society that is theocentric. That difference is that in a society whose moral roots lie solely in individual conscience, a certain diffidence inexorably results: You have your moral convictions, I have mine, who can tell who is right? Directly there follows, barring a great social transformation, a loss of will, of moral certainty, of direction. The Soviets have their system, we have ours, everything depends on your point of view, and so on—it is all, culturally speaking, devastatingly familiar.

At such a point as this, one's judgment of Solzhenitsyn becomes immediately personal. For myself, I think I have previously made clear (in *Belief and Unbelief*, 1965, and *The Experience of Nothingness*, 1970) my respect for the option of unbelief and my esteem for the secular saint. Yet as I grow older I do see the point of such ultimate warnings as those of Dostoyevsky: "If there is no God, everything is permitted" and G. K. Chesterton: "When a man ceases to believe in God, he does not believe in nothing, he believes anything." While brave and strong individuals continue to adhere to honesty, courage, liberty, and compassion, and even to give their lives for values they make central to their being, a *society* based systematically upon the nonexistence of God and upon man as the sole measure must, of human necessity, slide further and further into defenselessness and loss of will. For individuals vary. And if some say "You may prefer *x*, but as for me, I prefer *y*," tolerance demands that they be permitted so to believe. In the vast middle of society, what one generation learns as tolerance, another defines as indifference. Individuals are left to their own moral devices.

John Garvey, commenting upon Solzhenitsyn's Harvard address in *Commonweal* (September 1, 1978), cites the surprise of a college girl when, as a visiting professor, he tried to show how one value can be defended as superior to another. She refused to believe that he actually thought some values were better than others. One of the two professors who regularly taught the class agreed with her, even to the extent of refusing to say that Hitler's values were inferior to those of his opponents. In their minds, Garvey was exhibiting intolerance, arrogance, and cultural chauvinism.

In the vast middle ranges of our society, there are millions who have declared themselves incompetent to make value judgments. They insist that they can choose values only for themselves, and that it would be wrong (immoral? arrogant? coercive?) to "impose" values on, or even to apply one's own values to, others. But this is to refuse to ascend to the moral level, which if it is anything is universal and binding upon all. It is to remain on the level of personal feeling and personal preference. It is to legitimate those who *prefer* torture, rapine, systematic murder, authoritarianism, slavery. Of course, not facing such issues in their daily lives, protected by the defenses around this island of liberty, such defenders of nondiscrimination do not see the implications of their own moral vagueness. They believe in "freedom," in "non-coercion," in "keeping institutions off my back." They do not recognize how rare the capacity to enjoy such liberties has been for the human race, and on how profound a philosophical and moral base the system of liberty depends.

Solzhenitsyn diagnoses correctly the kind of silly optimism about the liberated individual that characterizes our culture. The word "evil" is not one that enlightened persons like to use. Excess, mistake, environmental influences, error of judgment, temporary loss of sanity— these categories feel comfortable. To attribute evil, or malice, or the demonic to human will seems to draw upon old-fashioned religious categories that are too harsh and unforgiving.

It is fascinating, indeed, to note that our nationally syndicated columnists, cultural leaders, and editorialists frequently castigate the American public in terms harsher than those used by Solzhenitsyn. They call our people too rich, soft, flabby, greedy, selfish, gluttonous, decadent, preoccupied, narrow, racist, imperialist, militant, corrupt. Eugene Ionesco recently described in *Le Figaro* what he discovered in America:

> Americans want to feel guilty. They have this need to be guilty. It is a masochism that we have already seen in France not so long ago. I found myself wanting to cheer them up, these Americans, I tried to do just that. . . . For the liberal anti-Americans, nothing good can come of the United States, even now. You have to call them Nazis, racists, and insist that their consumer society is worse than any of the underdeveloped societies. Call them names, insult them, that's their medicine. [Reprinted in the *Miami Herald*, January 7, 1979.]

Solzhenitsyn diagnoses the sources of this feeling: "This tilt of freedom toward evil has come about gradually. It is founded on the humanistic and benevolent concept that man—the master of this universe—has no evil inherent in his nature; all the defects of life are caused by wrong social systems that must be corrected."

In a strange way, departments of sociology and psychology all over America seem to teach, as do the newspapers, that the individual has no moral weight of his or her own but that all good and evil come from the social system. Individual morality is only a matter of therapy, as through such books as *Looking Out for Number One*, *Self-Assertiveness Training*, and *I'm OK, You're OK*. All moral questions become politicized. They have to do with being "liberated" from structures. Here, indeed, is the secret link of current liberal collectivism in the West with Marxist collectivism, about which Solzhenitsyn speaks so eloquently. Again Ionesco:

> Of 100 American students, 95 are apolitical and five are Marxists; but the latter are active, more effective. Those who go by the title of American intellectual—that is, journalists, novelists, actors, publishers, lawyers—are liberal, despite all the historical errors imputable to liberalism in the past fifty years. This state of mind exists in New York as well as Los Angeles. "God is dead, Marx is dead, and I don't feel too good either," as one of the street slogans put it during the 1968 student demonstrations in France. [*Le Figaro*, reprinted in the *Miami Herald*, January 7, 1979.]

Solzhenitsyn grasps with perfect clarity the secret bond between liberal humanism and Marxism. Citing Marx's assertion in 1844 that "communism is naturalized humanism," he comments:

> This proved to be not entirely without reason. There are common stones in the foundation of a humanism that has

been eroded and any of the varieties of socialism: bound-
less materialism, freedom from religion and from religious
responsibility (under communism driven as far as antire-
ligious dictatorship), and concentration on social structures trying to be scientific (the Enlightenment of the
eighteenth century and Marxism). It is not a coincidence
that all communist rhetoric concerns Man (with a capital
M) and his earthly happiness. A rather ugly comparison,
isn't it—common traits in the perception of the world and
the way of life in today's East and West! But such is the
logic of materialism's development.

Moreover, in the interrelationship of this kinship, the
law is such that the brand of materialism that is further
to the left and therefore more consistent always proves to
be stronger, more attractive, and victorious. . . . During
the past centuries, and especially in recent decades, as the
process became more acute, the alignment of the world
powers was as follows: liberalism was inevitably pushed
aside by radicalism, radicalism had to surrender to socialism, and socialism could not stand up to communism.
The communist regime in the East could endure and grow
precisely because of enthusiastic support from an enormous number of Western intellectuals, who (feeling the
kinship!) refused to see communism's crimes. When they
could no longer ignore them, they tried to justify them. So
it is: in the East, communism has suffered a total ideological defeat. It declined to zero. And yet Western intellectuals still look at it with considerable interest and sympathy.

Those who speak with the most moral conviction, the
most certainty, the most fervor in America today are
those who are vaguely Marxist. Ionesco notes it.
Solzhenitsyn notes it. The editorials of the *New York
Times*, even while seeming to be anti-Marxist, while pretending to a humble tolerance, a cautious pragmatism, a
liberal diffidence, do not often prevail against the harsh
moral claims of those farther to the left. In the face of

certainty, what can they do who, in principle, must deprive themselves of a contrary certainty?

It is true that religion in America—Protestant, Catholic, and Jewish—has been uncommonly unintellectual, narrow, and dogmatic. Perhaps in unconscious opposition, the enlightened have prided themselves on "not pretending to have all the answers," on being tolerant and pragmatic, on not arguing about moral principles or absolutes. A pluralistic society had to learn early that men and women of diverse backgrounds, moral convictions, and religious commitments need not come to explicit agreement on fundamental principles but could move forward by agreeing on practical courses of action. "Practical humanism," Jacques Maritain called this; "ecumenism," "pluralistic unity," "a common faith," others have called it.

But the deficiency in this arrangement is now becoming apparent, four generations after the great immigrations that thickened the nation's pluralism (making this effectively a Catholic and Jewish as well as a Protestant nation, and incidentally creating room for public nonbelievers). As long as diverse traditions are studied, nourished, and kept publicly effective, their divergence freshens the streams of faith and commitment that water our democratic institutions. But as the young of each successive generation learn less and less about their roots, and become (in principle) more tolerant and (in practice) more indifferent to the spiritual inheritance of which they are the carriers, the pluralistic arrangement degenerates into "do your own thing." Anything.

The "me decade" did not result from a sudden effusion of selfishness or decadence; it is the logical consequence of a public surface tolerance combined with a loss of individual historical depth. In a sense, people become more like one another (wear the same clothes, go

to the same schools, read the same books, are informed
by the same media, go to the same parties, are "liberated" into the same mores). In another sense, they lose
the social inheritances that, while differentiating them
from one another, also instilled in them profound common values. Inwardly, each is animated by nothing more
profound than personal preference and idiosyncrasy.
Homogenized yet fragmented, the society of the supreme
"me" (find yourself, be true to yourself) is the logical
expression of a materialistic humanism.

Against this trend, of course, are spiritual revivals of
many sorts as well as the continuing strength of many
inherited moral principles that are still upheld by countless families and individuals, by some writers and artists,
and in many churches, schools, and intellectual centers.
A free society necessarily exhibits contradictory patterns
of development, crosscurrents, and a paradoxical mix of
weaknesses and strengths. Solzhenitsyn, after all, is *here*;
he was invited to Harvard; many receive his words like
water in the desert: many have waited and prepared
themselves for an ultimate call to the deadly impending
struggle.

The positive antipathy to religion common among the
enlightened remains, however, a fundamental weakness
in our culture. If there is no God, no natural order, no
right and no wrong founded in the very nature of things,
then human beings are free to make of the world what
they will. Those who have confidence in the goodness of
the individual heart have not yet encountered the Beast.
They do not know what organized evil is. They cannot
defend themselves against it. For far too long a time they
try to "understand" it, to extend to it the sympathy they
desire for themselves, to tolerate it, to make excuses for
it, to evade its challenge. Then, after a time, beginning to
see (or, more exactly, to feel, in their dreams and hidden

fantasies) its strength, they become afraid, even paralyzed. Now they cannot move against it. First, they cannot easily admit how deeply they have been mistaken. Second, they lose heart at the prospect of how great a price they will have to pay to resist what has now become so strong. Some, fascinated by the sheer power of evil, join it. Others try to appease it.

This process has gone farther among us then we dare to admit. Our movies and television shows—the public record of our dreams—are filled today with images of disaster, flaming ruin, and devastation we dare not admit into public consciousness. We know well enough where we are headed. Paralysis grips us all.

Here religion ought to be a help, an awakener. But American religion has long relied upon a single chord: guilt. Accordingly, it strengthens in the public consciousness the very weaknesses Ionesco and Solzhenitsyn describe. In addition, American religion has been essentially privatistic. No theologian has yet created a theory of democratic capitalism, a religious theory that explains the basic institutions of the system that, at the cost of much historical struggling, finally appeared in human history, has had such spectacular and unprecedented moral and human successes, and now appears prematurely to be entering twilight.

Our preachers avoid institutional analysis. Those who take it up, evading the actual *history* of Marxism in the world these last sixty years, adopt a vulgar Marxist analysis. It is the organized churches that avert their eyes from the organized forces of repression in the imperial Soviet and analyze the world in terms of the private guilt of individual affluent Americans vis-à-vis the Third World, and that borrow Marxist propaganda to create a weapon of guilt for flaying their uncertain and predisposed followers. It is the churches that preach disarmament, urge tolerance for the Gulag Archipelago (not directly, of course, but in effect), support the forces of organized authoritarianism if only they will call themselves "liberation forces," and spread the doctrines of appeasement under the cloak of Christian charity. I invite Solzhenitsyn to inspect with care the pronouncements and policies of the National Council of Churches, the spiritual state and political perception of the leaders of "radical" and "liberal" religion (and even the sterility of "conservative" religion), the articles and editorials in our religious journals of opinion, and the utterances and deeds of our topmost political leaders who declare themselves publicly to be religious men—to inspect all this before he concludes that disaster will be averted through the agency of organized religion in the United States.

I can already hear his response. Perhaps, though, one must approach his final point by another route. Arthur J. Schlesinger, Jr., who claims to have learned much from Reinhold Niebuhr in politics, less so in religion, in his reply to Solzhenitsyn worried about "mysticism," and other secular critics called Solzhenitsyn an "enthusiast" or a "theocrat." But it is as much a matter of plain common sense, of down-to-earth reality, and even of cool pragmatism to speak of religion as not. It is true that Solzhenitsyn does not define the ideal institutional forms that would constitute his own conception of the good society. When he criticizes the society of the West and the society of the East—that "world split apart"—it is not clear what alternative he would propose. But his last few lines direct our gaze:

> If the world is not going to perish, it has at least reached a historic turning point, equal in importance to the turn from the Middle Ages to the Renaissance. This turn will demand a spiritual renewal from us so that we can ascend

to a new, higher vision, to a new level of life, where our physical nature will not be condemned as in the Middle Ages—but, even more important, our spiritual nature will not be trampled upon as in modern times.

This ascent is similar to climbing to the next anthropological stage. No one on earth has any other way left but—upward.

Two thinkers who move in the same world of vision as Solzhenitsyn and who have developed an intellectual model for a Christian humanism and a Christian culture are T. S. Eliot (see *Christianity and Culture*, Harcourt Brace, 1960) and Jacques Maritain (*Integral Humanism*, Notre Dame, 1973). Solzhenitsyn may at some point want to examine their work in order to differentiate from it his own vision. But I think we may use his own text to sketch a vision of a society worth building, a society whose heart is not so empty as that of our present civilization, a society that, while remaining pluralistic, is not relativistic. Every idea is not equal to every other, nor is every moral value equal to every other. There are actions that are good and actions that are evil. Dishonesty is not equal to honesty, nor cowardice to courage, nor apathy to compassion, nor degradation to dignity, nor slavery to liberty. A society that, in order to defend diversity and tolerance, permits everything equally will suffer the same fate as an individual who refuses to make moral choices, who merely shrugs, "What's the difference?" Even without a resolute enemy, such a person, like such a society, would have doomed himself. And a resolute enemy will find him thoroughly defenseless.

Religion itself is subject to many historical permutations. Like liberty, it is a dangerous part of human life; one without the other destroys itself. Moreover, religion has many forms: not only the various concrete traditions of Christianity and Judaism that have shaped the West, but also those several forms of classical "natural" religion, like stoicism and various forms of unclosed humanism, that have helped to form the legal and intellectual foundations of the West. The life of the spirit to which Solzhenitsyn calls us need not be sectarian, narrow, or lacking in ecumenical awareness. Indeed, he has taken pains to speak of it in words that belong to no one tradition alone, avoiding even the intimate symbols of his own beloved Russian Orthodoxy. He has raised the discussion to a pluralistic plane on which those of varying commitments may join.

A liberal, pluralistic, constitutional democracy would not in the least be falsified, moreover, by being rooted in institutions sharply defined by the vision of man that Solzhenitsyn sketches: imperfect, untrustworthy, requiring every sort of institutional check and balance. The Bill of Rights would not violate the civilization to which he beckons us. In such a civilization he surely would insist upon freedom of the press—but a press that operates fairly and responsibly. His complaint about the Western press is that its freedom has been paralyzed by the tyranny of fashion and the absence of a genuine competition of ideas. One who finds no substantial intellectual difference between the world of *Time* and the world of *Newsweek*, between the *Washington Post* and the *New York Times*, or between ABC, CBS, and NBC, would find it hard to object to his criticism of the present too-narrow reality. In a word, none of the institutions we so cherish in the West would be undone in the world Solzhenitsyn envisages.

But the spirit that inhabits them, infuses them, and directs them he most certainly asks us to change. From relativism and moral indifference (you follow your values, I'll follow mine), Solzhenitsyn calls us to moral choice and moral self-criticism, to *growth* in the values we claim to hold. His assumption here, if I follow him, is sound: on the surface, one value system (Christianity) seems to differ from another (Judaism), but at the depths the most serious seekers after truth come to unexpected and remarkable convergences.

The world split apart has at its center a powerful longing to draw all together. Solzhenitsyn's vision is not antithetical to the political institutions conceived, in part, under the aegis of the Enlightenment and anthropocentric humanism. But it does implant these institutions in their inmost center.

· 13 ·

THE CHRISTIAN
PHILOSOPHY OF JOHN
PAUL II

Unless many recent conversations around the country mislead me, intelligent Catholics in significant numbers seem not to be on the same wavelength as Pope John Paul II. In some ways this is odd, because intelligent Catholics usually like an intelligent and articulate pope, and this one is perhaps the most intellectually original, articulate, and prolific pope of the past one hundred years. Some of this discordance results (those who don't cotton to him sometimes suggest) from their very different reading of Vatican II. Some of it results, they say, from very strong feelings of disagreement about particular questions such as women priests, contraception, and celibacy. Many are willing to admit, however, that they simply do not see what this pope is up to—do not follow, and cannot recount, his arguments. To a remarkable extent, in rather wide circles of American Catholicism a certain resistance to John Paul II seems to be the expected attitude. It is sad, I think, to be alive during one of the great pontificates in history and to be in passive opposition to it.

First published in *America*, October 1997.

This general lack of insight into why the pope teaches and acts as he does is apparent in two popular, recent biographies, that by Tad Szulc and that by Carl Bernstein and Marco Politi, as well as in the recent account *American Catholic* by Charles R. Morris, not to mention the running commentaries of the late Peter Hebblethwaite.

Nonetheless, it should be possible to set out an account of John Paul II's method, and to assist readers in grasping the originality of several of his conceptual achievements, even without attempting to close the disagreements on particular questions that some Catholics express. I hope that even those who do not go along with the pope may find such an effort of service.

It has often been pointed out, of course, that the pope was a professional philosopher before he became a bishop, and that he is probably better identified as belonging to the school of phenomenology than, say, as a Neo-Thomist. People often said that Paul VI, for example, was an admirer and even follower of Jacques Maritain, but while there are points of contact with Maritain in Wojtyla's work one could not readily understand him within Maritain's framework.

One key to understanding Karol Wojtyla, I think, is that he is first of all a poet and dramatist. His sensibility is that of an artist. He is sensitive, feels things deeply, responds instantly to persons and situations through his emotions, takes things in as wholes, and learns quickly from concrete experience. He trusts experience more than words. He likes to reflect on concrete wholes, as an artist would, in order to allow their inner form to emerge subtly and slowly. He is not in a rush to slash, channel, contort, or ignore parts of these concrete wholes in concepts or systems. These dispositions led him at a very young age to find both release and congenial techniques

in phenomenological method, particularly as he found it
in Max Scheler (d. 1928), the philosopher par excellence
of the feelings.

It is a rare American, of course, who is helped by hearing the term phenomenology. I have seen even professional philosophers blanch on being asked to offer a
thumbnail sketch of phenomenology, and listened as
well-travelled journalists approached even the pronunci-
ation of the term the way they would approach a three-
foot-wide ditch: back up a few steps, take a deep breath,
and lunge.

Simply put, phenomenology is a sustained effort to
bring back into philosophy everyday things, concrete
wholes, the basic experiences of life as they come to us.
It wishes to recapture these quotidian realities from the
empiricists, on the one hand, who analyze them into
sense data, impressions, chemical compositions, neural
reactions, etc., and from the idealists, on the other hand,
who break them up into ideal types, categories, and
forms. When girl meets boy (as Rebecca in Genesis first
sees Isaac coming toward her across the field), the psy-
chologist may be interested in her prior relation to her
father, and Kant may be concerned that her attachment
to the categorical imperative may be going wobbly in the
face of teleological hedonism. But the phenomenologist
is interested in her experience of love as a concrete
whole, in the many strands that there move her. How
much is involved? How many elements make up the
whole? How does this whole of experience differ from
others she has known? What does her own heart tell her
is lacking—or fulfilling—within it? This example suggests why, despite its cumbersome name, phenomenological method has had some of its greatest successes in the
arts and aesthetics, as in the work of Wojtyla's friend
from Krakow, the philosopher Roman Ingarden. A cer-

tain dramatic texture is inherent within it, and it has a taste of "the real."

As an actor who had played men moved by both great and tender passions on the stage, and as a dramatist and poet who had tried to create scenes in which powerful emotions and rich experiences could be relived by others, Wojtyla found Max Scheler to be in part a wonderful guide to the panoply of meanings and values embodied in the rich world of human feelings. Perhaps a contemporary parallel on the American scene today might be the recent book by James Q. Wilson, *The Moral Sense*. In the end, though, Wojtyla found Scheler not a complete guide to human experience and feeling; in his own life, there were elements Scheler did not know of or explain.

I am not able to read the Polish texts of Wojtyla's Lublin lectures, in which as a young professor he recounted both his appreciation of and disappointments in Scheler's work. But I have been enormously helped by a brilliant doctoral thesis produced at Catholic University last year by a young Dominican from Krakow, Jaroslav Kupczak. According to Kupczak, Scheler was allergic to feelings of obligation, and determined to show that Kant was wrong in grounding morals in duty, rather than in feelings. Wojtyla knew from his own experience that feelings are very important to the moral life and wonderfully subtle teachers; they often lead us to insights that the intellect itself is at first blind to or resistant to. On the other hand, he had himself experienced moments when he felt the heavy hand of duty upon reluctant feelings, and knew he had to act even when he was afraid and experiencing dread.

More to the point, perhaps, feelings are something that "happen" to us; in a way, we are receivers of feelings, we suffer them, they come unbidden. But Wojtyla had also known moments when he knew he had to take charge of his own life, to will something, to make something new happen, to become the agent of his own decisions. Here, too, he found Scheler too passive.

Before studying Scheler, Wojtyla had also—during World War II and just afterwards—been introduced to the writings of Thomas Aquinas, through a textbook produced by a transcendental Thomist who had studied at Louvain with Desiree Cardinal Mercier and Joseph Marechal. For two long months Wojtyla struggled with the density and abstraction and complexity of the thing—what a way to meet both Aquinas/Aristotle and Kant at the same time, under Nazi occupation and after some years of hard manual labor and work in the clandestine theater! When Wojtyla had climbed high enough through the thickets to see where he was, and get a sense of the terrain, he had two very strong feelings: first, he had found a way of articulating some of his most important experiences (of inner searching and conversion, of will, of agency, of call and obligation, of growth and becoming, for example) and, second, he saw that Thomism was stronger on nature than on human nature—it lacked a full theory of consciousness, interiority, and even the feelings. It had strengths the moderns lack, but it was weak in some places where modernity demands strength. He thought it might be his task to contribute to bringing to the Thomistic patrimony a sense of interiority, a theory that included consciousness in its full range: somatic, vegetative, neural, emotional, passional, imaginative, intellectual, in the will.

At Lublin in the mid-1950s, then the freest and most independent university in the entire East, behind the Iron Curtain, Wojtyla lectured on Hume, Kant, Scheler, and other figures in the history of ethical thought, while slowly developing his own thesis on human agency and creativity, which was eventually published (more as notes-in-progress than as the rounded book he would have wished to produce—he was working on it even during sessions of the Vatican Council) under the title *The Acting Person*. If we now imagine Wojtyla working at his desk in St. Peter's as a young bishop during the years 1961–65, this might be a good moment to pause to introduce one other major strand in his way of thinking.

During his earlier stay in Rome for doctoral studies at the Angelicum from 1946–48, where he wrote a thesis on St. John of the Cross and St. Thomas Aquinas on faith, Karol Wojtyla was much taken with the argument on Christian philosophy launched by Etienne Gilson. According to Gilson, while maintaining its own methodological autonomy, philosophy had been and could continue to be enriched by questions posed for it by Christian faith. For example, the concept of "person" had first been developed in the context of the doctrine on the Trinity, and the concept of will arose from questions posed in the New Testament about doing what we will not, and not doing what we will. The notion of "conscience" and many other notions also arose because of difficulties that arose from reflections on Christian experience in the light of inadequate secular theories.

For Wojtyla, the most impressive problem posed for him by Christian experience in our time—a problem arising directly from biblical texts and from his experience of our time—is the question of freedom. For him, the question is first of all interior, but under the Nazis and the communists he could not help noticing that freedom also has a political, even an economic, dimension, and a cultural as well as a personal dimension. It is not easy to explain how some men seem to yield up their freedom to threats or even to the mass sentiment surrounding them, while others like Maximilian Kolbe are able to remain fearless masters of their own decisions.

Wojtyla has always been fascinated by the agency open to humans, the ability to—and the call to—take charge of one's own life. Ironically, of course, this "taking charge" often means remaining receptive to calls of grace, keeping oneself out of comfortable ruts so as to be disposed to going wherever God calls, even if one feels one has not the strength.

The point is, unlike kittens or dogs, human lives are not bound by iron circles of instinct and routine; our minds and wills are always open to fresh and immediate inspirations of grace, new calls to conversion and action, even if only in the manner and intensity with which we attend to everyday duties. In each staccato second the human spirit is open, free, creative, receptive, and ready to act in fresh ways.

Twice in his life, Wojtyla requested permission to enter the Carmelites, the order that nourished St. John of the Cross, St. Teresa of Avila, and St. Therese of Lisieux, three of the greatest doctors of the interior life, especially the life of inner darkness of spirit and naked, abandoned faith. All three, too, each in a different way, stressed the utility of humble daily routines and humdrum quotidian activities for poverty of spirit and acts of love for God and others. To fail to see the extent to which Wojtyla's soul is Carmelite is to miss a great deal, indeed. This means that he sees grace in all the things of nature, and all the things of nature as whisperers of grace. He tries always to be in the presence of God, even when (perhaps especially when) sharing a good joke. Like most Poles, he likes being made to laugh; and his friend Father Josef Tischner, for example, has a reputation of being one of the best joke tellers in a nation of joke tellers. Laughter, even more than sorrow, is part of the splendor of being; Poland knows more than its share of both.

At the Second Vatican Council, Wojtyla worked

closely with Henri De Lubac, and he and the famous Jesuit became good friends, as the latter testifies in his memoirs. Wojtyla also shares with De Lubac the conviction that the concept of pure nature—apart from the fall and grace—is a mere hypothetical, which does not and never did exist. Today everything that is is graced, wounded though it be by the fall. Both also share a vision of the church as a communion, a "we." It would not be right to say that the views of Wojtyla and De Lubac on these questions are identical, but Wojtyla's views on them are closer to De Lubac's than to those of any other theologian. This helps to explain why the pope sees so much sacramentality and grace in every land, historical event, and monument—as his talks in every part of the world demonstrate. He reads history and nature sacramentally.

To those brought up thinking about natural law in the way, say, that the great John Courtney Murray did, the pope's habit of insisting that the human being cannot be understood apart from Jesus Christ may at first seem disconcerting. Yet the pope is always thinking about the enormous impact of Jesus Christ upon concrete history, including huge geological shifts, so to speak, in the terrain of philosophy itself. To choose Anglo-American examples, even philosophers as disparate as Bertrand Russell and Richard Rorty have candidly admitted that key concepts absolutely central to their own philosophies, such as compassion and solidarity, respectively, derive from the heritage of Jesus Christ, not Greece or Rome or even the Enlightenment. Even such concepts as person, conscience, the dignity of every individual without exception, and individual liberty, Wojtyla notes, arose from sustained reflection on the gospels. In the pope's thought, the realm of "nature" is thin and hypothetical, indeed, compared to the actual workings of the fall and of grace in real history.

On the other hand, Wojtyla has never hesitated to speak a secular language to those who are secular. As a philosopher, he is quite accustomed to discussing problems without appeal to the language or premises of faith. In the old days during his debates with Marxist philosophers, he found it quite possible to turn the Marxist doctrines of labor inside out through a purely philosophical (phenomenological) examination of the concrete experience of the steelworker in Nowy Huit and the fisherman in Gdansk. He is not one of those Christians who cannot think unless he quotes biblical texts. When, as on his recent visit to Poland, the pope speaks privately to the communist president of the nation, one imagines that he can speak man-to-man in terms the president will have no difficulty understanding, terms that would not have required Christian faith.

In other words, it is not merely that Wojtyla has an unusual facility with many national languages; he also feels at home in and can communicate in a large number of quite different intellectual traditions and disciplinary contexts. One might say that in this way, by a different route, he also observes the protocols of the two different languages of nature and of grace.

The letters of advice that Bishop Wojtyla sent to the Preparatory Commission of the Second Vatican Council may have been the first to suggest the two axial concepts that later were to run through every document of the Council as if lettered in crimson, a kind of conceptual spine: *person* and *community*. These became the axial concepts not only of the document on religious liberty but also of *Lumen Gentium* (on the Church) and *Gaudium et Spes* (on the Church in the Modern World). Wojtyla remembers with special fondness his intimate collaboration on the drafting of the last. Yet Paul VI gave credit to the interventions of Wojtyla on behalf of the document on religious liberty for his last-minute decision that documents must be voted on before the Council closed, when the tactic of the opposition had been to work for irretrievable delay. Paul VI could not turn down the appeal of those suffering behind the Iron Curtain for a strong word about liberty; and the interventions of Wojtyla proved, he told the conservatives, that the issue arose not solely from restless bishops in the secular countries of the West.

As bishop and as pope, Wojtyla has been consistent in his belief that Vatican II was an immense grace and marks out God's will for the Church in our time. He rejects projective readings of the Council, however, by which some read into it their own wishes or even fantasies. He asks for a full, balanced, nonselective reading of its documents, rich in their balance and measured reflection. Many in the advanced countries, it seems, have an image of what Vatican II meant that is not based upon actual meditation on the written text. He urges serious inquirers to study the documents in a spirit of prayer and learning. He is not afraid to recommend an attitude of obedience to God, obedience of the sort that led many thousands of priests in his generation to accept martyrdom. The so-called "spirit of Vatican II," I have found myself, is no substitute for getting the doctrine of Vatican II straight from the texts. Rereading those documents brings surprises on virtually every page.

In the July 1997 issue of *Crisis*, John Crosby points out how much the pope's teachings on sexual ethics have in common with that of many "progressives"—but also the unnoticed premise that differentiates his teaching from theirs; namely, the phenomenological analysis of action that stresses the unity of body and spirit, and uncovers in consciousness pain at their separation. I do not wish to enter into these controversies here, for my aim is not to argue such matters of substance but, rather, to call attention to the originality of the pope's way of analyzing matters. Too many, I find, are reacting with resistance to something they do not recognize, without having any guide to help them clarify further the area of dispute. It is not right to allow unnecessary obscurity to persist. Some effort is required, but Wojtyla's reasoning is far more interesting and original than he is being given credit for. Some are judging him entirely within their own categories, a tactic they do not like when others use it against them.

A resident assistant at a supposedly sedate Ivy League university told me how, at freshmen orientation week, representatives of the university threw handfuls of condoms out into the gathered assembly of young men and women fresh from their homes and eager to learn about the university experience, and how the latter scrambled around on the floor picking up the condoms. Everyone was expected to carry one out, as their ticket to the university experience. Instructions were also passed out for a variety of sexual acts that some of them, at least, did not even care to know about. The rationale for the distribution of condoms was "safety." It was assumed that they would be having sex with people they did not know and could not trust, and probably with multiple partners. In other words, the university expected them to experience a radical separation between their bodily acts and their souls. The weeks to follow were made endurable by the ingestion of large quantities of alcohol and drugs before sex. (Three women in the dorm—a mixed dorm, naturally—were found nude and unconscious in various rooms, including common bathrooms, and in one case outside on the grounds during that term.) Hearing this story, others from other universities have matched it.

Yes, some will say, but within the bonds of matrimony and within a loving permanent relationship, the use of contraceptives is different. No doubt. Yet, Wojtyla points out, the alienation between body and soul remains detectable. However one finally resolves this question in one's own mind, one must say that Wojtyla's analysis hits a worrisome nerve. (It reminds one, too, of the empirical research describing young women who sometimes do not use contraceptives, not because they want to conceive, but because they do not want anything to come between them and the one they actually love; sometimes tragically, they intend this as a sign to him.)

On the question of a celibate clergy, too, it is useful to ask what Wojtyla thinks the priesthood is. When he became a priest and during the forty years afterward, Wojtyla knew that thousands of Polish priests were being killed, sent to labor camps, beaten, and jailed for years at a time, simply for being priests. To be a priest was to be a marked man. In such circumstances, the fact that priests did not have families to support was a blessing. To become a priest was actually, and was regarded as, a brave and manly act. The life to be led was one of poverty, uncertainty, physical discipline, and mortified flesh. A significant part of one's work would be clandestine. One would need to go out at all hours and in all weather. One priest would be clubbed by an anonymous band of thugs, in circumstances that made the act seem not unplanned; another would be approached after mass and struck on the head by a rock swung by a "madman," who would go unpunished. To see the large number of vocations to the priesthood in Poland today, and to witness the manly bearing and high morale of those who enter, is to see the harvesting of countless acts of courage and fidelity.

On matters of social ethics, one well-known U.S. theologian likes to describe Catholic social thought as a triad of "three S's"—Solidarity, Subsidiarity, and Social Justice. To these, John Paul II has added Subjectivity—the human person as subject, as agent, as center of imagination, initiative, and determined will. Against collectivism of all sorts, the pope counterpoises the self-conscious human subject who pours herself into all that she does. Here, too, he sees the ground for defending rights to private property and to private initiative; and, more basic still, rights to religious and moral liberty. Further, because he sees social justice as rooted in individual subjects, he is also able to defend it as a virtue, a habit of a new and specific sort proper to free men and women, a new seat of social responsibility. In this vein, too, the pope now places on families—what he calls the domestic church—the new locus of the royal power that the church once vested in kings, the royal obligation of building up the civilization of love. For him, the new *civis* is the married husband and wife, and it is they, not the state, who are the prime bearer of civilizing responsibilities. (Russell Hittinger of the University of Tulsa has tracked this turn in papal thought best.)

Those who wish to pursue further studies in the thought of John Paul II will now be tremendously helped by the magisterial, clear, and profound book of Rocco Buttiglione, *Karol Wojtyla*, the best study in any language. Buttiglione learned Polish and worked with Wojtyla before the latter became pope. He is much loved and trusted by the pope, who asked Buttiglione to write the brilliant introduction to the third Polish edition of *The Acting Person* (1994), which is reprinted in this handsome volume. Many American Catholics, I believe, will be stunned by the intellectual achievement recorded in Buttiglione's study. Like Wojtyla, Buttiglione also shares a great love for America and its tradition of practicality and common sense, and is able to show connections between phenomenological method and typically American habits of thought.

Since Pope John Paul II has the large vision of a philosopher, he is a little like Leo XIII (1878–1903) in the broad range of the subjects he writes about. It looks now, too, as if his papacy may run as long, or longer. Indeed, if John Paul lives as long as Leo, he will celebrate Easter of the year 2013 in the papacy. Beyond sharing years and range of views, however, I think it can be fairly argued that John Paul II is more professionally trained in a variety of contemporary disciplines than Leo XIII was, more penetrating, more original and—perhaps for that reason—more disturbing.

I know that my friend Hans Küng thinks that Pope John Paul II is very bad for the church, according to Hans's vision of the church. Yet, affection for Hans aside, I think that John Paul II is very good for the church. The church as Hans wants it is not a church I would wish to belong to nor is it, by Hans's own testimony, the church it has always been.

I hope all my progressive friends will forgive me if I close with the ancient Polish prayer, on behalf of Karol Wojtyla: *"May he live a hundred years!"*

· III ·

AFTERWORD

· 14 ·

Errand into the Wilderness

Since at least second grade, I have wanted to become a writer. From ages fourteen to twenty-six, I studied for the Roman Catholic priesthood until, six months before ordination, in 1960, I decided not to become a priest. Not long after I first began publishing in earnest, the Second Vatican Council (1962–1965) brought the Catholic Church to more favorable public attention than it had earlier received in America. From about 1967 until 1971, those who knew my writing had reason to describe me as a "progressive, left-of-center Catholic," and even as one who sided with the radical left, over against the "corporate liberalism" (as I then called it) of the mainline left. I liked being thought of in that way. Nonetheless, a left-wing friend described me to her colleagues in 1968 as one whose "temperament is conservative but who thinks himself into left-wing positions." (That taught me a new way of thinking about myself.)

First published in John H. Bunzel, *Political Passages: Journals of Change Through Two Decades 1968–1988* (New York: Free Press, 1988). Reprinted as one in a series of *Presidential Essays* selected by Edwin J. Feulner, Jr., President, Heritage Foundation, December 1989.

Slowly, though, I also thought my way out of left-wing positions.

My first published book was a novel, *The Tiber was Silver* (1961). I was long uncertain whether I wanted to be a scholar, a novelist, a social critic, or an engaged activist. The French tradition of Mauriac, Sartre, Camus, and others taught me that an intellectual could properly do all four, each in its season. Aristotle counseled that until he is at least fifty, a philosopher should engage in a broad range of activities at first hand. In my own poor way, I have given that a shot, more or less systematically involving myself in and reflecting upon various dimensions of American life.

During the three decades of my adulthood, political and cultural changes have occurred rapidly. "Movements" of many kinds have swept through the consciousness of readers and writers. On these changes swift judgments are often required. Making them, one can often lose old friends. Families—even spouses—have been driven apart by answering them in different ways. Those who were once allies often become, almost overnight, bitterly estranged. Too often these days, dinner parties erupt in loud and angry disagreement. All this happens because new forms of "consciousness"— concerning American "imperialism," detente, feminism, homosexuality, liberation theology, the rebels in Nicaragua—have confronted our generation with a relentless series of fundamental decisions. *What should we think? What should we hope for? What should we do?*

There is a "vulgar Marxist" way of answering these questions. There is a "line." In fact, other progressives often bully one another into becoming "sophisticated." (There is in our society a deep, although disguised, hunger for orthodoxy, especially among persons who think of themselves as progressives. Most do not wish to appear to be orthodox, only sophisticated. It is the same thing.) With unprecedented speed, the literate are urged to adapt to new ideas, to new ways of thinking, and to new standards of judgment. Theology is done, again and yet again, "in a new key." I have come to call it neodoxy: obedience to the new.

At a certain point, one wants to get off the train; at least, I wanted to get off the train. The progressive "line" draws strength from many diverse cultural feeders but always runs in one direction. It is consistent in the disciplines and inhibitions it wishes to destroy, and in which direction it wants to move. (Near the top of the book of Genesis, for example, we are told, "Man and woman He made them." That is one of the differentiations to be destroyed.) The climate becomes ever more utopian, ever more dreamy. The mildly Marxist analysis that is the vanguard of left-wing consciousness is not random or undirected. It is an analysis of a quite distinctive type. But this is to get too far ahead in the story.

I wrote some years ago that life is in some equal measure self-discovery and self-invention. In part we discover—over time and through much darkness—who we are. In part, through trial and error, we choose to be who we are; we give ourselves our own identity. In mobile and free societies such as ours, with access to an almost infinite range of experiences, books, and thought, it is not so easy as it once was to live a life of straight-line logic. Experiences occur that call into question earlier certitudes. Fresh insights and new paradigms allow us to break through earlier established horizons, sometimes from heights (or depths) that alter our vision of the entire landscape round about. In my case, I once had a vision of political economy that I have since come to discover was mistaken.

Like many young Catholics and Jews, I had imbibed

from an early age a set of suspicions concerning big business, capitalism, Marlboro man individualism, and Anglo-Saxon ethnic superiority. While never seriously tempted to join a socialist party, I rather liked socialist analyses that attacked the complacency of America. The anticapitalism of such writers as R. H. Tawney on Protestantism and the acquisitive instinct appealed to me. One need not be a socialist or a Marxist to be fairly systematically anticapitalist (and radically critical of American society). For all practical purposes, though, one usually becomes thus the ally of socialists and Marxists.

Today, some of my best friends remain far to the left. *Remain* far to the left? During the past twenty years, by their own admission, they have moved ever farther left. Like me, they are voyagers. Their voyages in recent years have taken them into three specific desert fastnesses: that the United States is an imperialist nation oppressive to people in the Third World; that capitalism is an evil economic system, propelling imperialism abroad and multiple ills at home; and that the combination of imperialism and capitalism is fed by patriarchy, machismo, and male domination.

Although twenty years ago I was poised to journey into that wilderness myself, such friends now look around to find me not only absent from their caravan but among their nagging critics. Some have expressed hurt. Others find my own change of direction (even though it was not sudden, but protracted; and not secret, but argued out step-by-step in print) puzzling, troubling, and—when they are angry enough to say so—a mark of disloyalty, betrayal, and downright moral corruption. Their own deepening involvement with the left seems to them so correct, so commanded by the evidence, and so morally obligatory that it is truly difficult for them to understand my "defection." They know that their own views are moral. (I once thought so too, but no longer.) They feel themselves impelled by Christian faith and moral obligation. For them, it is a matter of *Saying Yes and Saying No* (the title of a book by one of my closest former colleagues, Robert McAfee Brown). If they say yes, while I say no, it is virtually impossible for them to allow that I am moral, or even to be open to argument that *their* position is immoral.

Around them, socialist experiments crumble. The most publicly uncelebrated fact of the late twentieth century is the death of the socialist idea, especially in economics. (Why, I often wonder, did it take me so long to discover this myself?) The 3 percent of the land allotted to private farming and to market transactions within the USSR yields roughly 33 percent of the foodstuffs that reach the Soviet table, as Secretary General Gorbachev has been obliged to note—and to hold up as the standard for the "new" Soviet economy. Weary of being both socialist and poor, the Chinese have recently turned to private property, markets, and other capitalist techniques, thereby doubling their food production within two short years (an achievement which in a country of one billion citizens carries a certain clout).

Perhaps sensing the ground shift beneath their feet, my old colleagues on the left are most reluctant to enter into debate concerning the empirical record of the idea they have made central to their moral vision: socialism as a means of liberating the poor. They are unwilling to point to any existing socialist society as the model toward which they aspire, or even to specify the institutions they believe essential to the socialism of their dreams. The dreamier, the better. I think they sense the verdict that history will pronounce upon them, for their tone is increasingly shrill and anxious. They have internalized the neo-Marxist analysis of oppression and dependence.

Their paralysis springs from the shame they feel at being Americans. They have the right idea: to help the poor. But they have chosen methods bound to disappoint them. Slowly many will see that.

Not all, though. The older among them are fully grown adults who have formed their views deliberately, and are fully culpable or (as they think) praiseworthy on that account. Many of them believe that capitalism is inherently evil, that business is based on greed, and that Americans ought to live in shame for living as they do. They are alienated grown adults, who think that their alienation is a higher form of virtue, rather than a form of bad faith.

It is not they, then, who are likely to be persuaded through reason and an analysis of cases. They have made their commitment. It is, rather, the younger ones, still openminded and searching, the questioning and the self-affirming, who know in the depths of their minds that self-hatred, alienation, and resentment are signs of illness of the spirit, and that a falsely learned alienation is a lie. It is to the latter, not the former, that argument is usefully addressed. The former do not dialogue, I have sadly learned. They excommunicate. There is nothing to fear in that. It is a blessing.

In August 1947, I travelled by train to South Bend, Indiana, to begin my studies—a long course of studies—leading, I hoped, to ordination as a Catholic priest. I will never forget my first sight of the dome of Notre Dame or, once at the heart of the campus, of St. Mary's Lake, still and leaden in the hot late-summer air, and across it on a grassy mound the gray stones of Holy Cross Seminary, which was to be my home for four years. I was then just a few days short of my fourteenth birthday, about to become a high school freshman. I said a prayer of commitment. I would give it my best.

My parents had tried to dissuade me from entering the seminary. My father was in those days a touch anticlerical. "Remember, you're a Novak," he said in our last embrace at the Pittsburgh train station, as if we were of noble lineage. He said one more time, "Don't let them put you on a pedestal." He then talked vividly about how lonely the life of a priest could be; he told me of a priest friend of his who had described how many achingly long evenings he had sat alone at the piano. My father had also described the many symbols—the cassock and collar, the being set apart, the eager deference of the people toward the clergy—that could relentlessly and steadily go to a young man's head. (I do not think now that he was right about that. In this generation, many priests are quite modest; a crisis in self-confidence is apparent now.)

A few weeks earlier, when I was out of earshot, my father had responded to my uncle, who strongly objected to my going to the seminary at such a young age, that I was unusually mature, that he had made his objections known, but that I had thought it out and was determined to go. "Besides," I heard him say, "the more I would say no, the more Mike would say yes."

I had long loved getting up early and walking a mile and a half across the iron-squeaking snow to serve the 7 A.M. Mass, arriving early enough to kneel before the tabernacle in our parish church, with the red sanctuary candle flickering, where no one could observe me. I wasn't certain I would become a priest, but I was perfectly sure that I should try; the call was strong. At last giving up on his objections, my father said: "If you go, give it a good shot; stay at least a full year, don't give up easily. But when you want to come home, we want you here."

One afternoon, he and yet another uncle of mine had watched me play eighth-grade football (we had no

league, nor any equipment but what we bought for ourselves). During the first half I scored five touchdowns,
until I had to leave with my father. "Pretty good, Mike,"
Uncle Johnnie said at the car. "He's not well coordinated
for this game," my father said matter of factly as he
closed the car door on the other side. He had never said
I should not play football in high school, although the
local coach (famous in that area) had already stopped
by to watch me play and to encourage me to come and
see him. It is odd that part of me accepted my father's
assessment of my abilities, although another part of me
was exhilarated by the success on the field that I usually
experienced.

There was no doubt in my mind, on arrival in South
Bend, that I should enter the seminary *then, there*. I was
not sure that I would manage to finish all four years in
that gray building across the sky-reflecting lake. But I
knew it was my inner destiny to try. I knew that if I did
not try now, before high school, then football and
girls—I was prematurely crazy about girls—would fate-
fully distract me. Now was the time, Notre Dame was the
place. I had tried to enter the Jesuits and had inquired of
several other communities. The Jesuits didn't take candi-
dates until after high school, and the Holy Cross Fathers
(who run Notre Dame) offered the broadest scope of
priestly activities, from teaching and research, through
television and journalism, to foreign and domestic mis-
sions. My eighth-grade yearbook suggested that I would
be an anchorman or journalist (I wrote the prediction
myself), but I was uncertain what I wanted to do, and
wanted room to experiment. Holy Cross was perfect.

So it turned out to be. I loved my years of study, including Latin, Greek, French, and (much later) Hebrew
and Italian. After graduating from high school, I chose
to leave the Notre Dame province to join the newer and

more pioneering venture of building up the new Stonehill College in Massachusetts. First, though, came a concentrated year of prayer and a more strictly monastic life in the novitiate at North Dartmouth, Massachusetts. The years at Stonehill were happy and fruitful (to my joy, our seminary team in the intramural football league lost only two games during four years). After graduation, my superiors selected me for study at the Gregorian University in Rome. I had been having doubts about becoming a priest. I wanted to do so many things that I didn't know how I could do them all, bound under obedience. I wanted and needed to be a free-lance writer. But that conflict took a while to become intense.

Over the years, I had almost quit several times. (All one had to do was say the word and go; of the thirty-nine I started with in 1947, I was the last to go; none of the "original class" made it into the priesthood, although of course others who entered along the way did.) But I basically loved the study, the prayer, the atmosphere of charity and learning.

After two years in Rome, in 1958, I finally asked to leave. My superior back in Massachusetts, a marvelous priest (a missionary in Chile and Peru for many years), agreed that I should leave. "Still," he said, "you've put in so many years. Perhaps Rome got you down. Graduate studies in literature here may refresh you. Why don't you be a little more patient, make certain what you're doing, then decide? Either way, I'm with you."

It did seem reasonable to be certain that later I'd have no regrets. For another year and a half, I gave it all I had. Then I knew. Contrary to custom at the time, my superior allowed the whole seminary—in Washington, D.C., at Catholic University—to hold a good-bye party for me. That was a warming gesture. He also gave me money for a suit, my first in twelve years that wasn't clerical black. After a visit with my family, disappointed but supportive, I set off for New York City in January 1960 to make a career as a novelist, with $100 from my father. I found the garret of my dreams and worked hard.

By the time my first novel was accepted, late in the summer of that year, I had also won a fellowship in philosophy at Harvard. Not knowing better, I had applied only to Harvard and to Yale; Harvard offered more support. After having lived in Manhattan on $35 a week, earned by writing, I enjoyed the relative opulence of a Harvard dormitory and regular meals. But Harvard philosophy—heavy on logic and language analysis—was more narrow in its intellectual range than Stonehill or Rome had been, and it seemed to me terribly inadequate to the century of the Holocaust, to the turmoil in Europe (the Hungarian revolution of 1956 had occurred just as I arrived in Rome), and to the spiritual quest many had been experiencing in the late 1950s. *Harper's* asked me to do a piece for a special issue on the universities; it came out as "God in the Colleges," and was later reprinted in several anthologies of the New Left. Its basic theme was that behind the logic and the pragmatism, behind the cloverleaves and the swift, finned automobiles, there was growing a hunger to ask, "Who are we, under the stars, with the wind on our faces?"

In the seminary, I used to admire the intellectual leaders of the religious and philosophical left most of all. One of the first models around whom I wished to fashion my own career was the young Michael Harrington, then of the Catholic Worker movement, who used to write in *The Commonweal* well before he became famous for *The Other America*. In the generation following Reinhold Niebuhr and John Bennett, Robert McAfee Brown and

Harvey Cox were personal friends. In the mid-1960s, I was invited to serve as the first Roman Catholic on the editorial board of *The Christian Century*, and also on the board of *Christianity and Crisis*, Niebuhr's own journal. And, of course, I cherished my outlets in *The Common-weal* and the *National Catholic Reporter*, the two major lay Catholic journals. (There was a time, the joke went, that no religious magazine of the left could publish without Michael Novak on its board.) Gradually, I could no longer avoid seeming adversarial within these journals because they were moving leftward, while I no longer believed in left-wing visions.

How did that conversion happen? If I had been knocked down from a horse by a blinding light on a single memorable day, it would be easier to say. Instead, it was quite gradual, through examining my own left-wing presuppositions one by one. Underneath this questioning, perhaps, lay a pursuit of self-knowledge, a drive to be faithful to my family and roots, to be myself.

Half of my grandfather's family remained behind in Slovakia when four brothers came to America just before the turn of the century. Part of our family still lives behind the Iron Curtain. Socialism to me was not, therefore, merely an intellectual symbol, but a family matter. Nonetheless, my education was as anticapitalist as that of any other liberal arts major who took seriously the anticapitalist reflections of English literary critics and of most literary giants in America and Britain. As a Catholic, I was perhaps somewhat more Euro-centered than my fellow students in my intellectual interests. I especially loved Albert Camus, but also read a great deal about the worker-priests of France and Catholic Action in Italy. I read the early (anticapitalist) writings of the Christian Democrats; Graham Greene, Heinrich Böll, Alberto Moravia, Ignazio Silone, and others. Following

Michael Harrington (although suspicious of the scholasticism of his Marxism), I thought I could be a social democrat or democratic socialist—a democrat in politics, a mild socialist in economics, a blend of conservative and modernist in culture. It seemed there must be a "third way" between oppressive socialism and laissez-faire capitalism, probably something like democracy plus a cooperative economy gently directed in some new way.

It has never been difficult for me to identify with the poor. I was born among them. Johnstown, Pennsylvania, its steel mills strung out for a dozen miles along the valley floors of the Conemaugh and Stony Creek rivers, flanked by steep green hills, was a good place to grow up, among plain, solid people. The countryside is beautiful round about; deer are seen frequently, large bears occasionally, and ring-neck pheasants and rabbits are abundant. I used to marvel at the thick red smoke from the open hearth at Bethlehem Steel, and the white-hot ingots brought out in toy-solider rows to cool. Watching the thick clouds of smoke billow over the hilltops, I felt sorry for the almost naked Indians who once camped upon the Conemaugh, near the point where the two rivers join. (The Point Stadium still sits there, from which Babe Ruth once hit a home run fifteen feet above the 406-foot mark in right field, my father says, and still climbing.) The poor Indians had no industry, no heated homes, no wheels, no iron stoves. I was an admirer of progress. It did not surprise me later to learn that the Germans sent the Graf Zeppelin over Johnstown, for espionage purposes, in about 1936, when I was three; and I think I faintly remember it. I certainly remember the vast formations of aircraft—especially the P-38s—winging overhead on their way to Europe from 1942 on, and the hulks of tanks, German and American, shipped back to the Johnstown mills for meltdown from the African campaign.

My father had to leave school during the sixth grade to help support the family. His father had died when a carriage overturned on him at a funeral, when my father was two. His mother, who had been sent to America as a girl of sixteen with a sign "Passaic" around her neck, now supported six children by taking in washing and housecleaning. They lived on Virginia Avenue, which clings to the side of a steep hill above the mills, its narrow frame houses almost two stories higher on the back side than on the street side; you have to see Virginia Avenue to believe it.

One uncle, on my mother's side, went to college, until the bank collapse in 1933 forced him to withdraw. Practically all the men went off to war. My father was all packed and ready for the navy, when on the day before the train departed a telegram brought word of a new ruling exempting men of his age and number of children (then four). Later, in December 1944, another telegram announced the death of his best friend, Mickey Yuhas, in the Battle of the Bulge. On the same day I was hit by a car while sledding and, the doctor said, came within an inch of having my skull crushed and an eye lost (my head smashed the headlight at its edge, and I went up over the fender). Three weeks later at midnight Mass, marching in the choir in the darkened church with a candle in my hand, I was the eleven-year-old whose black eye made people in the pews cover smiles and whisper.

Marriage and a honeymoon in Rome in the fall of 1963, to cover the Second Vatican Council, interrupted my Harvard studies. The stunning new "openness" of the Catholic Church fulfilled many of my seminary dreams of what ought to happen. I was glad to be able to report on it, with all the freedom of a layman but with an insider's knowledge. Lord Acton's account of the First Vatican Council a century earlier was my model. From Stanford, Robert McAfee Brown came to Rome as a Protestant observer; soon enough, he proposed a teaching position at Stanford, where in 1965 I became the first Catholic in the religion department. It was there that my radical phase began.

Stanford in 1965 was just becoming alive with radical politics as Karen (big with our first child) and I arrived. Until early 1967, I was in favor of the Kennedy-Johnson commitment to South Vietnam, for Niebuhrian "realist" and anticommunist reasons. The cause was just. Gradually, though, I became convinced that the strategy and tactics of the conduct of the war were not likely to lead to success, and began to oppose it on just-war grounds.[1] This measured judgment did not satisfy the left, but did persuade many moderate people. I spent a month in Vietnam during the election period of August 1967, and came back with a sharper grasp of the concrete setting, a deeper appreciation of the complex antagonisms among the Vietnamese, and a confirmation of my modulated—but clearly antiwar—views. I was not, I could not be, an anti-American. "To love one's own country is not a sin," I used to paraphrase Camus. To stop the war was one aim; to negotiate a safe period during which to secure a free and mutual reunification of Vietnam over the long term was another, at once more complex and more honorable.

In the spring of 1968, after campaigning vigorously for Robert Kennedy and being devastated by his murder, I moved back east to the idyllic campus of Old Westbury, the newest branch of the State University of New York. Two things attracted me. First, Old Westbury was to be an experimental college, and education reform was clearly a coming priority. Second, the president, Harris Wofford, had helped begin the Peace Corps, and his interests in Democratic Party politics and his enthusiasm for whatever he undertook were terribly winning. Given my seminary background, I felt I very much needed more experience of the world, especially in politics. At Old Westbury, we would be in the vanguard of educational reform, and I would learn a lot from the Peace Corps style of Wofford. My expectations were abundantly fulfilled, although as usual not in the way I expected.

So radical were the first hundred students admitted to Old Westbury for its first year in 1968–1969 that, in one survey, all students except one thought electoral politics was a bourgeois fraud and only that one planned to participate at all; he was for Eugene McCarthy. Both Harris and I went to the Chicago convention; that was a searing experience, amid stink bombs and tear gas, ignorant armies clashing by night.

Back on campus, the students soon turned against Harris; there were endless demonstrations, grievances, protests, and bizarre behaviors. The fact that the bookstore was open only during assigned hours was interpreted as "bourgeois"; one of the faculty members smashed the door down with his foot, and students took what they wanted. Another professor, to demonstrate the rigorously egalitarian atmosphere, met his seminar under the large classroom table, all squatting and ducking their heads at egalityrannical levels. Think of this as childish vulgar Marxism; the grown-up version has uncannily repeated itself in every Communist Party victory. At Stanford, the small proportion of radicals were (until violence erupted in the year following my departure) like a little salt sprinkled over a large roast. At Old Westbury, there was little else besides salt, and I very soon rebelled.

Most students wanted total liberty, meaning no standards, no restrictions, no differentiations, no authorities, no requirements. Against this, a few of us established a second college within the college, which quite deliberately we called the Discipline College. Assignments, authorities, standards, requirements. We were said by some to be—what else?—fascists.

One of my favorite moments at Old Westbury was an invitation I extended to Herbert Marcuse to hold a seminar. Prussian to his fingertips, Marcuse said no student should feel competent to rebel against a teacher until he had mastered what his teacher knew; until then, revolution must mean discipline. *Delectatio morosa*: Marcuse plunged in the estimation of our most vocal radicals, and I enjoyed their discontent.

The very word "radical," of course, began to make me queasy. The entire vocabulary of the far left—which sounds the more plausible the less likely it is to be realized—assumes an entirely different significance when a dominant majority begins to act it out and to impose it. Some really *do* mean "paranoia is true perception." I began to understand the disbelief that many millions in this century have experienced when totalitarians actually began to put into practice the assault upon "bourgeois standards" that once sounded merely clever and literary. At Old Westbury, some really *did* mean that Shakespeare is "crap" and burned his books to dramatize their feelings. Someone even carefully placed human excrement on a piece of cardboard and put it in the desk drawer of a woman on the faculty. What some didn't like they simply disrupted. Anarchy and tyranny, contempt for disciplined intellect and a fascination with "the ferocious exercise of will"[2] are not so far buried in human consciousness that they cannot easily be released.

All the words of the far left began to sound new chords

in my head. Like all words, each of them has an Orwellian double meaning. If one understands them in a decent, bourgeois liberal way, they have an attractive sound. (Who can be against freedom or equality?) If one grasps what these same words mean when they are acted out apart from the restraints of checks and balances, and through the coercions of a majority willing to throw tantrums in order to get its way, their true force is to dehumanize those who use them and to imperil any who get in the way. Played in the classic liberal key, words such as "freedom," "equality," "justice," and "the poor" have had a powerful meaning for my family and for many others. (The United States is like a Broadway hit, with immigrants lined up around the block by the millions waiting to get in.) Played in their naked vulgar Marxist key, the same words intend only one thing: a rationale for naked power. Wherever they are around the world, at the fringes of Britain's Labor Party or the German SDP, at feminist caucuses or among the Sandinista turbas, extreme leftists do whatever is necessary to get their way. My wife was told our house would be bombed; we took care to keep close track of both our children, then ages three and one.

The hard lessons learned from living in a "total community" with the fervent radicals of Old Westbury, who brooked no opposition and shouted down appeals to reason, were like a vaccination. What Kolakowski wrote of the relation between Marx and the totalitarian USSR might also be said of the relation between the ideas of the serious left and the infantile leftists of Old Westbury: while one could not predict from the words of the former what the latter would make of them, neither was there anything in the former that would prevent the worst from happening. And everything done by the new left could be justified by quoting amply from the old left.

At Stanford, the year after my departure, buildings were bombed. Elsewhere, the radical left turned to kidnappings, bombings, and bank robberies. The decline of the universities was in full swing. Many of my associates who had been hesitant were rapidly now becoming radicalized, just as I was moving in the opposite direction, becoming deradicalized. But disaffection with the left is not enough to constitute a true conversion.[3]

In 1975, American involvement in Vietnam ended with an irrational, irresponsible abruptness. The vision of hundreds of thousands of boat people, preyed upon by pirates who raped and looted and murdered, afflicted my conscience. As I read about the sufferings of the Vietnamese people left behind in Vietnam and (still later) of the systematic deceptions practiced by the North Vietnamese upon those of us in the antiwar movement, I dreamt at night of blood on my own hands. The situation in present-day Vietnam is a rebuke to the antiwar movement, as is the continuing expansion of Soviet air and naval power in the South Pacific.

More to the point, as I surveyed the economic record of the socialist nations of Eastern Europe, Asia, Africa, and Cuba, I could find none that I admired, or would choose as a model for the world. The socialist *economic* ideal clearly did not work in practice, not anywhere. Upon sustained reflection, it also became clear to me that its flaw lay not only in its practice, but in its fundamental ideas. Socialism as an economic ideal is not designed to create new wealth, but only to mobilize envy. Idealists say that its aim is to distribute wealth evenly. Realists must observe that socialist elites retain uncommon powers, privileges, and wealth. Socialist idealism is a deception.

The great advantage the socialist ideal brings to an

intellectual, however, is difficult to do without. Socialism is essentially a vision for organizing history. Cosmic in its attraction, it offers security and solid footing. Through its gaze, we know that capitalist institutions are destined for the dustbin, that to favor freer markets is "ideological," and that the growth of collective power is inevitable in history. Therefore, faced with any event or proposition, one must only analyze whether it furthers the collapse of capitalism or enhances the growth of collective power. If so, it belongs to the future, gains its *truth* from that, and ought to be applauded and supported. If not, we know that it is to be despised as out of date and doomed.

When I ceased relying on socialist methods of analysis, therefore, I felt a significant inner emptiness. If one is not a card-carrying socialist, but a pragmatic leftist, one can of course employ many forms of socialist and Marxist analysis without being ideologically careful about the full sweep of their logic. Still, losing faith in socialist methods of analysis is like losing an inner compass, a chart, a vision. Fortunately, there fell into my hands, among other writings, some of the essays of Irving Kristol, recalling me to an intellectual tradition I had hitherto avoided: that of the American Framers and that of British and French liberals of the early nineteenth century. I trusted former persons of the left more than conservative intellectuals; the fact that others (soon to be labeled by Michael Harrington "neoconservatives") had doubts and questions similar to mine much strengthened me.

Both as a Slavic Catholic and by temperament, I am partial to thinkers who are somewhat skeptical of a merely geometric logic, of rationalism. I am attracted to thinkers who love the unpredictability of fact, who respect the ambiguity of history, and the concreteness of ethical reasoning and ethical perception—to Aristotle and Aquinas, for example, and to the Whig tradition. I respect those who give due weight to the ethical role of the family, to tradition, to religion, to the tacit wisdom built up through the social experience of the human race. For such reasons, the sheer individualism of some Anglo-American thinkers (from Bentham to Rawls) has always less than satisfied me. But such writers as Adam Smith, Edmund Burke, John Stuart Mill (despite my allergy to his socialist inclinations), Montesquieu, Bastiat, Lord Acton, and John Henry Newman awakened deeply responsive chords in me. When I read Hayek's postscript to *The Constitution of Liberty*, "Why I Am Not a Conservative," I responded as one who finally grasped a way of stating what I am. I belong to what used to be called the Whig tradition; its vision of progress is quite different from that of the "progressives"—a term captured by socialist ways of thought. In offering an alternative to the socialist dream of the future, it has captured the idea of the future. It is more realistic, more likely to work, proven in its successes. In these respects, this vision (for which I would have preferred the name "neoliberal") is a much greater threat to leftists than conservatives have ever been. That is why it infuriates leftists.

Meanwhile, on another front, another stage in my conversion began in 1970, continued through the process of writing *The Rise of the Unmeltable Ethnics* (1972), and culminated in my efforts on behalf of the McGovern campaign in 1972. In July 1970, just after I had set aside a report in the *New York Times* that Sargent Shriver, recently resigned as ambassador to France, was launching a national campaign to help elect Democrats to Congress, and just after telling my wife that I would love to be involved in that, my telephone rang. It was Mr. Shriver, telling me that he had just finished *The Experi-*

ence of Nothingness, and wanted me to write for him in his campaign. Could I come down to Washington? I didn't even shave my long beard.

There followed three splendid months of living with the Shrivers at their home in Rockville, Maryland, and flying out on fascinating campaign trips to some thirty states. We had a marvelous time. I don't think I have ever met a man with so much energy, so much enthusiasm, and such a serious practical interest in philosophical and religious ideas. We had so many good laughs, doing the zany things media campaigns force politicians to do (being pulled by speedboats on inflated tractor-tire inner tubes on a lake in South Dakota, for example), and so many long and happy conversations that those months are a kind of highlight in my memory.

Most of all, though, by election day in the congressional year 1970, I felt I had a far better grasp of the diverse neighborhoods of America than I had ever had before. I had seen at first hand the true significance of ethnicity and localism in American life. On the same day, we once met with black ministers for whom "quotas" mean being brought *in*; a Jewish woman's group for whom "quotas" mean a history of being kept *out*; and an electrician's union (mostly Italian Catholic) for whom "quotas" mean "they never include us." Political symbols have their own geography. A speechwriter needs to know which words mean what to whom, where, and when. Moreover, I learned to respect the great openness, yearning, generosity, and hope of all those ordinary people that we met along the way, hands rough or smooth, faces beautifully kept or weathered, speech cultivated or rough. Words that I had written about the American majority—complacently drinking beer in front of television—in *Toward a Theology of Radical Politics* now made shame color my cheeks. I met the American people

in the flesh; my literary imagination had been calumni-
ous. But this had not been my vision only. In rejecting it,
I was rejecting the leftist vision of America (or Amerika),
the anti-Americanism so common among my intellectual
colleagues.

I noted, too, that the great political commentators
often had things wrong. In poor black neighborhoods,
we avoided speaking of crime, which we took to be a
"code word"; but the local black politicians who spoke
before Mr. Shriver attacked crime far more heatedly
than anyone I had ever seen on television. In working
class neighborhoods, we often spoke in bars near factor-
ies or in union meeting halls that were far better inte-
grated, whites and blacks in obvious camaraderie, than
I had ever seen in any other social location. And why
not? In major cities such as Philadelphia and Pittsburgh,
Cleveland and Gary, Newark and Detroit, the great
Democratic politicians such as Jack and Robert Kennedy, Lyndon Johnson and Hubert Humphrey, rang up
great majorities among blacks and white ethnics alike.
The more highly educated observers, I learned (most political journalists these days have graduate degrees),
were nowadays less in touch with working class Americans than I had imagined.

Ed Muskie was my candidate in 1972, but neither he
nor his chief speechwriter, Robert Shrum, thought much
of my thesis about whites and blacks together in *The
Rise of the Unmeltable Ethnics*. Muskie struck me as an
admirable man, as quick to irascibility as a Slav ought
to be (I know it in myself), and genial and warm, too;
but he seemed to think of himself as a Maine Yankee and
patrician. In any case, McGovern won the nomination.
And the instant Senator Eagleton pulled out, I knew
Shriver would eventually be nominated for vice president, and began writing his acceptance speech. Without

waiting to be invited, I showed up on his doorstep in Rockville the day the decision was announced. Although he already had a team of veteran Kennedy speech writers hard at work, I labored quietly over my own draft of his acceptance speech. He slowly read all the drafts (unsigned), then accepted mine, and gave it hours later, on television, at the "mini-convention" hastily summoned to present him to the public.

There followed some ten or eleven hectic weeks on the Shriver campaign plane. We actually thought the crowds were getting bigger and more supportive toward the end; perhaps they were only compensating for being sorry they would not vote for us. In any case, as I saw more and more "sparklies" and "trendies" operating in the campaign—and heard the media appeals to the "new vote" of the blacks, the young, and women—I felt the Democratic Party changing its allegiance, away from working people and toward the symbol-making class around the universities, the news media, and the industries of culture. Partly as a consequence of their new class allegiances, since 1968 the Democrats have lost all but 21 percent of the electoral votes in the past five presidential elections.

Even before the campaign, I had begun to see that I was caught up in a new form of class warfare. During 1972, I published an essay in *Commentary*, "Needing Niebuhr Again," describing the "new class" of symbol makers who were wresting leadership within the Democratic Party from the labor unions, big city mayors, and traditional politicians whose electoral base lay among the poor and working classes. This essay occasioned an editorial by Norman Podhoretz, the distinguished editor of *Commentary*, that led to a fresh burst of "new class" criticism chronicled by B. Bruce-Biggs in *The New Class* (1979). The more highly educated, more utopian "lifestyle" liberals were gaining salience throughout society, and the Democratic Party was quickly seduced by their glittery power. There was much evidence of this in the campaign of 1972. Mr. Shriver was greeted with scarcely veiled disdain, I thought, by workers at the gates of the Homestead Steel mills—my own kind of folks, who would normally be with us by upwards of 89 percent. In Joliet, Illinois, on a factory floor where I encountered dozens of Slovak faces that made me think of my cousins in Johnstown, workers did not want to shake McGovern-Shriver hands. Trying to find out why, I met with our "advance person"—a young woman wearing a mini-skirt, high white boots, and a see-through blouse, with a large pro-abortion button on her collar. On that factory floor in 1972, the clash of social classes and cultural politics could scarcely have been more discordant.

After the campaign, I gladly joined with other traditional Democrats in founding the Coalition for a Democratic Majority, under the leadership of "Scoop" Jackson, Hubert Humphrey, Pat Moynihan, Tom Foley, and others. Foreign policy most worried me, but so did the efforts by upper class liberals to separate blacks and Hispanics from white ethnics and from labor, discarding the latter (so blind they were) as reactionary and racist. I had requested a leave of absence from Old Westbury, precisely to campaign against Nixon in 1972 (a promise I had made myself when Humphrey lost in 1968). Fighting for the soul of the Democratic Party, I saw the other side gain control of it.

Now I understand that there were two "power elites" in this nation: (1) the "old elite," whose base lies in the business sector, and whose vision of what makes America great looks to her economic and political freedoms, and (2) the "new class," whose base lies in education and the new communications industries, and whose vision of what makes America great is a compassionate (therefore, large) government. (The so-called "Yuppies" of later years are divided between these two elites, tending now one way, now another.) Unknowingly, until now, I had been supporting the politics of the new class, out of an uncritical acceptance of "progressive" ideology. What would happen if I turned against the new class the same intensity of critical fire that I had earlier learned from my education to turn against the old elite? Didn't the new one deserve it more? The imbalance of criticism in the academy and among intellectuals is a scandal. The naked ambition of the new class for power, its self-interest, its lack of self-knowledge, and its moral arrogance are transparent. So are its resentments.

Even though I slowly was becoming deradicalized, the information in my head during these years was very often exclusively derived from writers of the far left. In *Ascent of the Mountain, Flight of the Dove* (1971), for example, I wrote that "a huge bureaucracy with an unparalleled budget has grown up around the Department of Defense." Again: "The economic, bureaucratic interests represented by that budget tend to govern the direction not only of American foreign policy but also of American domestic life. They determine what 'the realities' of American life are." The footnotes to such wildly exaggerated passages refer to such authors as Fred J. Cook, *The Warfare State*, Richard J. Barnet, *The Economy of Death*, a book of essays called *American Militarism 1970*, and Seymour Melman, *Pentagon Capitalism*. I had not been educated in the left wing radical tradition, and I thought of myself here as being open minded. What I did not do was to submit such partisans to rigorous cross-examination. As a percentage of gross national product, for example, military budgets in 1970 (not far above 5 percent) were a very small tail to be wagging a very large dog. Moreover, the relatively low spending on arms qua arms during the 1970s placed the nation in considerable peril, as even Jimmy Carter slowly realized. Far from being "militaristic," the American people were about to secure a long series of years of declining defense budgets. This was to happen just as the Soviets were rapidly expanding theirs. The new thrusts of Soviet expansion and the upsurge of terrorism were a vivid consequence. Less spending brought greater violence, not less.

For most of the 1970s, I was of two minds. Philosophically, I was slowly turning away from the radical left. Informationally, my mind was stuffed with uncritically accepted information from highly partisan sources. Furthermore, I was painfully eager to maintain my credentials on the left. I remembered Maritain writing (in defense of his support of liberal Christian Democratic movements) that he always wished to be "a man of the left." That seemed to me too, at that time, to be the only moral alternative. My will to be on the left was stronger than any intellectual reasons I could assemble for being there. What the heart wills, the mind for a time finds reasons for. Until, one by one, those reasons turn to ash.

Yet even my first tentative criticisms of the left brought down upon my head passionate assaults, less given to answering my arguments than to questioning my morality. Some reviews of *The Rise of the Unmeltable Ethnics*, which I thought would help inspire the left to a base-broadening realism, were so unfair and so hostile to my person that, on at least one occasion (I was less thick-skinned then), I took to my bed until I could gain composure to get back to work. I had to call upon the intellectual guidance I had established for myself in *The Experience of Nothingness* (1970)—namely, the calm knowledge that one had to be prepared to go forward "with no supports," relying on no one.

Reinhold Niebuhr had taught me to weigh powers, interests, and facts carefully *before* pronouncing moral judgment; so I knew I had to do some long rethinking. About all the left wing information in my head, I began to ask, Is it actually well founded? No longer relying upon socialist forms of analysis (with their predetermined outcomes), I began to ask, What fair-minded evaluation can be made of capitalism? My first essay on this latter subject suggested that, at the very least, capitalism is among intellectuals "an underpraised and undervalued system." By contrast, I had learned that socialism, although highly praised for its "ideals," is quite disillusioning once the facts about any instances of its practice are examined. I backed into a more positive judgment of capitalism very, very slowly, having to fight against my broadly anticapitalist education.

On the theological side of the question, I found, one has to do most of the work oneself. Perhaps von Mises, Hayek, and others do persuade those who are already liberal (in the classical sense). But for those of us who were taught to think through anticapitalist analysis, such arguments can only be conducted in highly moral terms that present a comparable historical vision. Seven or eight new insights are necessary. It takes time and patience to achieve them. Cardinal Newman was correct: one can drive out a powerful idea only in the light of a still more powerful idea. It took me until 1982, with the completion of *The Spirit of Democratic Capitalism*, to begin to get that intellectually stronger set of ideas in my head. That vision remained critical of flaws in all three systems of American life—political, economic, moral-cultural—but in a systematic way I kept asking, *Compared to what?* At last, I was thinking empirically in a sustained way.

Slowly, I saw that being on the left had been a sort of

"bad faith," a learned ideology that was false to my own experience, to that of my family, and indeed to that of millions of families all around the world. I had been teaching myself to debunk the American system, and by means of arguments whose plausibility lay, not in themselves, but in their conformity to a prearranged mental scheme: capitalism is of the past, immoral, and doomed, whereas steps toward a more socialist economy are "progressive," right, and predetermined by history to be victorious. Recently, I have encountered a slogan of the Sandinistas that shockingly expresses the relevant mental scheme, although in terms so gross that they would have repelled me even in my most progressive days: "To learn from the Soviet Union is to advance; to learn from the United States is to retreat." Supply "progressivism" for "Soviet Union," and "capitalism" for "the United States," and that is how I had earlier interpreted history. Reality does not support such blind faith.

The great and liberating interpretive idea, I have come to think, is Jefferson's: "The God who gave us life gave us liberty." Human beings are made in the image of God: creatures of insight and liberty, of intelligence and responsibility. The only social systems worthy of creatures of such gifted dignity are those that allow them to be relentlessly inquiring, creative, and responsible: a free polity, a relatively free economy, and a free moral-cultural order. All systems that secure such individual rights and that are now empirically available have predominantly capitalist economies.[4]

A story of this sort necessarily has two tracks, one consisting of a record of experiences, the other a record of newly acquired insights. During my left-wing, or radical, period (1967–1971), bounded by the antiwar movement on the one end and the experience of "radical culture" at Old Westbury on the other, I had become adept at trying to explain my radical ideas in liberal terms. "Liberal" is the cover that most socialist-minded leftists employ to make their ideas seem continuous with those of the pragmatic, mainline left. I had to learn the hard way the discontinuity between "socialist" and "liberal," just as an earlier generation (Sidney Hook, for example) had learned to see the sharp divide between "communist" and "socialist." In that earlier generation, the dividing line had been commitment to democracy. Communists accepted Party discipline and were radically undemocratic. Democratic socialists and social democrats insisted upon the primacy of democracy and free personal inquiry. A generation later, the deplorable economic record of socialism since World War II is more in evidence; and the dependence of social democracy on capitalist institutions (markets, incentives, private property, and openness) is more transparent. In our generation, the dividing line between liberals and socialists is how much freedom to allow a free economy. "Socialists" (the word has lost much of its practical meaning) tend to favor greater political controls; liberals (classical liberals) tend to favor greater economic liberties. At its best, this argument is pragmatic and experimental.

Some years after the fact, I have come to see the role played in my own thought by the gradual acceptance of several key ideas. As a matter of intellectual biography, it seems worthwhile to state a few of them, even without space to argue against the objections my earlier way of thinking had employed to block them.

Utopianism v. Realistic Morality

By nature, I tend to be idealistic and wholehearted; to respect ambiguity, irony, and tragedy is a tendency I have always wanted to strengthen in myself. But the discovery of the systematic biases of my own class, the new class, taught me that I must make a still sharper distinction between reasoning about moral ideals and reasoning about political realities. When I was on the left, I found myself looking down upon the American people, upon "vulgar" business activities, upon capitalism. I implicitly pictured my friends on the left and myself as more "pure" than all the others. In *Toward a Theology of Radical Politics* (1969), I had unmasked the "Myth of the Pure Protester," the contemporary version of Dostoyevsky's "Myth of the Grand Inquisitor." But it is one thing to detect a mythic structure in one's colleagues, and another to drive it out of one's own habitual practice. The Pure Protester loves his or her own moral purity, sacrificing all else to that. To overcome it, I learned, one has to distinguish more sharply between one's high moral claims and the actual effects of one's ideas and actions on the plain of battle.

To begin with, one must grant that others, too, make high moral claims. One must compare moral claims to moral claims. But one must also examine *what happens in history because of those moral claims*: one must compare *practice* to *practice*. Sometimes those who make high claims bring about results more evil than the results achieved by those whose moral claims have been more cautious. In practice, this meant for me that I must stop having contempt for those (to my right) with whom I was in moral disagreement. And I must take greater responsibility for the actual results of my own moral claims. For example, after the Democratic Convention of 1968, I was so hostile to Hubert Humphrey (because of a disgraceful speech he had made on the war at Stanford that spring) that I wrote in favor of abstaining from voting, even if Richard Nixon won the election. I added that those who followed such an injunction would incur an obligation to work that much harder to defeat Nixon in 1972—which explains my taking an unpaid leave of absence in the fall of 1972 to do so. This was moral purity masked as practical politics. I learned from such an error that I must never again seek moral purity at the expense of responsibility for the results.

As a result, I have striven to conduct argument with those with whom I disagree on two separate levels: to argue against their moral claims, on one level, and to argue against the probable practical consequences of their moral claims, on yet another. One effect of this resolution was to free me from the grip of the moral vision of the left, in the many forms in which I had encountered it. I began to examine its consequences more closely and to experiment with a better vision that might have better consequences. In short, consequences matter.

"Bad Faith"

One of the features of being on the left that most disquieted me was the "bad faith" in which it placed me. In arguing for left-wing positions, I found myself putting down other Americans, trying to shock "the complacent" (as I thought them) and writing of U.S. "militarism" and "imperialism." But who was I to be anything but grateful to this country that had taken in an impoverished and much oppressed family of former serfs from Slovakia, and that had given to me and countless others opportunities unprecedented in history? I had always tempered my radical criticism with explicit patriotism and gratitude, but still, I had conceded far too much to an unwarranted anti-Americanism. The more I examined the neo-Marxist analysis of oppression and dependency, the less tenable it was. Its main substance is emotional, not intellectual. It begins with feelings of guilt, awaits no evidence, and includes the final verdict in the method of analysis. Eventually, I could not stomach this bad faith. I understood the anger that union workers felt when they saw privileged university students burning American flags, for which so many in their own families (like Mickey Yuhas) had gladly given their lives. Working people shamed me into abandoning my bad faith.

Future as Truth

The first insinuation of a Marxist-Leninist way of thinking into one's mind is through epistemology: "The tide of history is on the side of revolution." Here is how it happens. The first temptation is to hold that "the correspondence theory of truth" is Aristotelian and old-fashioned. One should not examine claims to truth in the light of empirical evidence. Empiricism is static and reactionary. Instead, one must keep one's eye upon the goal of the future. Truth is what brings the revolution of the future into power. What helps the revolution belongs to the future and is true. What blocks the revolution is reactionary and against the stream of history, so it is false. The dynamic course of history has been scientifically discerned; history is driven forward both by the "contradictions of capitalism" and by the triumphant logic of egalitarianism, the end of alienation, and the common good, i.e., socialism. "To learn from socialism is to advance; to learn from capitalism is to retreat." Only "progressives" grasp the larger picture. Appeals to empirical fact regarding the failures of socialism are signs of bourgeois reasoning. To be a progressive is to be ennobled by an inner vision of a superior truth. It is to belong to a secular religion. If only one holds tightly to that shining vision, the imperfections of the present will be enveloped in the soft light of ideals that drive one on-ward. How much progress has been made already!

Having long fought against "cheap grace"—having been chastened by my own "dark night of the soul," as suggested in *The Experience of Nothingness* (1970)—I had long since fled from an adolescent Christian faith to an adult one. So I resisted the soft light of socialism. No Robert Heilbroner or Irving Howe "visions" for me. I had Catholicism, a much tougher faith—tested by fire—and had no vacuum in the religious depths of my soul that socialism could possibly fill. If one doesn't need socialism as a religion, then it must stand or fall by its record in historical praxis. One advantage of a capitalist economy, indeed, is that it asks to be judged on no other than empirical and practical grounds. It is asymmetrical with socialism; it offers no comparable "vision."

Thus, as I mentally toured the horizon of the twentieth century, I could see less and less reason for any serious mind to believe—against the overpowering evidence—that actual socialism matches socialist claims. On the contrary, from the USSR to a communist Vietnam, from communist Albania to Cuba, socialism is a human wasteland. As for the "socialism" of Sweden, Israel, and France, many of their own socialists have come to see that what is most vital in such nations is their commit-ment to democracy, and what are most retardant are the state controls that drag down their market economies. In economics, democratic socialists are democratic capital-ists who argue for slightly larger governmental initiatives and controls at the margin. In practice, democratic so-cialists and social democrats live as parasites upon dem-ocratic capitalist systems while claiming to have purer and larger hearts pulsing with "compassion." To some extent (when it works), this is a useful leaven and I sometimes support them. To a great extent, however, socialist visions serve the interests and ambitions of large segments of the educated class (who in Europe staff government-owned media, universities, and the massive welfare administrative apparatus) and paralyze the poor. In addition, many democratic socialists tend toward an unhealthy preference for the foreign policy of the USSR over that of the USA in virtually every concrete circumstance. Most leftists are ritualistic anti-Stalinists. In practice, however, they nearly always oppose American policy. Sometimes they may be correct; the issue rests with exact judgment, case by case. Underlying ideological support for Cuba and Nicaragua, for example, is an epistemology that holds that socialism will prevail over capitalism, left-wing progressives over right-wing reactionaries, the vision of a shining future over the sad realities of Cuban prisons and fervent Sandinista Leninism. When one's vision is of paradise, the dungeons in which prisoners are tortured cannot be seen.

The Factual Record

Once one sets aside vulgar Marxist epistemology and tries to see the world whole and factual, one is free to judge socialism by its record—and to reexamine capitalism afresh. It is difficult to get socialists to name a socialist experiment on which they rest their case. Their touching faith in each successive project lasts only so long as the full story has not come out—in China before Westerners could freely visit it; in Albania before "socialist youth brigades" from Western Europe came home with shocking tales; in Cuba before Armando Valladares awakened the poets, essayists, and novelists of the outside world.

In Western Europe, socialists in power turn increasingly to capitalist techniques because they work better than socialist techniques. Once socialist economies are submitted to the same rigorous tests as capitalist economies, the jig is up. As an economic idea, socialism has died a thousand deaths by qualification. Markets, incentives, private property, and openness work better in the humble history of fact. Since it is basically an empirically derived set of techniques, one does not have to give capitalism even two cheers; still, in an imperfect world, it wins hands down. Chinese and Soviets pay it the sincerest form of flattery.

What is Capitalism?

The liberal arts tradition of Britain and the United States owes much to the aristocratic traditions of the distant past, and keeps alive the resentment of aristocrats against the "philistinism" of the rising business class and the nouveaux riches. The social sciences are profoundly anti-individual, collectivist in spirit and in method, and often antithetical to the tacit wisdom of tradition and the indirect "spontaneous order" (Hayek) of many traditional social institutions, including markets. Thus, most of us grow up being taught to think ill of capitalists and capitalism. Some reasons are aesthetic. Some are class-based: aristocratic tastes preferred to business-inspired tastes. Some are radical. We may not hold that "property is theft" or fully accept the "labor theory of value," according to which all value derives from labor and any profit not distributed to labor is ill-gained. Nonetheless, socialists such as Tawney have taught us that capitalism is rooted in acquisitiveness, in selfish as opposed to public interests, and in vaguely tainted "profit." There are some on the left who regard capitalism as an essentially evil system that must be replaced. Perhaps a larger number have made peace with capitalism which, though vulgar and disreputable, is a necessary practicality. (Not even Adam Smith held actual businessmen in high regard.)

It took me a long while to recognize in myself just how much of this received wisdom I had uncritically received. Beyond that, there is also a taboo against assessing capitalism seriously and fairly. Within the horizon of progressivism, to approach the morality of capitalism as an open question is regarded as selling out. To render a favorable empirical verdict upon capitalism while recognizing its defects where they undeniably exist makes socialist analysis totter on its foundations. These foundations are mainly anticapitalist, negative rather than positive. (And insofar as they are positive, they are utopian.)

Those who remain attached to socialist methods of analysis, of course, do not give up even when they lose particular arguments.

Progressivism is a closed system. It has an answer to everything. It does not rest upon empirical verification; it does not employ the criterion of falsifiability. It insists upon "vision," upon "perspective," upon "point of view." Once one is within that horizon, nothing can penetrate it. It is reinforced by everything that happens. It is more like a religious faith than like a scientific theory subject to falsification. But it lacks one key constitutive element common to Jewish and Christian religious faith. Jewish and Christian faith hold each believer personally responsible for the reasonableness of the act of faith; both engage the unbeliever (present within every believer) in argument. The progressive never takes the doubter seriously; to doubt progressivism is considered to be not an intellectual but a moral act. For Jew and Christian, God is truth. For the progressive, history is a tale of irresistible power, to which truth is secondary. Progressives do not argue; they attack the bona fides of doubters.

That is why the first battle of the soul in rejecting the progressive horizon is to subject it to tests of empirical falsifiability. Since the first of all moral maxims is to think clearly, this struggle is a moral one. Does truth stand outside of history, as a judge upon it, or within it, as a subject judged by history? Some prefer to be "on the side of" history. Others choose to subject historical movements to the judgment of truth. Castro had Valladares under the thumb of history, naked in an unlit cell; but Valladares clung to a truth beyond the power of history.

Once one begins to examine the historical record of capitalist societies—the paradigm case is the United States—one learns that the received wisdom about the nature of capitalism is erroneous. Far from being theft, private property is (as even Leo XIII said) the necessary condition for individual freedom of action in history. The right to private property supplies the wherewithal for self-determination. This important empirical claim is subject to tests of falsifiability: An order that respects rights to private property is more likely to result in the improvement of nature, the advancing of the common good, superior creativity, and social vitality than any collectivist order. In the practical sphere, the proper question is, compared to what? Compared to traditionalist and socialist orders, the capitalist economic order has empirically shown superior results.

In my first ruminations, following Max Weber, I thought of capitalism as essentially consisting in a regime of private property, markets, incentives, and profits. But all traditional societies (such as Jerusalem in the biblical era, and most Third World regimes today) have had these. Still they were (or are) precapitalist. Only slowly did I come to the precise capitalist insight: creativity is more productive than rote labor; therefore, the primary form of capital is mind. The cause of the wealth of the nations is mind. Capitalism is not constituted solely by private property, incentives, markets, double-entry bookkeeping, or any other social techniques (though all of these are necessary elements), but rather by a social order favorable to alertness, inventiveness, discovery, and creativity. This means a social order based upon education, research, the freedom to create, and the right to enjoy the fruits of one's own creativity. Thus, all the American steps to protect the rights of citizens to exercise their own practical judgment—i.e., Article I, Section 8, of the U.S. Constitution, asserting the rights of "authors and inventors"; the Homestead Act; the Land Grant College Act; and an immense national commitment to universal private and public education— were indispensable stages along the road to a civilization that favored invention and discovery more than any other in history. "The first developed nation" owes its development chiefly to the cultivation of intellect, both practical and theoretical.

The Nature of Communism

For intellectuals, the most divisive event of the twentieth century has been the rise of communism. How should communism be judged? For many intellectuals of a generation ago, communism was a profound temptation. Most attributed this to their own idealism, rather than to their lust for power or their envy of the business class. To others today, to seem friendly and unconcerned about the rise of communism seems to be more idealistic than to be anticommunist. Even before the era of Joseph McCarthy, to be anticommunist was thought to represent a failure of idealism, imagination, creative sympathy, and broad-mindedness. Besides, anticommunism seemed vulgar. It represented a middlebrow or lowbrow reflex, worthy perhaps of the *Reader's Digest* but scarcely of the academy. Thus, even today many who have refused to become communists would prefer not to be known as anticommunists—indeed, would prefer to be less anticommunist than anti-anticommunist.

This tendency has effects upon foreign policy debates. Many intellectuals today grasp the failure of the *Marxist* component of Marxism-Leninism—recognize, that is, the rebuff history has given to the nineteenth-century economics of Marx. But many of the same persons continue to accept, perhaps unconsciously, the *Leninist* doctrine that imperialism is the natural expression of capitalism. And they interpret American foreign policy (not Soviet foreign policy) accordingly. American foreign policy in Southeast Asia, in Central America, and elsewhere, they say, is driven by business interests. These consist either of malign multinational corporations or of the military-industrial complex. These accusations are fair enough; but it is only fair to hear the other side of the evidence, not merely to give in to reflexive feelings of guilt. The evidence does not support the accusations. Nonetheless, what is left of Marxism-Leninism is Leninism. The Leninist doctrine of imperialism satisfied deep anti-American longings.

There is no excuse for serious men and women not to have an exact and accurate picture of the power controlled by the Communist Party USSR: in offensive nuclear might and strategic defense against nuclear attack; in naval power on (and under) every ocean surface; in conventional arms massed near the European frontier and along the borders separated from the Persian Gulf solely by Iran; in a covert intelligence force larger and more versatile than any in history; and in a capacity for ideological penetration, both in the West and in the Third World, unrivaled in human history. According to the Brezhnev Doctrine, where communism begins to govern it never surrenders. (The single minor rollback has been Grenada.) By the end of the Carter administration, the boundaries defended by this doctrine had been extended far beyond those of 1945. Nicaragua, ripe as a plum, seems to be next in line.

Pure Leninism is about power, naked power, brutal power, power through terror. To the dictator within a Leninist system, anything is permitted. To appeal to values beyond naked power in the hands of a Leninist vanguard, one must go outside of Leninism. Thus, belief in Marxism-Leninism as a set of substantive doctrines has waned, especially in communist nations. Ironically, though, utopian progressivism, the marshland in which communism incubates, thrives happily among the privileged in the affluent West. The resentments of intellectuals against the business class nourish it far more than any evidence warrants. Meanwhile, the naked military power of the USSR is stronger than that of Adolf Hitler at the peak of his power. And Marxist-Leninist ideology, even in decline, still awakens an echoing resonance among intellectuals that the Nazi ideology, based upon race, never could.

The capacity of Western intellectuals to deny the reality of Soviet power, the scope of Soviet ambition, and the record of Soviet deception is one of the marvels of history. It represents a triumph of intellectual dishonesty and massive self-contempt. To refuse to take part in this "treason of the intellectuals" is said to be troglodytic, reactionary, the work of a cold warrior, bellicose, and a sign of reflexive anticommunism. It is none of these things. It is a refusal to go on being complicit in intellectual dishonesty and self-contempt. An exact and accurate picture must be argued out empirically. So also the strategic response. On concrete matters, honest persons may disagree. But resistance to communism, principled and militarily effective, is morally obligatory.

Openness

How can I explain to myself the attacks upon my own work by former colleagues on the left once I began to move from concentrating my criticism on the right to directing some of it onto the left? Persons who had written that I was brilliant began to find my work—which was far more penetrating than it had been—evidence of a bad character. No doubt, my positions of today have faults, which I would be glad to correct. Virtually never do my critics respond with argument, however. Only seldom have they met the case I have made head on. Their main advice to their faithful flock is not to read my work. Their technique is ridicule in a falsetto voice; consult the reviews of *The Spirit of Democratic Capitalism* in religious left-wing journals. True, elsewhere the more open among them have accepted several basic points, and this process continues.

Knowing that I was wrong once, I would be glad to be shown again where now I am in error. I fear no arguments from the left. I welcome them eagerly. Having expanded my views before, to meet overpowering evidence, I would gladly do so again. To admit that one has been wrong is, after the first time or two, joyful work, because it demonstrates a willingness to follow inquiry where it leads.

I see, of course, that intellectual conversions, or "raisings of consciousness," still move some persons to the left. The left, given its epistemology, regards such conversions as signs of natural growth. Nonetheless, the numbers of those on the left who are embracing more and more of the "Whig" (realistic, democratic capitalist) analysis are growing yet more rapidly, for sound empirical reasons. In intellectual life, there is no determinism. Honest inquiry has its own power, its own laws, and its own respect for time.

The Ironic Law of Small Differences

It is an odd feature of arguments about political economy, I have found, that small differences in *the balance of judgment* have very large consequences for action. In the world of practice, judgments are necessarily probabilistic. Manicheanism is out. There are almost always some reasons for most (but not all) systemic positions. (Hitler's maniacal efforts to eradicate Jews, like Stalin's earlier deliberate starvation of some eight million Ukrainians, have come as close to pure and massive evil as the world has ever seen.) Thus, consider the judgment that, on balance, the United States is a force for good in the international arena. To interpret that judgment in numerical terms, one person may judge that by 51–49, or 55–45, it is correct; another, by 49–51, or 45–55, the other way. But this relatively small margin of difference between the acceptance and the rejection of that proposition may involve extremely large differences in further judgment and action. One may still wish to make judgments case by case. But one is *likely* to give the benefit of the doubt one way or the other: thumbs up or thumbs down. History demands action. Playing Hamlet is certain tragedy. Once a judgment is reached (by however small a margin), action must be wholehearted.

Moreover, judgment about political economy evokes high passion. Even if one disagrees with those on the other side of a question for action by only 2, 5, or 25 percent, still, that difference has the effect that a civil war does in dividing the consciences of even close brothers within a family. At the extreme, killing one another may result (as in the American Civil War; among Vietnamese, Nicaraguans, and others). Far short of that, even in an argument over dinner, passions are likely to rise. The temptation of those on opposite sides to paint each other in extreme colors, to demonize one another, is extremely hard to resist.

In action in history, small differences in the balance of judgment often lead to dramatic, passionate, and life-and-death opposition. To recognize this helps to diminish fanaticism. But it does not alleviate the need to go into opposition. Civility is then an almost heroic achievement. Still, civility remains necessary.

Whether to the left or the right, in any case, those inquirers for whom I have the greatest admiration are willing to continue facing argument, to stay in dialogue, and to rethink things again. Surprisingly, one does not find in life many open minds. There are not multitudes whose3drive to question is virtually unrestricted. When you find one whose views are radically different from yours but who is willing to discuss such differences openly and at length, you find a pearl of great price.

Where, then, am I today? As before, I remain both a Democrat and a member of the Democratic party in politics ("republican" in the early American sense, a biblical or civil republican). In culture, I am, as Lord Acton was, that loneliest of breeds, a liberal Catholic; not a conservative one because Catholicism is a living force, ever ancient and ever new. In economics, I am in favor of the mind-centered, creative, inventive system—in short, capitalism. I have come to see that these are the *three* liberations symbolized by the classic liberal tricolor: liberation from tyranny and torture, through *democracy*; the liberation of conscience, association, and expression, through *pluralism*; and liberation from poverty, through *capitalism*.

No one who holds faith with such commitments, Hayek wrote, is properly to be called a "conservative." For each of these three liberations names a *dynamic* principle as deep as human nature itself, the powerful propeller of history. These are the principles that will be decisive in the future, the principles at the heart of every form of progress. In practical cases, some will favor government intervention, others will favor a freer economy; in an open society, there is ample room for pragmatic argument and closely watched experimentation.

And yet, of course, to hold fast to such principles as these is not to have sprung as innocent and naked as Venus from the sea. It is to stand on principles one's forebears have wrested over centuries from the ambiguities and ironies of human history, and is, in that sense, conservative (a conservative is one who believes that his forebears were at least as intelligent as he). To hold to principles dynamic in their nature and yet ancient and traditional in their gradual elucidation is to be simultaneously a person of the future and of the past, a conservative and a progressive—in short, a Whig. Alas, that name seems no longer to be retrievable. But the principles it signals are everlastingly available, rooted as they are in the natural liberty (and its tendency toward historical progress) that our Creator has endowed in us.

And so I end my story. Having begun life in the bosom of a good family in an out-of-the-way steel town, best known for the tragedies it has endured by flood in 1889, 1936, and 1977; having had an excellent classical education in philosophy, literature, and theology; having from the start declared my intention to create a philosophy of the distinctively American experience; having begun by seeking a "third way" between capitalism and socialism, as a result of the typical anticapitalist biases of the humanities (not least in Catholic thought); having long looked for this "third way" in the direction of socialist thought and radical politics—after all this, during my forties, I came to find the socialist and radical paths destructive of truth, and signs of bad faith. And I came back to rediscover the power of the American idea, "man's best hope" as Jefferson called it in his First Inaugural. I came back in short, to the tradition of Aristotle, Cicero, and Aquinas; of Madison, Hamilton, Jay, Jefferson, and Lincoln; of Montesquieu, Smith, Burke, and Acton—i.e., to the Whig tradition. Many call me a neoconservative. I prefer neoliberal. Yet the name matters less than the reality: a threefold commitment to democracy, capitalism, and pluralism, whose premise is liberation—from tyranny and torture, from poverty, and from oppression of intellect, art, and conscience. To be where I am, I judge, is a good place to be—for which thanksgiving be to my Creator, merciful to those who wander in the wilderness.

· Appendix ·

MICHAEL NOVAK:
A READER'S GUIDE

Brian C. Anderson and Derek Cross

Over in the shadows of the darkened lots of the Beth-lehem Steel Company, across the river from the Point Stadium in Johnstown, Pennsylvania, where he grew up, the young Michael Novak often saw molten red ingots cooling in the night air. That image burned into his memory as a metaphor for the way God's love penetrates the world and the incarnation suffuses itself into history. Thus, Novak's work has from his earliest days pressed the edges of new issues, exploring, pioneering, advancing Christian thought into various corners of contemporary culture in which theology has seldom gone. In *Belief and Unbelief*, he tried to advance a new method for approaching the presence of God through inquiry and reflection. In *The Experience of Nothingness*, he tried to meet the challenge articulated by Albert Camus: that anyone writing today about ethics must pass through the problematic of nihilism. His books were also the first to reflect theologically upon sports and on "the new ethnicity." So, too, in the economics area. He has constantly attempted pioneering work, to open up new territories for others.

Novak's major works can be divided into five categories: preparatory studies; statements of method and horizon; religious explorations in American culture; a trilogy on capitalism and socialism; the cultural ecology of liberty. A sixth category, faith for a new generation, points to the future.

I. Preparatory Studies

1. SETTING THE AGENDA. *A New Generation: American and Catholic* (New York: Herder and Herder, 1964). In this first collection of essays, Novak set out the aims of his lifetime work, as he then saw it: to deal with the two great, overriding facts of his time and place: being Catholic and being American. The United States is the creative land of this century, he held; the center of the struggle between the free human spirit and technology is fixed in her daily life. Respect for the person is not preserved by the insights of British empiricism and American pragmatism, but by inarticulate traditions in American and British life; our philosophy lags behind our living. We must extend the empirical and pragmatic temper into neglected experiences of human consciousness. Sustained reflection on new experiences, in the light of the open traditions of the past, seems also to be the most adequate philosophy for finding the vital relation of Christian faith to contemporary life.

2. CONTEXT AND STAGE: STATE OF THE QUESTION. *The Open Church: Vatican II, Act II* (New York: Macmillan, 1964). This report on the second session of the Second Vatican Council, tells the story of an apparently immobile Church finding its way back into the living sources of contemporary history. The conservative men who loved the splendor of papal Rome, the clarity

of Roman law, and the absoluteness of nonhistorical theology, Novak found, are not despicable, mean, or uncouth men. They are men who have tried to live outside of history. Having shown how a nonhistorical orthodoxy is unable to come to grips with history, the Council began proposing another way: through an open Church. In opening the Church, the Second Vatican Council spoke afresh to the world, changing centuries-old alignments and probabilities.

II. Method, Horizon

3. *Belief and Unbelief: A Philosophy of Self-Knowledge* (New York: Macmillan, 1965). This book is an attempt to work out some of the problems of self-identity, and some of the problems of belief and unbelief. The roots of the two sets of problems are entangled. For in deciding who one is, one places oneself in relation to others, to the world, and to God. This study begins to elucidate those experiences of human intellectual life in which belief in God is rooted; that is, the experiences of "intelligent subjectivity." Its aim is to provide empirical tools for sorting out the elements of belief and unbelief in one's own experience. Under certain conditions, in the quality of experience they engender, belief and unbelief are quite close.

4. *The Experience of Nothingness* (New York: Harper and Row, 1970). The first philosophical problem of our time is how to interpret the experience of nothingness, how to plunge deeper into it and wrest from it a humanistic, revolutionary ethic. The experience of nothingness arises only under certain conditions. To notice them, to reinforce them, and to build one's life upon them is a choice which does not falsify the experience of nothing-

ness. The experience of nothingness arises when we consciously become aware of—and appropriate—our own actual horizons. What seemed certain, necessary, and stable suddenly seems arbitrary and unfounded. We do not know who we are. Yet we continue to throw up symbols against the dark. This book does not intend to remove, cover over, or alleviate the experience of nothingness. It unmasks one piece of ideology only—that the experience of nothingness necessarily incapacitates one from further action. Granted that we have the experience of nothingness, what shall we do with it?

5. *Ascent of the Mountain, Flight of the Dove: An Invitation to Religious Studies* (New York: Harper & Row, 1971). Religious studies are primarily the taking up of successive standpoints, from which one may assimilate a fresh horizon. Progress in religious studies is not a logical progression, within one fixed and unchanging standpoint. It is a series of "conversions" from standpoint to standpoint, of breakthroughs, of perspectival shifts. In our actions, intelligence is always intermixed with the work of the imagination and the sensibility—with experience, image, symbol, myth, and narrative context. The concept story allows us to treat all parts of the self in one unified concept and to approach the problem of belief and unbelief in a fresh and more illuminating light.

III. Explorations in American Culture

6. CULTURAL PLURALISM. *The Rise of the Unmeltable Ethnics: Politics and Culture in the Seventies* (New York: Macmillan, 1972). The "new ethnicity" of the 1970s is a form of historical consciousness. This book is not a call to separatism but to self-consciousness. It does not seek division but rather accurate, mutual ap-

preciation. For it is in possessing our own particularity that we come to feel at home with ourselves and are best able to enter into communion with others. The point of becoming ethnically alert and self-possessed is not self-enclosure, it is genuine community. This book maps the shape of long repressed sentiments of Southern and Eastern Europeans in cultural collision with British-Americans. Ethnicity, Novak predicted, will be an increasingly important dimension of social life around the world.

7. PRESIDENTIAL POLITICS, SYMBOLIC GEOM-ETRY. *Choosing Our King: Symbols of Political Leadership* (New York: Macmillan, 1974). The American presidency is the most dramatic expression of America's civil religion. Two presidential roles can be distinguished: the president as personification of the nation and the president as political leader. Symbols possess decisive power in American politics. Americans, lacking a king, necessarily invest kingly majesty in the office of the presidency. They seek and choose a man with whom they can identify—as they are and as they want to be. The president mirrors the people that elect him. There is a geography of the soul to be learned in understanding this continental nation. Sets of symbols that "work" in one place seem in another off-key. To communicate credibly with Americans about America, one must grasp a good many secrets of this symbolic geography.

8. LABOR UNION HISTORY, SLAVIC HISTORY. *The Guns of Lattimer: The True Story of a Massacre and a Trial, August 1897–March 1898* (New York: Basic, 1978). On September 10, 1887, in the hamlet of Lattimer Mines, Pennsylvania, an armed posse took aim and fired into a crowd of oncoming mine workers, who were marching in their corner of the coal-mining region to call their fellow miners out on strike. The marchers—Poles,

Slovaks, and Hungarians, most of whom could not yet speak English—were themselves armed only with an American flag and a timid, budding confidence in their new-found rights as free men in their newly adopted country. The mine operators took another view of these rights and of the strange, alien men who claimed them. When the posse was done firing, nineteen of the demonstrators were dead and thirty-nine were seriously wounded. Some six months later a jury of their peers was to exonerate the deputies of any wrongdoing. The "Lattimer Massacre" is not only a powerful story in its own right (and an invaluable key to the history of the growth of the United Mine Workers), but an allegory of that peculiarly American experience undergone over and over again throughout the land, and down to this very day: the experience of new immigrants, still miserable with poverty and bewilderment and suffering the trauma of culture shock, being confronted by the hostility and blind contempt of the "real" Americans. The incident at Lattimer was a tragedy brought on not so much by inhumanity as by profound intercultural suspicion. The victims were not attracted to socialism, and did not denounce America even when they were denied justice; they believed doggedly that their children would do better. Injustice was not to them a new experience; liberty was.

9. *The Joy of Sports: End Zones, Bases, Baskets, Balls, and the Consecration of the American Spirit* (New York: Basic, 1976). Far from feeling guilty over the hours spent in front of the television set watching grown men play games, American sports fans ought to recognize that they are engaging in an important public liturgy—it is not just "mere entertainment." For sports bring to human beings—whether as players or spectators—experiences more akin to natural religion than to diversion. Particularly in America, where religious forms

have tended to fade, such indispensable aids to the spirit as sacred time and sacred space are found within the innings or quarters of a game and inside the park or stadium. It is play, not work, which truly civilizes people, touching them with the qualities of beauty, truth, and excellence. Each of the three games invented in America (and beloved by all social classes)—baseball, basketball, and football—has its own distinctive mythic content. You can't understand America unless you understand its public, liturgical sports.

IV. Trilogy on Capitalism v. Socialism and Catholic Thought

10. THREE SYSTEMS. *The Spirit of Democratic Capitalism* (New York: Simon & Schuster, 1982). Of all the systems of political economy which have shaped our history, none has so revolutionized ordinary expectations of human life—lengthened the life span, made the elimination of poverty and famine thinkable, enlarged the range of human choice—as democratic capitalism. And yet, for two centuries now, democratic capitalism has had little appeal for the human spirit. To invoke loyalty to it because of the prosperity it brings is regarded by most Western intellectuals as simply materialistic and, at worst, even corrupt. The moral high ground has been regularly conceded to socialism. The practice of democratic capitalism has been informed by presuppositions that until now have remained largely unarticulated. Democratic capitalism is a novel unity of political democracy, a market and incentive economy, and a liberal and pluralistic culture. The idea of this threefold social system, based on respect for the inalienable dignity of

the individual, the rule of law, and compassion for the poor, has an inherently greater moral and spiritual power than the idea of socialism. This book is about the life of the spirit which makes democratic capitalism, as well as its vision of high moral purpose, both possible and spiritually fruitful.

11. *Freedom with Justice: Catholic Social Thought and Liberal Institutions* (San Francisco: Harper & Row, 1984). Although the Catholic church during the nineteenth and early twentieth centuries set itself against liberalism as an ideology, it has slowly come to admire liberal institutions such as democracy and free markets. Between the Catholic vision of social justice and liberal institutions, there is a profound consonance (but not identity). One may cherish liberal institutions without embracing the philosophies of the liberal thinkers who first promoted them. Institutions have a life of their own in history, that permits genuine but often unpredictable development from the germ of earlier intuitions. One may, indeed, undergird liberal institutions with the more adequate Catholic philosophy of the human person, its deep sense of community, and its long-experienced respect for "intermediate associations" or "mediating structures."

12. *Will It Liberate? Questions About Liberation Theology* (New York: Paulist, 1986). "Liberation theology" presents itself as an alternative to the sterile theoretical thought of the Old World. It offers a vision of history and human salvation that borrows heavily from a Marxian analysis of society. This book offers the empirical hypothesis that the liberal society, built around a capitalist economy that promotes discovery and entrepreneurship among the poor will succeed more quickly, more thoroughly, and in a more liberating fashion, than the socialist societies so far conceived of by liberation theologians.

Liberation theologians seem to misunderstand systematically the spiritual resources and economic dynamism of liberal societies. Of course, a pluralism of theologies entails serious disagreements. Identifying those disagreements exactly requires each participant in the debate to "cross over" into the point of departure and dynamic of the other points of view, both with sympathy and with alert skepticism, but in the end with a painstaking desire to understand. Novak tries to read the liberation theologians with seriousness and dogged inquiry, to understand and to raise further questions. The main question: what will actually work to help the poor out of poverty?

V. Cultural Ecology

13. SOLVING A KEY PUZZLE: HOW TO RECONCILE THE INCOMMENSURABLE VALUE OF PERSON WITH THE COMMON GOOD? *Free Persons and the Common Good* (Lanham, Md.: Madison Books, 1989). This work seeks to bridge the gap between liberalism and the Catholic notion of the "common good" by showing that the liberal tradition includes a vision of the common good, a vision both historically original and crucial to its defense of the human person. Too often, the liberal tradition is discussed wholly in terms of the individual, the rational economic agent, self-interest, and something like the utilitarian calculus. On the other side, too often the classical view of the common good is presented as though it did not respect the freedom of the human person, the rights of the individual, and the unique properties of the many different spheres through which the common good is cumulatively realized. Yet the liberal tradition has in fact greatly expanded and enriched the concept of the common good. And the Catho-

lic tradition—through its distinctive concepts of the person, will, self-deception, virtue, practical wisdom, the dark night of the soul, and insight itself—has thickened and enriched our understanding of the individual. On matters of institutional realism, the liberal tradition has made discoveries that the Catholic tradition sorely needs; reciprocally, regarding certain philosophical-theological conceptions, the Catholic tradition has achieved some insights (into the nature of the human person, the human community, and mediating institutions, for example) in which many in the liberal intellectual tradition are now expressing interest. The two traditions need each other, each being weaker where the other is stronger.

14. *This Hemisphere of Liberty: A Philosophy of the Americas* (Washington, D.C.: AEI Press, 1990). To call attention to the distinctive complex of mental tendencies that speaks to the Latin American condition, in this book Michael Novak coins the phrase "the Catholic Whig tradition." Lord Acton called Thomas Aquinas the first Whig. The ancient Whig pedigree, far older than the now defunct British and American parties of that name, includes Bellarmine, Alexis de Tocqueville, Acton himself, Jacques Maritain, Yves R. Simon, and others. Catholic Whigs, like Progressives, believe in the dignity of the human person, in human liberty, in institutional reform, in gradual progress. But they also have a deep respect for language, law, liturgy, custom, habit, and tradition that marks them, simultaneously, as conservatives. With the conservatives, the Catholic Whigs have an awareness of the force of cultural habit and the role of passion and sin in human affairs. With the liberals, they give central importance to human liberty, especially the slow building of institutions of liberty. The Catholic Whigs see liberty as ordered liberty—not the liberty to do what one wishes, but the liberty to do what one ought. Working

within this horizon, this book shows how institutions of liberty may be built in this hemisphere (and the other). The liberation of Latin America, especially its economic liberation, has not yet been accomplished. In the precapitalist mode, Latin American economies are characterized by markets, private property, and profits. These do not, contrary to Marx, suffice to constitute a capitalist system. Latin America offers few legal or cultural supports for the essential mark of the capitalist economy: enterprise, innovation, creativity. Only from the dynamic energy of moral striving (through ideas, habits, and institutions) can a political economy take life. Economies work better when human persons are given institutional support to become creators of wealth, not merely dependents on government. Development means empowering the poor to incorporate their own businesses, to own their own land, to improve their education and skills, and to exercise their God-given right to personal economic initiative.

15. SUMMARIZING THE WORK OF LAST DECADE AND POSING QUESTIONS FOR REMAINDER. *The Catholic Ethic and the Spirit of Capitalism* (New York: Free Press, 1993). This book offers a fuller theory of the Catholic social ethic and capitalism, a practical agenda for addressing the critical problems of poverty, race, and ethnicity, and an approach to the problem yet unaddressed: the ecology of liberty. Out of a hundred-year debate within the Catholic Church has come a fuller and more satisfying vision of the capitalist ethic than Max Weber's Protestant ethic. No other religious tradition has wrestled so long with, or been so reluctant to come to terms with, the capitalist reality. This book chronicles the Catholic opposition to capitalism and the beginnings of modern papal social thought, including an account of how Pope John Paul II's commitment to

human liberty came to include economic as well as religious and political liberty. Novak offers a new and practical definition of social justice, designed to rescue this central concept of papal social thought from the powerful objections of Friedrich Hayek. It reinterprets social justice as the distinctive virtue of free persons associating themselves together, cooperatively, within a free society. It also delinks social justice from an uncritical reliance on the blind leviathan of the state and links it, instead, to the concrete intelligence of individuals and their free associations within "the civic forum." This new definition of social justice, which emphasizes "civil society," not the "state," gives rise to a new approach to government and social activism, which Michael Novak calls "the civil society project." This project addresses several social perplexities of the near future, including the desperate condition of many of the world's poor, ethnicity and race, and the new factory in cultural ecology, the omnipresent media of communications. The combination of democracy and capitalism can do more to free the poor from poverty and tyranny when the welfare state is redesigned to open up the sphere of free associations and "little platoons" that express the social side of human nature. In matters of race and ethnicity, a wise focus is the development of "human capital" among the most vulnerable, as the chief ground on which an individual can build a sense of dignity, achievement, and pride. Finally, the primary flaw in free society today lies not so much in its political or economic systems, but in its moral-cultural system. Today, one must scrutinize especially the cultural elites who create the stories, images, and symbols of the nation's self-understanding and moral direction. The new frontier of the twenty-first century is likely to be contestation for the soul of the moral-cultural system. Building up civilizations that respect the true and nature-fulfilling "moral ecology," in which the virtues of ordered liberty flourish, is a demanding task which will occupy the human race throughout the coming century. Novak calls this "the ecology of liberty."

16. A NEW LOOK AT DEMOCRATIC CAPITAL-ISM—FROM WITHIN. *Business as a Calling: Work and the Examined Life* (New York: Free Press, 1996). Drawing on interviews with men and women who work in business, as well as published accounts and wide-ranging research, this book brings us inside the everyday world of business. What unifies Novak's account is the conviction that, *pace* the treatment it usually receives from Hollywood, the news media, and counterculture intellectuals, business life is morally serious, and it constitutes what religious believers (and even a few secularists) recognize as a calling: unique to each individual; requiring talent; revealing itself by the pleasure and sense of accomplishment its practice yields us; and not always easy to discover among the false paths life presents. Novak begins his discussion of business as a calling by examining the ideals and possibilites inherent in industry and commerce, considering both the virtues internal to business and the myriad ethical responsibilities of businessmen and women. He then discusses democratic capitalism as a system, underscoring the two most powerful arguments for capitalism: that it better helps the poor to escape from poverty than any other economic system, and that it is a necessary (though not sufficient) condition for democracy. But while Novak is clear about the virtues of business life, and the moral legitimacy of democratic capitalism, he is also acutely aware of the threat posed by modern culture to the moral capital of the West. Both intellectual elites and the national media have been remarkably incurious about virtue and religion for some years, threatening our nation's moral ecol-

ogy. Because business is dependent on the moral and cultural institutions of the free society, corporations cannot afford to ignore this threat to a healthy public ethos of virtue. What becomes clear by the end of Novak's study is that, as in all human affairs, one can do both good and evil in business—whether one owns a small coffee shop or works in a large telecom corporation—but that to do evil corrupts the inner telos of business as a calling.

17. *The Fire of Invention: Civil Society and the Future of the Corporation* (Lanham, Md.: Rowman & Littlefield, 1997) This book evolved from three lectures at the American Enterprise Institute on three distinct but related topics: the history and distinctive nature of the business corporation; the animating force that gives birth to the business corporation, "the fire of invention," and patents and copyrights; and questions of structure and governance of the corporation. It looks at the business corporation's influence on civil society and, in the postsocialist era opening before us, assesses some of the principal new threats to the corporation appearing on the horizon. Novak presents a brief history of the corporation, tracing its roots back to medieval monastic life, and argues that it is a primary institution of the free society, second only to religion (the corporation is the major material, while religion is the major spiritual, institution of civil society). But Novak's analysis is prescriptive, too. The business corporation has come under fire from a new set of enemies, including those, like the British financial journalist Will Hutton, who call for a "stakeholder" society in which political elites will set out vast new corporate responsibilities under the heading of "corporate governance." Much of the discussion surrounding corporate governance, Novak argues, misapplies categories of political philosophy—designed for political institutions—to the corporation, which is not a political com-

munity. It is therefore crucial, Novak argues, for the corporation to take account of its own identity and its central role in the building of the chief alternative to government: civil society. One of Novak's principal themes in this book is the trade-off between risk and security in the free society. Americans have traditionally been more open to risk than Europeans—as Tocqueville already grasped in *Democracy in America*. Hence the greater dynamism of American economic life, the flourishing of the corporation in American soil, and the vast sums of venture capital invested by Americans in risky new firms. This emphasis on dynamism and creativity is perfectly captured in the American respect for intellectual property. Accordingly, Novak illumines the complex field of patents and copyrights with the help of Abraham Lincoln, for whom "all of nature is a wholly unexplored mine." Patent regimes grant inventors and authors the fruit of their labor, and thereby serve the common good through the inventions and works of the spirit they promote. *The Fire of Invention* opens a new and exciting field of inquiry, the business corporation, to scholars in humanistic studies.

VI. Faith for a New Generation

18. *Tell Me Why: A Father Answers His Daughter's Questions About God*, with Jana Novak (New York: Pocket Books, 1998) Beginning with a fax of honest and pressing questions about religion sent by his daughter Jana, Novak launches into a discussion with her on crucial issues of faith, religion, and meaning. At once autobiographical and philosophically and theologically searching, the book reveals that, far from being an opiate of the masses, as Marx held, true religion cuts to the core

of existence, and that, in the dark night of the soul, it can be of little short-term solace. What the exploration of faith is finally about, Novak explains, is truth. The book is written as a dialogue, with each chapter framed by a question from Jana on God, religious institutions, and morality. While answering his daughter's often skeptical queries on such issues as the decision to have faith, the variety of organized religions, and the nature and importance of God, Novak explains both the many ideas that different world religions have in common and the central beliefs and principles of Catholicism. Following Chesterton, who described the Catholic faith as "the democracy of the dead," Novak stresses the importance of tradition and ritual in giving continuity and substance to life's most important events. More, Novak rejects the view that it is unrealistic to expect modern men and women to adhere to church teachings on sex and morals. On the contrary, the challenge those teachings offer serves to intensify experience, to make life richer for those who adhere to them. No controversy is skirted here: Novak addresses the role of women in the Church, abortion and contraception, charity, science and faith, and religion and the free society. *Tell Me Why* is a return, thirty years on, to the existential and theological concerns that first animated Novak's thought.

Notes

Introduction

1. *The Spirit of Democratic Capitalism* (Lanham, Md.: Madison Books, 1982, 1991); *Business as a Calling: Work and the Examined Life* (New York: Free Press, 1996); *The Fire of Invention: Civil Society and the Future of the Corporation* (Lanham, Md.: Rowman & Littlefield, 1997). It has been Novak's defense of market institutions, embedded in a thick world of moral norms and constrained by democratic political institutions, that has led to the great interest in his thought in Latin America, Italy, and in Eastern and Central Europe. Against the backdrop of Catholic cultures, long distrustful of economic freedom, his work has resonated loudly. See, e.g., Gianni Baget Bozzo, "Mettiamo insieme S. Tommaso e Adam Smith," *Liberal*, February 1997, pp. 58–59.

2. John Gray, *Post-Liberalism: Studies in Political Thought* (London: Routledge, 1993), p. 73.

3. See Francis Fukuyama, *Trust: The Social Virtues and the Creation of Prosperity* (New York: Free Press, 1995) for a learned look at different kinds of capitalism; for a bleaker view of the coming millennium, which predicts the immolation of global capitalism from self-contradiction, see John Gray's fiery—and intermittently brilliant and frustrating—*False Dawn: The Delusions of Global Capitalism* (London: Granta Books, 1998). Novak's *The Fire of Invention*, by no means

blind to the perils Gray warns us of, offers a more measured and empirically grounded look at where we're headed.

4. See Michael Novak, "How to Make a Republic Work," *The Kansas Journal of Law and Public Policy*, Vol. 2, No. 1, Spring 1992, pp. 67–78.

5. See Pope John Paul II, *Evangelium Vitae* (New York: Times Books, 1995), particularly numbers 3 and 4.

Chapter 1

1. See Michael Lewis on Woody Allen, "The Very Last Lover," *The New Republic*, 28 September 1992, p. 11.

2. *Planned Parenthood v Casey*, 505 U.S. 120 L Ed 2d 674 (1992). Russell Hittinger parsed the destructive notion of liberty at the heart of *Casey*: "One would seem to have a right to do or not do whatever one pleases" ("What Really Happened in the Casey Decision," *Crisis* [September 1992], pp. 16–22).

3. In view of his earlier defense of nihilism, Camus sets forth, with some difficulty, his argument against Nazism in "Letters to a German Friend: Second Letter," *Resistance, Rebellion and Death* (New York: Alfred A. Knopf, 1961).

4. Schlesinger wrote, "The American mind is by nature and tradition skeptical, irreverent, pluralistic and relativistic. . . . People with different history will have different values. But we believe that our own are better for us. They work for us; and, for that reason, we live and die by them" ("The Opening of the American Mind," *New York Times Book Review*, 23 July 1989, p. 26). A good statement of Rorty's views on democracy can be found in "Taking Philosophy Seriously," *New Republic*, 11 April 1988, p. 22, where Rorty writes, "No specific doctrine is much of a danger, but the idea that democracy depends on adhesion to some such doctrine is."

5. For the testimony of Vaclav Havel and other East and Central European dissidents on the culture of the Lie, see Havel et al., *The Power and the Powerless: Citizens Against*

the State in Central and Eastern Europe (Armark, NY: M. E. Sharpe, 1990).

6. Solzhenitsyn was quoting, in his 1970 Nobel prize lecture, an old Russian proverb: "One word of truth outweighs the world." *Nobel Lecture* (New York: Farrar, Straus & Giroux, 1970), p. 34.

7. Berlin defined negative liberty as "not being interfered with by others. The wider the area of non-interference the wider my freedom." See Berlin's famous "Two Concepts of Liberty," in *Four Essays on Liberty* (Oxford: Oxford University Press, 1969), pp. 118–72.

8. See my *Morality, Capitalism and Democracy* (London: IEA Health and Welfare, 1990), originally delivered as an IEA Health and Welfare Unit lecture in the Queen Elizabeth II Conference Centre in 1990. The lecture's original title was "Christianity, Capitalism, and Democracy," and it so appears in the Czech and Polish translations.

9. Still, note the neat connection between the third concept of liberty and the liberal concept of "negative liberty." The American regime *permits* liberty even to those who do not practice self-government, but are slaves (as all of us are in part) to their own passions. But it cannot survive unless a sufficient proportion of its citizens do practice self-government in their private lives, and so are prepared to practice it in public as well. If all are slaves to passion and interest, free institutions cannot stand. The state cannot command or coerce self-government in private life, but it can do two things: (a) it can avoid undermining it by its laws, its regulations, and its taxes; and (b) it can support it by structures of incentives and punishments.

10. For Russell, see *Why I am Not a Christian* (New York: Simon & Schuster, 1957), particularly pp. 14–15; Sartre's views are developed in *The Words* (New York: George Braziller, 1964); on Strauss's relationship to Judaism, see David Novak, ed., *Leo Strauss and Judaism: Jerusalem and Athens Critically Revisited* (Lanham, MD: Rowman and Littlefield, 1996).

11. Tocqueville wrote: "While the law allows the American people to do everything, there are things which religion pre-

vents them from imagining and forbids them to dare. Religion, which never intervenes directly in the government of American society, should therefore be considered as the first of their political institutions, for although it did not give them the taste for liberty, it singularly facilitates their use thereof" (*Democracy in America*, ed. J. P. Mayer, trans. G. Lawrence [New York: Anchor Books, 1966], p. 292).

12. In Niebuhr's words, "Man's capacity for justice makes democracy possible; but man's inclination to injustice makes democracy necessary" (*The Children of Light and the Children of Darkness: A Vindication of Democracy and a Critique of Its Traditional Defense* [New York: Charles Scribner's Sons, 1944], p. xi).

13. During the constitutional debate of 1788, Madison asked: "Is there no virtue among us? If there be not, we are in a wretched situation. No theoretical checks, no form of government, can render us secure. To suppose any form of government will secure liberty or happiness without any virtue in the people, is a chimercial idea. If there be sufficient virtue and intelligence in the community, it will be exercised in the selection of these men; so that we do not depend on their virtue, or put confidence in our rulers, but in the people who are to choose them" (Jonathan Elliot, ed., *Debates in the Several State Conventions on the Adoption of the Federal Constitution* [Philadelphia: Lippincott, 1907], Virginia, 20 June 1788).

14. Washington declared that "Virtue and morality is a necessary spring of popular government" ("Farewell Address," 19 September 1796, in *The Early Republic, 1789–1828*, ed. Noble E. Cunningham, Jr. [Columbia, SC: University of South Carolina Press, 1968], p. 53). For two recent studies of Washington's exemplary character, see Richard Brookhiser, *Founding Father: Rediscovering George Washington* (New York: Free Press, 1996), and Harrison Clark, *All Cloudless Glory: The Life of George Washington from Youth to Yorktown* (Washington, DC: Regnery, 1996).

15. C. F. Adams, ed., *The Works of John Adams*, vol. 9 (Boston: Little-Brown, 1854), pp. 609–60. (emphasis added)

16. See St. Thomas Aquinas, I *Politics*, lect. 1; *Aristotle*,

1252b5; see also Thomas Gilby, *Between Community and Society: A Philosophy and Theology of the State* (London: Longmans, Green and Co., 1953), p. 93.

17. See Friedrich Nietzsche, *The Will to Power*, ed. Walter Kaufmann (New York: Random House, 1967).

18. Lord Acton, *Selected Writings of Lord Acton*, ed. J. Rufus Fears, vol. 3 (Indianapolis: Liberty Classics, 1988), p. 491. See also pp. 29–30.

19. Pope John Paul II, *Centesimus Annus* (Boston: Daughter's of St. Paul, 1991), #46.

20. Pope John Paul II, *Veritatis Splendor* (Boston: Daughter's of St. Paul, 1991), #101.

21. Friedman's comments were part of a symposium on *Centesimus Annus* in *National Review* (24 June 1991). They were reprinted as "Goods in Conflict?" in *A New Worldly Order: John Paul II and Human Freedom*, ed. George Weigel (Washington, DC: Ethics and Public Policy, 1992), p. 77.

22. During the conference at which this paper was presented (at the Henry Salvatori Center of Claremont McKenna College, 18–20 April 1996), Professor Friedman emphatically renounced relativism: "I have no doubt that there is an absolute standard of truth, and that in any particular matter there is a truth to be recognized. But I don't know what it is. The overlooked element here is humility. We have to know we don't know." And later, "I am not an atheist. I see the importance of religion, I respect it, I believe it has an important place in life, but I just do not see, I do not have belief myself, open as I am to it." (Conversation with the author.)

23. Blaise Pascal, *Pensées*, with an introduction by T. S. Eliot (New York: Dutton, 1958), #277.

24. See, *e.g.*, Niebuhr's discussion on "Having, And Not Having the Truth" in *The Nature and Destiny of Man* (New York: Macmillan, 1943), p. 243: "The truth remains subject to the paradox of grace. We may have it; and yet we do not have it. And we will have it the more purely in fact if we know that we have it only in principle. Our toleration of truths opposed to those which we confess is an expression of the spirit of forgiveness in the realm of culture. Like all forgiveness, it is possible only if we are not too sure of our own virtue."

25. Tocqueville quotes Cotton Mather: "Nor would I have you mistake in the point of your own liberty. There is a liberty of corrupt nature, which is affected by men and beasts to do what they list; and this liberty is inconsistent with authority, impatient of all restraint. . . . But there is a civil, a moral, a federal liberty, which is the proper end and object of authority; it is a liberty for that only which is just and good" (*Democracy in America*, p. 46). In the succinct formulation of Lord Acton, liberty is not to be defined as "the power of doing what we like, but the right of being able to do what we ought" (*Selected Writings of Lord Acton*, p. 613).

26. John Bunyan, *Pilgrim's Progress* (New York: Viking Penguin, 1965).

Chapter 2

1. With respect to the State, liberal doctrines in the United States appear to embody at least four overlapping premises, and all four seem to be contrary to indispensable characteristics of human liberty. Despite their inadequacy, these four premises reign supreme:

(a) that government should be neutral as between various ways of life, operating thus in a non-moral way (or, as Gertrude Himmelfarb puts it, a de-moralized way); e.g., government must regard homosexual couples as morally equivalent to traditionally married couples;

(b) that government must try to lessen existing inequalities between citizens (economic redistribution, affirmative action for minorities and women);

(c) that government properly bases itself on procedures rather than on substantive moral conceptions; and

(d) that substantive moral convictions are inherently conflictual and must, therefore, be banned from the public square as unreasonable and undemocratic. Thus, the political liberal Amy Guttmann has proposed gag rules for certain (nonliberal) parties in public debate, and John Rawls in a celebrated footnote in *Political Liberalism* urges exclusion from public debate—as too unreasonable—of anyone who opposes abortion during the first three months of pregnancy. These premises seem to describe quite well the totalitarian temptation in certain forms of liberal intolerance. The intolerance of secular liberals, who pride themselves on their openness, flies beneath their own radar.

Chapter 5

1. *Democracy in America*, tr. by George Lawrence, ed. J. P. Meyer (New York: Anchor Books Ed., 1969), vol. II, Part IV, Ch. 6, p. 692.

2. A useful conspectus of the dimensions of the coming welfare crisis, in its demographic and fiscal dimensions, is proffered in a special issue of *The American Enterprise*, "Fixing Social Security," January/February 1997, p. 6.

3. Robert Bork, *Slouching Towards Gomorrah* (New York: HarperCollins, 1996). See also William Bennett's *Index of Leading Cultural Indicators: Facts and Figures on the State of American Society* (New York: Simon & Schuster, 1994).

4. Tocqueville, *Democracy in America*, pp. 691–692.

5. *Gaudium et Spes*, #69, *The Documents of Vatican II*, Walter M. Abbott, S.J., ed. (Piscataway, N.J.: New Century Publishers, 1966).

6. In Britain, see David Green, *Reinventing Civil Society* (London: IEA, 1993), and Ralph Harris and Arthur Seldon's *Welfare Without the State* (London: IEA, 1987); in the U.S. see Marvin Olasky, *The Tragedy of American Compassion* (Wheaton, Ill.: Crossway Books, 1992).

7. Peter L. Berger & Richard John Neuhaus, *To Empower People: From State to Civil Society*, 20th anniv. ed. by Michael Novak (Washington, D.C.: AEI Press, 1996).

8. Irving Kristol, "The Spiritual Crisis of the Welfare State," *Wall Street Journal*, February 3, 1997.

9. *Centesimus Annus*, sect. 48.

10. Over 50 percent of all children born in Sweden are born out of wedlock compared with about 31 percent in the United

States. This difference is due in large part to the fact that 25 percent of all couples in Sweden are living in consensual unions, compared with about 5 percent in the U.S. However, the divorce rate in Sweden is still surprisingly high—36 percent compared with 42 percent in the U.S. See David Popenoe, "Family Decline in the Swedish Welfare State," *The Public Interest*, Winter 1991, 66–67. For further statistics on the United States, see *Report to Congress on Out-of-Wedlock Childbearing* (Washington, D.C.: Dept. of Health and Human Services, 1995). On Great Britain, whose illegitimacy rate has reached over 30 percent, see Charles Murray, et al., *Charles Murray and the Underclass: The Developing Debate* (London: IEA Health and Welfare Unit, 1996).

11. See *The New Consensus on Family and Welfare*, ed. by Michael Novak et al. (Washington, D.C.: AEI Press, 1987).

12. For examples of the ways in which centralized governmental regulations and administrative rulings now stifle local initiatives, see the essays by David Green, Michael Horowitz, and Marvin Olasky in *To Empower People: From State to Civil Society*, op. cit.

13. Robert Pear, "Moynihan Offers Proposal to Preserve Social Security," *The New York Times*, March 15, 1998, p. 24. Moynihan would allow workers to pay only 12 percent (instead of 14 percent) of their income into the existing social security system; the other 2 percent would be invested in a private investment vehicle.

14. Presidential candidate Steve Forbes first brought the proportional income tax—or "flat tax"—to prominence in the campaign of 1996, but Representative Dick Armey has introduced actual legislation for a flat tax plan of his own. Details in all such plans vary. The original proponents of the idea were Alvin Rabushka and Robert E. Hall in *The Flat Tax* (Stanford: Hoover Institution Press, 1985).

15. Robert E. Hall, Alvin Rabushka, Dick Armey, Robert Eisner, and Herbert Stein, *Fairness and Efficiency in the Flat Tax* (Washington, D.C.: AEI Press, 1996). See also Robert E. Hall and Alvin Rabushka, *The Flat Tax*, op. cit.

16. It seems patently more fair for everyone to pay at the

same rate (the poor exempted) than at "progressive" rates (higher rates as incomes rise). Those who think it more fair to have higher rates for higher incomes have never really justified that claim. They must face the fact that their odd sense of justice is frustrated by the sense of unfairness it raises in its targets and the wasteful search for tax shelters it encourages. For taxes to be paid fairly they must be perceived to have been levied fairly. I've been unable to locate good arguments for "progressivity," although obviously the "gut feeling" in their favor is widespread.

Chapter 6

1. When Carter asked to see me on his first precampaign trip to New York City that summer, I proposed such a conference to him.

Chapter 8

1. "Thomas Aquinas, the First Whig: What Our Liberties Owe to a Neapolitan Mendicant" in *Crisis*, October 1990, pp. 31–38, reprinted in a longer version with notes as the Appendix to Michael Novak, *This Hemisphere of Liberty* (Washington, D.C.: AEI Press, 1992), pp. 107–123. See also chapter two above.

2. See "The History of Freedom in Christianity" in Lord Acton, *Essays on Freedom and Power*, selected with a new introduction by Gertrude Himmelfarb (New York: Meridian Books, 1955), where Acton argues that Aquinas provided "the earliest exposition of the Whig theory of revolution" (p. 88).

3. See Jacques Maritain, *Scholasticism and Politics* (New York: Doubleday, 1960), particularly "The Thomist Idea of Freedom," pp. 117–138; *Christianity and Democracy and The Rights of Man and Natural Law* (New York: Ignatius Press, 1986); and *Man and the State* (Chicago: University of Chicago

Press, 1951); Thomas Gilby's *The Political Thought of Thomas Aquinas* (Chicago: University of Chicago Press, 1958); and John Courtney Murray, *We Hold These Truths: Catholic Reflections on the American Proposition* (New York: Sheed and Ward, 1960).

4. David Abulafia, *Frederick II: A Medieval Emperor* (London: Allen Lane, 1988).

5. Abulafia evokes this fascination in "The Ghosts of the Hohenenstaufen," chapter 13 of *Frederick II:* "Sibylline oracles, still circulating in 1250, spoke of the mysterious return of him in whom man's hopes rested: 'he lives and he lives not'; a phrase that one modern historian of Frederick II, writing in the days of Weimar, unfortunately saw fit even to apply to the yet-to-be resurrected Germany of his own time." p. 432.

6. "Nor, again, is it surprising that usury follows heresy, treason and sacrilege in the order of laws. Here the influence of canonistic thinking is plain: an opposition based on the idea that money which grows simply by lapse of time, without any contribution of labour, grows unnaturally, since it is immoral to receive money without investment of work. The papacy saw in widespread usury a threat to moral conduct and to the fabric of society comparable to that of heresy; papal denunciations of the Albigensian heretics usually included reference also to moneylenders." Ibid., pp. 212–213.

7. Bede Jarrett, O.P., notes that actual heretics were well known to medieval theologians; what was dangerous about them in their view was the fact that they were propagandists and leaders of movements. See *Social Theories of the Middle Ages 1200–1500* (New York: Ungar Publishing Co., 1966).

8. See Ralph McInerny, *Aquinas Against the Averroists: On There Being Only One Intellect* (Indiana: Purdue University Press, 1993).

9. *Titus*, 3, 10.

10. Jerome, *In Galat*, III, On *Galatians* 5, 9. PL 26, 430. Gratian, *Decretum* II, 24, 3, 16. RF I, 995.

11. *Summa Theologica*, 2a2ae. X. 8.

12. The text continues: "For this reason the Church has at times, when infidels were in great number, tolerated the rites

even of heretics and pagans." *Summa Theological* 2a2ae. X. 11.

13. On this subject, see Bede Jarrett, O.P., op. cit.

14. Paul Johnson, *A History of Christianity* (New York: Atheneum, 1980), pp. 252–253.

15. Louis de Wohl, *The Quiet Light: A Novel of St. Thomas Aquinas* (New York: Doubleday, 1958).

16. See the important study by James M. Powell, *Albertanus of Brescia: The Pursuit of Happiness in the Early Thirteenth Century* (Philadelphia: University of Pennsylvania Press, 1992).

17. See *The Declaration of Religious Liberty, Dignitatis Humanae* in *The Sixteen Documents of Vatican II with Commentaries by the Council Fathers* (Boston: St. Paul Books, 1967), pp. 395–413; e.g., "In faithfulness therefore to the truth of the Gospel, the Church is following the way of Christ and the apostles when she recognizes and gives support to the principle of religious freedom as befitting the dignity of man and as being in accord with divine revelation. Throughout the ages the Church has kept safe and handed on the doctrine received from the Master and from the apostles. In the life of the People of God, as it has made its pilgrim way through the vicissitudes of human history, there has at times appeared a way of acting that was hardly in accord with the spirit of the Gospel or even opposed to it. Nevertheless, the doctrine of the Church that no one is to be coerced into faith has always stood firm." #12.

18. See my Krakow lecture of July 7, 1994, "How Christ Changed Political Economy," in *Crisis*, February 1995, pp. 4–7.

19. Pierre Manent, "Christianity and Democracy" trans. by D. Mahoney and P. Seaton, part I, *Crisis*, January 1995, pp. 40–44; part II, *Crisis*, February 1995, pp. 42–48.

Chapter 10

1. *From Marxism to Judaism: The Collected Essays of Will Herberg*, ed. David G. Dalin (New York: Markus Wiener, 1989), pp. 39–40.

2. Ronald Preston, "Reinhold Niebuhr and the New Right," in *Reinhold Niebuhr and the Issues of Our Time*, ed. Richard Harries (Grand Rapids, Mich.: Eerdmans, 1986), pp. 88–104.

3. David Halberstam, *The Powers that Be* (New York: Dell, 1986).

4. Peter L. Berger, *The Capitalist Revolution: Fifty Propositions about Prosperity, Equality, and Liberty* (New York: Basic, 1986), pp. 72–89, 212–13.

5. Reinhold Niebuhr, *The Irony of American History* (New York: Scribner's, 1952), p. 93.

6. Reinhold Niebuhr, *Christian Realism and Political Problems: Essays on Political, Social, Ethical and Theological Themes* (New York: Scribner's, 1953), pp. 67–68.

7. Michael Novak, John Cogan, et al., *The New Consensus on Family and Welfare* (Washington, D.C.: American Enterprise Institute for Public Policy Research, 1987).

8. Irving Kristol, *Reflections of a Neoconservative: Looking Back, Looking Ahead* (New York: Basic, 1983).

Chapter 14

1. Decisive in my thinking was Theodore Draper's article in *Commentary* in January 1967, which asserted that in December 1964, the North Vietnamese had moved 400 regular troops into South Vietnam—a tiny "invasion," it seemed to me then. We now know that many more troops than that had been coming south and from a far earlier time.

2. Mussolini used this expression to define the essence of the new type of system in history, totalitarianism. In Mussolini is found the *locus classicus* of the "totalitarian/authoritarian" distinction.

3. Political conversions are not as deep as religious conversion. Psychologically, as Gordon Allport once observed, they occur on different levels of the psyche. But they are deep enough, since they affect all one's judgment and actions as a citizen. Different visions of political economy embody different

senses of reality, different views of human nature, different senses of historical narrative, and quite different forms of self-knowledge.

4. Peter Berger's *The Capitalist Revolution* (New York: Basic Books, 1985) assembles the empirical evidence in an easily accessible way, in the form of fifty falsifiable theses.

INDEX

ABOUT THE AUTHOR AND EDITOR

MICHAEL NOVAK holds the George Frederick Jewett Chair in Religion, Philosophy, and Public Policy at the American Enterprise Institute, where he is also director of social and political studies. In 1986, Mr. Novak headed the U.S. delegation to the United Nations Human Rights Commission in Geneva. Mr. Novak has won the Templeton Prize for Progress in Religion, the Anthony Fisher Award, the Wilhelm Weber Prize, and the International Award of the Institution for World Capitalism, among others. The author of more than twenty-five books, he is also a cofounder and former publisher of *Crisis* and has been a columnist for both *National Review* and *Forbes.* His most recent book is *Tell Me Why: A Father Answers His Daughter's Questions About God,* written with Jana Novak.

BRIAN C. ANDERSON is senior editor at *City Journal* and author of *Raymond Aron: The Recovery of the Political* (Rowman & Littlefield). His reviews and essays have appeared in *First Things, Review of Politics, The Wilson Quarterly,* and many other publications.